Clarence Shuler has been
tute, bringing a wealth of exp
to bear on the issue of racial
desiring to move boldly into
without schism—fit for heaven

**Joseph Stowell**
**President, Cornerstone University**
**Former president, Moody Bible Institute**

Clarence Shuler's book is a must-read for people of every race and culture who are confused about the term racial reconciliation, and frustrated with the current state of race relations. It is an equipping, challenging, healing, and compelling book! Through powerful personal stories, we are led to a singular conclusion—only by following the healing power of the Word of God can we build what he calls racial partnerships as a way of life. Clarence Shuler's message is clear. There is no middle ground. White believers must take the initiative to remove the pain and injustices caused to people of color by racism, but everyone must act. The bottom line is— the Church must choose between Christ and culture in order to bring about unity within the body of Christ.

**Dr. Barbara Williams-Skinner**
**President,**
**Skinner Leadership Institute**

It is time for all of us in the body of Christ to be serious about loving one another, regardless of race or ethnicity. This is a life message and a burden that I believe God has placed on the heart of my brother Clarence Shuler. As you read this book, pray that God will speak to your own heart about what you can do to help bring about true biblical unity among Christians.

**Bob Lepine**
**Co-Host,**
**FamilyLife Today**

DISCARD

I heartily endorse Clarence Shuler's book *Winning the Race to Unity*. I have read several books on the subject and this one spoke to me more deeply than most. Clarence is helping the Christian community understand what biblical diversity looks like and how we can take practical steps toward an authentic unity through his writings and seminars.

**Dr. William J. Hamel**
**President,**
**Evangelical Free Church of America**

The church cannot focus too aggressively on the need for transethnic sensitivity and spiritually motivated therapy for our wounds in this arena of separation. If Christians can gain ground in racial unity, maybe we'll be able to learn to win the big battle—the one that separates the church attitudinally, as our sectarianism biases divide us.

**Jack W. Hayford**
**Pastor Emeritus,**
**The Church on the Way**

Clarence Shuler has captured through his life experience the principles that lead to deeper dialogue and practice in race reconciliation. I encourage the reading of this important book.

**Matthew Parker**
**President,**
**Institute for Black Family Development**

Shuler challenges us to hunger for the nations in our own communities. With thought-provoking questions and biblical principles, Shuler breaks down the communications barriers among God's people.

**Myrna Gutierrez**
**President/CEO,**
**Integrated Solutions**

Clarence understands both the black and the white communities with striking depth and compassion. He challenges us in this book as few could. Clarence is helping us to move forward with vision and hope.

**John and Susan Yates**
**popular writers and speakers in the area of family life**

Clarence's book raises crucial questions concerning authentic racial unity in the body of Christ. His chapter on how to relate to the Black community is an instant classic. For those tired of playing the same old games, I heartily recommend this book.

**Chris Rice**
**Senior Fellow, Northeast Asia Reconciliation Initiative**
**Duke Divinity School**

Finally, a thought-provoking book that asks readers to discern racial reconciliation from an African American perspective! Clarence Shuler challenges Christians to examine the misuse of culture, power and ethics within the body of Christ and to work for the fair treatment of all humanity regardless of their social status. A must read for all who wish to transcend racial and cultural barriers.

**Dr. Alvin Sanders**
**Senior Vice President, World Impact**
**Author of** *Bridging the Diversity Gap*

*Winning the Race to Unity* by Clarence Shuler is perhaps the best book on race relations in print! It deals with difficult, sensitive matters in a Christ-like, graceful and sensitive manner. While one is convicted of his past and present sins of prejudice, discrimination and racism, one is moved to positive Christ-centered response in dealing with issues for the glory of God. I have distributed this book widely in various parts of the world through our missionaries, but also in North America to key pastors and Christian leaders. It has helped me immensely in my personal walk with God!

**Doug Nichols**
**Founder of ACTION**

God has used Clarence Shuler to speak to the greatest hindrance to the influence of the church today. Until Christians can genuinely love one another as Clarence teaches in *Winning the Race to Unity* we will be unable to effectively reach our world. This book is a must-read for everyone who is serious about expanding the kingdom of God in America. If we don't win the race to unity we will lose the race!

**B. Courtney McBath, D. Min.**
**Founding & Senior Pastor,**
**Calvary Revival Church**

Clarence writes with love and compassion for the victims of racial bias as well as for those persons or groups who perpetuate it. This prophetic book is rare in its honesty and practicality. Reverend Shuler provides several illustrations of real problems as well as tangible steps to ameliorate them. As a sociologist who has worked in evangelical settings for nearly three decades, I think that Reverend Shuler has written one of the very best books for helping evangelical Christians understand the subtleties of racial conflicts.

**Henry Allen**
**Ph.D., Professor of Sociology,**
**Wheaton College**

Dr. Martin Luther King, Jr. rightly criticized the church, stating that eleven o 'clock Sunday morning was the most segregated hour in America, revealing the historical trend of God's people to be last in efforts of racial unity. Clarence's book is very insightful in explaining why the church has been slack in the race. This is a must read book for God's people who are no longer content to bring up the rear, but rather determined to win the race for racial unity.

**Vernard T. Gant, D. Min.**
**Director of Urban Ministries**
**Association of Christian Schools International**

Clarence Shuler uses his gifts as a researcher and communicator to bring home some much-needed truth. His honest use of his personal history combined with the eye-opening glimpse into our nation's past allows us the opportunity to run a race free of the burden that has weighed us down for so long. I believe every member of the body of Christ should be ready to run this race, and this book will give us the courage and freedom we need to win.

**Jerald January Sr.,**
**Author, and Senior Pastor**
**Vernon Park Church of God**

Clarence Shuler writes with integrity. I was surprised at how superficial my understanding of race is. A continuing dialogue is necessary, for there is such a long way to go for both sides. He has started us on the difficult journey.

**Fred Smith Sr.**
**Former Businessman and contributing editor,**
**Leadership Journal**

Clarence Shuler's book is sorely needed. It is a creative and thoughtful discussion of the issues of racial reconciliation in the evangelical church. This book should be read by all who are involved in building relationships between evangelical institutions and minorities.

**Dr. H. Malcom Newton**
**Founding Director of Globalization**

Clarence Shuler's book is a gift for those willing to hear hard truths gleaned from his familiar storytelling technique which stirs the conscience and sharpens our perception on reconciliation.

**Dr. Cynthia D. James**
**Director of Northern California, Nevada, Hawaii Association of the Churches of God**

# Winning the Race to Unity

## Is racial reconciliation really working?

*Dr. Clarence Shuler*

*forewords by Dr. Willie Richardson
and Gary Chapman, Ph.D*

MOODY PUBLISHERS
CHICAGO

Editor: Cheryl Dunlop
Cover Design: Penny Hunter, Hunter Communications
Interior Design: Ragont Design

Library of Congress Cataloging-in-Publication Data

Shuler, Clarence.
 Winning the race to unity: is racial reconciliation really working? / Clarence Shuler.
    p. cm.
Includes biographical references
 ISBN 978-0-8024-8159-7
 1. Race relations—Religious aspects—Baptists. 2. Reconciliation—Religious aspects—Baptists. 3. United States—Race relations. I. Title
 BT734.2.S53 2003
 261.8'348'00973—dc21

                                                          2002156572

5 7 9 10 8 6

*Printed in the United States of America*

# Contents

*This book is dedicated to June Runyan, who touched so many lives, representing so many cultures. She had no fear, only energy to make things better. It didn't matter to her if she was the only white person sitting in the middle of an African-American Gospel concert or in a predominantly white church with a person of color, she was comfortable because of her love of Christ. She was a doer. Thanks for touching my life. I miss you. See you soon.*

# Foreword

Clarence Shuler has written a significant book that is a great source for those who are concerned about race relations, especially among Christians. This book is inspiring and gives hope that things can change. You are motivated and encouraged to believe that, as Christians, we can truly experience the fact that "in Christ we who are many form one body, and each member belongs to all the others" (Romans 12:5).

*Winning the Race to Unity: Is Racial Reconciliation Really Working?* gives insight into and understanding of the differences in racial cultures. It certainly appears that God has prepared Clarence through his unique cross-cultural life experiences. These experiences enable him to approach a sometimes controversial subject with fairness and objectivity. He faces the issues with godly passion and gives us hope for change and progress in the body of Christ. By the time you complete the last chapter of this book, you will realize that you have been exposed to Clarence's spiritual maturity because of the way he handles such a tough topic.

Clarence gives biblical principles and practical directions for joining him in his crusade for Christians to face sinful and deplorable situations. For more than one hundred years, these situations have existed in America without forthright spiritual leadership from evangelicals. Recently, during a lecture given at the National Conference on Expository Preaching, sponsored by E. K. Bailey Ministries, Dr. Gardner Taylor expressed his confusion about the national priorities of white evangelicals. He stated: "While leadership of the country can't discover how drugs get into the country or how to stop its distribution that is destroying the African-American community, the evangelicals have declared a war on Mickey Mouse."

This book takes you back in history to learn new facts you did not know and causes you to reexamine what you thought you knew—and then move forward, not repeating the mistakes of the past. Clarence focuses on historical facts some will find shocking and sometimes threatening because of what they have been taught. Nevertheless, Jesus said it best: "The truth will set you free."

When Clarence challenges his readers concerning the use of the term *racial reconciliation,* I find what he says refreshing and a demonstration of his wisdom. This will help some white Christians understand why some African Americans are cool when asked to join in racial reconciliation efforts. Personally, I have always had problems with the term *racial reconciliation.* However, I have made every effort to be part of the solution and not part of the problem in improving race relations with white Christians. For the last thirty years I have worked diligently with white pastors, most major parachurch organizations, and white denominations, trying to help give racial understanding and use harmony so that we would serve as a team to carry out the Great Commission. Repeatedly, although the project, program, crusade, or event was accomplished, there has never been lasting reconciliation or a commitment from the white Christian community beyond what they wanted to do for the moment. So it has become a liability for me as a leader in Philadelphia (and for other leaders) to use my influence, which has taken more than thirty-five years to build by the grace of God, to recruit other pastors and churches to work with white Christians, who, after making unsolicited statements of brotherly love and commitments that "our hearts beat as one," have literally "pulled up their tents" and disappeared overnight. Of course I realize that they decided to leave and to stop ministering with us for weeks or months before their departure. However, they did not think us worthy of being part of the decision-making process, nor did they have the decency to inform us of their departure. However, I have not given up on obeying the Lord by trying to be "one body in Christ" with white Christians because it is God's will.

Clarence goes into great detail chronicling the mistakes Christians have made that have hindered and impeded progress in race relations between white and African-American Christians. He also gives direction and leadership concerning what you can do to avoid making the same mistakes, and he expresses the positive actions and attitudes you should take now to move toward a brighter future in glorifying Christ through better race relations. It has taken courage and deep conviction for Clarence to write such a book and put his future at risk when he believes God has called him to minister with and make a living working alongside white Christians. If Christians take Clarence's book seriously, we will have revival in the church of Jesus Christ. They will know that we are "His disciples because they can see that we love one another."

DR. WILLIE RICHARDSON, SENIOR PASTOR
CHRISTIAN STRONGHOLD BAPTIST CHURCH
PHILADELPHIA

# Foreword

I first encountered Clarence Shuler in the late 1960s when both of us lived in a community that was caught in the throes of racial turmoil. I remember the morning I awakened to see the National Guard stationed along the street outside my house in an effort to keep peace. I was on the staff of an all white church which had recently built a new gym for "our" young people. One Saturday night, Clarence and his friend James showed up to play basketball. Their presence was obvious.

To the credit of our young people, they received Clarence and James into the events of the evening. I'm not sure that Clarence realized that he was building bridges that night or if he was simply motivated to play basketball. However, from that night Clarence Shuler has been a part of my life. He became a regular at our youth events and shortly thereafter received Christ and we became brothers.

At the death of his father, Clarence invited me into his house to meet his mother and sister. They too became a part of my life. The early days of our relationship were difficult. I remember the night I went to his house to take Clarence and James to an event. I got out of my car as they walked out onto the porch. Innocently, I said, "Are you boys ready to go?" James who was the bigger of the two bristled and said, "I ain't no boy!" I was shocked at his response, but I held my composure. I had no idea at the time that this reference had such a negative connotation to males in the African American community.

That night after the meeting Clarence, James and I talked, and talked, and talked. I listened as they shared their perspective and they listened as I shared mine. By the end of our three hour conversation, I think we all had a genuine respect for each other.

From those early beginnings, and many conversations later, I have deep appreciation for Clarence's impact on my life. He taught me that when we treat others with respect, racial differences need not be divisive. I have watched with joy at the hand of God upon the life of Clarence Shuler. Through college and seminary and into ministry, I have observed his heart for discipleship, and his desire to bring brothers and sisters together across racial lines in order to experience the unity which we have as members of the same family.

It is my desire that this revised edition of *Winning the Race to Unity* will open to the reader the heart of God who loves all of His children with an everlasting love; and that in response, we will learn to love each other, more overtly.

Gary D. Chapman, Ph.D.

# Acknowledgments

This book is dedicated to many people, but first and foremost are the four special ladies in my life. I am ever grateful to God for Brenda, my gorgeous wife, and my three beautiful daughters, Christina, Michelle, and Andrea, who graciously allowed me to work on this manuscript, which took precious time from them that can never be replaced. To the four of you ladies, "Thank you" for your sacrifice.

Jean Shuler, I couldn't have asked for a better sister. I thank God for our relationship. "Thanks" also for my nephew, Jonathan, and my niece, Jennifer.

Gary and Karolyn Chapman, Derek, Shelley, and John, "Thanks" for being my family. Without you, there would be no book. God used you to keep me from becoming a racist. There is no way to thank you for all you have done for me over the last thirty years. Thanks, also, for what you have done for Brenda and the girls.

Jerald January, "Thanks" for the example and encouragement you provided for me (going where I have yet to go). Jerra, "Thanks" for the many timely and necessary sermons.

Tim and Katie Price—Tim, "Thanks" for being a Jonathan to me.

Herb and Wanda Brisbane, my prayer partners, my brother and sister. Your timely, godly words of encouragement are like no other. I feel God often speaks to me through you.

Coach Mac, Alvin Simpkins, and Chuck Lane, "Thanks" for praying for Brenda and me every day. Please don't stop.

Bev Sullivan, you are indirectly responsible for the writing of this book. You provided me with the first opportunity to write an article, which was published by a Southern Baptist magazine and in Dr. Joseph Stowell's book *Following Christ*. This experience encouraged me to try to write this book.

Jo Kadlecek, my blue-eyed, blonde soul sister who lives in Harlem, I can say that without you I definitely would not have written this book. "Thank you" for your many hours of editing this work. God has gifted you with *incredible insight and wisdom*. "Thanks" also for your work on the proposal and advice for the order of the chapters. "Thanks" for praying for me each week. The Lord knows I need it. Dear Jo, thanks so much for taking time to help me write and edit the last two chapters of this book. Thanks for encouraging and challenging me to write when I didn't feel like it. Without question, your skills, experience, and insights makes it a better book. Jo Kadlecek is a writer in New York City whose most recent books include *Fear: A Spiritual Navigation* and *Winter Flowers and Other Signs of Redemption*. She also teaches writing at Columbia University.

I am also indebted to Cheryl Dunlop, Moody Publishers' in-house editor, who as Jo did, provided different points of view, refining and finishing the additions to the first edition of this book. I think this book is much stronger because of her input. She is also the author of *Follow Me As I Follow Christ: A Guide for Teaching Children in a Church Setting*.

Joyce Dinkins, Thanks seems so inadequate for the incredible help you gave me at the last minute, when I was so overwhelmed from counseling and trying to finish this manuscript. "Thanks" for the editing, especially reducing massive sections as well as blending other sections of the manuscript together for a smoother flow. NavPress is blessed to have you.

Pastor David Guy, "Thank you" for the many prayers for this book. Thanks also for getting Living Stones Fellowship to pray for my family, this book, and me.

Bob and Jean Cook, Jack and Judi Harrison: "Thanks," Bob, for being one of my mentors. Thanks also for the *incredible amount of time* you devoted to this book, for the use of your computer, for your help in editing, and for getting much of your family involved. Jean, "Thanks" for sharing him with me and for letting me sleep over in order to meet one of my deadlines. Jack, "Thanks" for your computer wizardry and for your help in putting this book together to give it a "professional" look before it got to Moody Press. Judi, "Thank you," too, for sharing him.

Darryl Moore, without you, this book could not have been written. I "Thank God" for your technical computer skills and for the grace by which you have shared them with me on *numerous* (and I do mean *numerous*) occasions. You never laughed at all the dumb questions I asked; you just patiently solved my many problems. As grateful as I am for your technical skill, it seemed the true blessing was and is your Christlike servant spirit. You are one of the people I want to be like when I grow up. "Thanks" for teaching me so much when I was under pressure. Stephanie, "Thanks" for letting me borrow him.

Carlton Sherbert, blessings on you for your *tremendous* assistance in gathering the research and documentation for this book. "Thanks" for being such a patient and understanding brother during the writing of this book.

Dr. Malcolm Newton, "Thanks" for opportunities to speak at Denver Seminary and your various workshops to see how people would respond to this book. Thanks for being someone on whom I can always count.

Greg Thornton, "Thanks" for taking a chance on this book. Thanks for your and your staff's patience as I missed most of my deadlines. Thanks most of all for your friendship.

"Thanks" to Rudy Perkins, for our many talks laid the foundation for much of this book.

Representative Sharon Weston, "Thanks" for the timely prayer phone calls and being a great younger sister.

Matt Parker, "Thanks" for being a visionary for much of the black Christian community; without your vision and influence, there would be many fewer published African-American authors.

Ron Ritchie, "Thanks" for helping me to edit this book so it won't kill people as they read it—or at least won't kill as many people.

Glenn and Janna Powell, "Thank you" for the *unbelievable gift* of a laptop computer. It was on this computer that much of the rough draft of this book was done. Your generosity blows me away. Thank you for your example of giving.

Pastor Don Sharp, you are always challenging me to think. "Thank you" for mentoring me. "Thanks" for being one of my earthly "dads."

"Thanks" to Urban and Loretta Gree, Uncle Matt and Sweet "D" Aunt Vi Daniels, Dwight and Barbara Morrison, Bob and Sharon Matthieu, Willard and Elrena O'Neil, and Bill and Rushella Latimer for adopting me into your families.

"Thanks" to my prayer partners: Myrna Gutierriez, Pastor Calvin and Deborah Johnson, Alvin Sanders, the Lee Paris family, Corwin and Kim Anthony, Patrick Burke, the Bill Delvin family, Keith and Karen Colvin, the late Vince Guillory, Bob and LeAnne Miller, Phil Williams, Calvary Baptist Church, Front Range Alliance Church, Dave and Tami Thornton, Mike and Monica Kessler, Bill and Vickie Markham, Small Group from Front Range Missionary Church, Don and Rosa Tilton, Tom and Vickie Griffin, Tom Phillips, Jerome Simpson, Mike Jones, Bill Weedman—your mentoring helped me prepare for what I am doing today. "Thanks," Brenda Wright, Mark Boateng, John Bass, Gordon Loux, Fred Smith, Ben and Wanda Anderson, Dr. Willie Richardson, Dr. Lloyd Blue, Dr. Jerry Buckner, Dr. Carl Ellis, Roz Caldwell, Mr. and Mrs. Will Chevalier, Dr. Emmitt Cooper, Dawn Corthell, Pastor Phil Davis, Mike De'Vine, Dr. Paul Fowler, Michael Geer, Mr. and Mrs. John Girton, Carl B. Herrick, Mark and Susan McCartney, Manny and Barbara Mill, Dr. William Pannell, Bishop Dantley, Pastor Ray McMillian, Sam Huddleston, Dick Mason, Tim Doyle, Allen Belton, Mychal Wynn, Rev. Linda Woodall, Doris Logan, Patricia Merritt,

Rosemary Harris, Steve Nakamura, Mr. and Mrs. Glen Kehrein, Dr. John Perkins, Chris Rice, the late Spencer Perkins, Dick Bruso, Judith Welker, Bo Holland, Ray Pokorny, Steve Hixon, Robin Cook, Peter and Darlene Poirson, Pastor Michael Thurman, Jim and Kim Turner, Spence Nelson, Bishop Courtney McBath, Lee Jenkins, Bishop Wellington Boone, Dr. Myles Munroe, Bishop Eddie Long, Stan and Debbie Senft, Gordon and Cherise Selley, Chuck and Diane Dade, Dr. Vernard Gant, Bruce and Sydney Barber, Dan Reeve, Mark Pollard, Stan Long, Travis Jones, Scott and Whitney Emerick, Ron Tilley; to my prayer partners and friends at Focus on the Family; to Dr. Dobson for airing some of my projects; and to the more than one thousand people who have committed to pray for Brenda and me the last three years.

Anne Scherich, "Thanks" for doing the extra research for me. Thanks for working through this project with me.

Lou Prioleau, "Thanks" for all of the tennis lessons, which helped to keep my stress level lower and improved my game. "Thanks" to my other tennis buddies: Jim McAnally, Steve Branch, Dale Halling, Susan Swarmer, Luis Cuadras, Pete Anderson, Rey Figueroa, Rich and Kaye Schlueter, Terry Snow, Don Haller, Tom Zamborelli, Steve Sicola, and Kelly Whitehead.

# Introduction: "Change Has Got to Come"

## The Race Problem Won't Go Away by Itself

*When you have a problem, don't fight it, solve it.*
—Millard Fuller

**M**ost of my life I have watched the problems poor race relations have caused throughout the history of our country. And much of my life I have looked for ways to solve them. Three hundred years of injustice and indifference cannot be changed easily, nor can they be changed overnight. But I'm convinced change is possible. I've seen changes and know there is hope!

### POOR, BUT I DIDN'T KNOW IT

God blessed me to be born into a family full of love. My father (now at home with the Lord) was and still is my hero because he worked two, sometimes three, jobs to provide for my mother, sister, and me. My mother (also in heaven with my father) worked equally hard. She was a college graduate, schoolteacher, and saleswoman. She taught me that if I worked hard enough I could achieve anything, even if the cards were stacked against me. This attitude is a great gift to give to a child. Lord willing, I hope to teach it to my girls. Then there was Jean, my older sister by nineteen months. She kept me from receiving many a spanking. I wasn't a "bad" kid, just inquisitive. Jean was a straight A student, which made it difficult for me, for the teachers who had taught her expected the same results from me. I disappointed more than a few of them.

Home life was pretty simple. Dad and Mom worked very hard. No Cs were allowed on report cards without consequences (spankings). My dad was only allowed to finish the eighth grade because his father made him quit school to work on their farm full-time. Dad was determined that Jean and I would have a college education and therefore he expected the best from us in our schoolwork.

We were in Mt. Zion Baptist Church every Sunday morning and evening. We never missed. We did not have much in the way of material treasures. Our treasures were each other. We spent a lot of time together. Jean and I often went with our parents on their jobs. Mom was a saleswoman for Stanley Home Products (similar to Avon), and Dad was a janitor for thirty-eight years for the R. J. Reynolds Tobacco Company and also had many part-time janitorial jobs. We played a lot of games together and spent hours "just talking." I was surrounded by three people who loved me very much—and I loved them just as much.

Materially, I was poor. But as I look back on my past, I was rich.

## DIFFERENT WORLDS

When I was thirteen years old, I would sneak into Wake Forest University's gym in Winston-Salem, North Carolina, to play basketball against the college players in order to hone my skills. This athletic facility actually housed five regulation basketball courts as well as a gymnastic facility, racquetball courts, and a weight room. During this time I met Denny, the son of the athletic director for Wake Forest sports. Denny was a short, blue-eyed, blond white guy. He introduced me to his basketball buddies, all sons of Wake Forest faculty members. This was North Carolina in the late 1960s, which meant if you were black, you didn't go into white settings without at least one black friend. So I introduced them to Russell, one of my good friends.

All of us went to summer basketball camps at Wake together. I was fortunate to make the All-Star teams, with the help of some personal coaching by Billy Packer, the assistant coach at Wake, and Jack McCloskey, the head basketball coach. I was already good friends with Coach McCloskey's kids. I had met them through Russell because he attended an integrated school whereas I went to an all-black school.

We could never get enough basketball. One summer, former Harlem Globetrotter Joe Cunningham formed a summer basketball league at the black YMCA. One day between pickup games Denny heard Russell and me talking about making up a team for the thirteen- to fifteen-year-olds' league—and it didn't include him or our new white friends. He asked us why we hadn't asked them to play.

"You guys are white, and it is a *black* 'Y,'" I said, matter-of-factly. What I meant was that he couldn't play with us there. But he didn't back down. He insisted on playing with us. He convinced Russell that they should play, which made me the bad guy. I tried to tell Denny and the other guys what they were getting themselves into, but he refused to withdraw his plea.

The red-bricked, fifteen-year-old "Y" where we would play was special to me because I had been involved in its activities since I was five years old. Our church had used the building on Sundays for worship services until our new church was built. (I was not a Christian at this time, but church is usually a part of the black experience, so I went with my parents. Religion is often prominent in the lives of people who are oppressed or feel they are, as James 2:5 tells us.) Our church basketball league games were played there. Many of the black social events were hosted at this prestigious, tradition-graced facility. So, for me, playing there was like going home.

We entered the summer league as an "integrated" team. All of us were nervous (scared is more accurate) as we walked into this well-lit-around-the-baskets-but-dark-at-other-places gym. The rims were "shooters." This meant they were a little loose, which helped the ball go in even if it was a little off center if the shooter had a soft touch. The floor was a good, old wood one, which gave the ball a true bounce so a player could dribble without looking at the ball. Naturally, the gym had that special aroma, the smell of sweat! There was no air conditioning, so the doors in the back of the gym were always open.

I'll never forget the first time our team entered the gym. Complete silence fell as the white guys became the center of attention. That silence was accompanied by equally intense stares that said "What are *you* doing here!"

As the game began, my worst fears were realized. When any of the white guys were fouled, it was not called. In fact, the white guys would normally be knocked down hard to the wood floor if they attempted to shoot or rebound. The message was simple: "You whites don't belong here. Go home." Refusal to heed this message meant continued hard fouls. Every time this happened, Russell and I fought with whoever committed the foul against our teammate. (The refs never gave me a technical because I was a "homeboy.")

For the first time in my life I saw in that gym something I never had expected to see: reverse racism.

Finally, during another game early in the season, Denny said to me, "You can't keep fighting everyone trying to protect me. I can take it." My respect for Denny went through the roof. Here was this slow, short, as pure a jump shooter as I've ever seen, tough white boy. I think it was at this point that we became brothers without ever saying it. Reluctantly, I agreed, for I knew he was right. He would have to earn respect on the court, just as I had had to earn respect because of my lack of height.

It was difficult for me to watch Denny and the other guys get nailed every time they shot the ball or went for a rebound. They were more than my teammates; they were friends for whom I had developed great love. Skin color was no longer a major issue for me.

I understood why the black guys were protesting having white guys play in the league. They knew they could never play in a white league. They had also heard or watched their parents experience racism from white people without any chance at justice, just like I had. Things were pretty intense in the late sixties in America. Winston-Salem, North Carolina, was no exception.

Yet, I still knew that the way my white friends were being treated was wrong. I also knew that my black friends who were beating my white friends didn't have any white friends themselves. Racism for them was both personal and impersonal. It was personal in that they had seen and heard of their parents' experiences. It was impersonal in that they did not have close relationships with any white kids. They had no way of knowing that not all whites were the racist types who had hurt their parents.

As the summer league progressed, our team began to gel. To everyone's amazement, we even got into the championship game— in spite of our lack of height and all these "crazy" rich white boys. Believe me, this was no small miracle! The officiating and the smiles that accompanied certain calls told me there was no way the refs were going to let this integrated team beat the "home 'Y'" team. And indeed we lost the championship game. But I felt we *did* win the respect of many of those associated with the league. By the end of the season, if our white players were fouled, the refs even called some of them.

When the All-League team players were about to be announced, we waited to hear who might have earned the coveted spots. Three of the players from the champion "Y" team made the All-League team. So did I. And so did one of our white players, Jimmy Williams. We were thrilled! We had lost the championship, but we had won something much more important—team unity—and that meant the most to me. All on our team learned that you can effect change in life if you are willing to sacrifice yourself in order to pay the price. It was a powerful experience for me. Even though none of the people involved were Christians, they showed me that with hard work, a lot of patience, and sheer determination, we could at least begin to address the racial problem.

Having been in the ministry for more than thirty years, I wonder why it is that non-Christians seem to deal with the racial situation more effectively than we Christians? As Christians, we have the Holy Spirit, whereas non-Christians don't, so we shouldn't have so much trouble with race. What's our problem?

## ENTERING THE GAME

When I think about that summer in North Carolina and the way people respond to the racial tensions that have long plagued our country, it seems to me that the Christian community of which I am a member has settled for watching the race problem from the sidelines instead of seeking to solve it by entering the game. Consequently, as early as 1972 during my freshman year at a prestigious Christian college, God revealed to me the need for a book such as this.

Yet I write this book with reluctance and regret—reluctance because of the very real possibility that I will receive a negative response as a minority speaking out on racism among black and white Christians; regret because Christians have not been able to have victory in the area of racism and move on to show the world a compelling unity.

I hesitated to write for another reason. I hoped (naively, perhaps) that the Christian community would not have allowed the sin of racism to persist in its midst for so long. But I've learned otherwise, especially as I've talked with and spoken to believers around the country about the subject.

The race problem in our country is getting worse, not better. And the discussion involves not just the black-white confrontation, but the conflicts all ethnic groups have with the white culture.

Native Americans object to the naming of sports teams after Indian personages—the chiefs and braves, for example. They feel it is demeaning to them. They also have expressed concern about the annual observance of Columbus Day. It's not a time of celebration for them. Hispanics are the fastest growing group of people in America, yet they are often not even mentioned in talks regarding race relations. In this book I will primarily address the plight of the African-American Christian, but I will also include the term *minority,* referring to Native Americans (First Nations), Hispanics, Asians, and other ethnic minorities in this country.

Beyond the obvious racial tensions we've seen in response to the O. J. trial and the L.A. riots, I hear the concerns of blacks employed by churches and parachurch ministries that say they want to minister to blacks. When a black joins such a group to help it minister effectively to the black community, that person discovers that he or she is not given the authority needed to actually do the job. By "lack of authority" I am in no way saying that what is requested is unlimited authority or not being accountable to authority (extremes discussed in 1 Peter 5:1–5). I realize that in order to *have* authority, one must be *under* authority. What I'm talking about is not being allowed to do what is necessary to affect those whom the black was hired to reach. Many blacks who have been through this experience have told me they never want to work in a white Christian organization again. Some of them are even looking to the Minister Louis Farrakhan, the leader of the Nation of Islam, because, they tell me, they would rather fellowship with a nonbeliever who understands their racial struggles than a believer who does not. Until this problem is resolved, or at least until there is major improvement, I fear what might happen. That is why I am convinced that the time is now for Christ's church to respond to the Gospel message of unity, love, and justice.

## CAUGHT IN THE MIDDLE

As my mental movie screen reviews my life, it seems that God has been preparing me all my life to confront the race issue in the body of Christ. When I was young, God sent a white Christian man into my life to begin to teach me the ways of Christianity. When I was fourteen years old, Dr. Gary Chapman showed me what it means to live a Christian lifestyle. God used Gary two years later to introduce me to Himself, when I accepted Jesus Christ as my Lord and Savior on May 8, 1970, in Hillsville, Virginia, on a youth retreat. I didn't realize it at the time, but I'm sure that Gary may well have risked his job by having a friendship with a young black boy in Winston-Salem, North Carolina, in 1968. Racial tension was high.

Soon after Gary introduced me to Jesus, he left the Southern Baptist church he was serving. Not long after his departure, the church hired a new youth minister. One night the new youth minister—who was short, bald, and had a "serious" military attitude—told us it was God's will for blacks and whites to worship separately. I was devastated! How could Gary have reached out to me when this man was telling me I couldn't worship with him? Besides, I had brought my best friend, James, to the youth group. James was not yet a Christian. I thought he would never accept Christ after hearing that statement. (Eventually he did so on his own. God is good!)

I continued to try to grow in my new faith. And—despite what that youth pastor had said—I continued to maintain friendships with whites and blacks alike. It just felt like the right thing to do.

When I was sixteen, the father of one of my white basketball friends asked me to take his daughter and her friend to a Friends of Distinction concert being held on the Wake Forest University campus. The girls were fourteen years old, but they looked like college freshmen—they were extremely attractive. Both were blue-eyed blondes. I told my parents, and they had a fit! They were concerned that I would be attacked by white guys. I was concerned too, but I didn't admit it to them.

My father told me that in South Carolina more than forty years before he had seen one of his boyhood friends lynched because he dared look at a white girl. I tried to understand his fear. I could only guess how that horrible experience had affected him. But I tried to reason with him—the lynching was forty years ago. Things had changed. He stared at me with fatherly concern as he listened to me.

I was finally able to talk my parents and my aunt into allowing me to take the girls to the concert. I wasn't sure what to do or how to act. The girls made it easy because they appeared to really want to be with me. When we arrived, I led them to the balcony because fewer people would see us there. As I got into the concert and the dance, I saw the girls trying to learn my moves (steps). For some reason, maybe basic survival, I turned around to see the lay of the land behind me. To my pleasant surprise, I saw Charlie Davis, the NCAA basketball All-American, sitting behind us with his white girlfriend. We knew each other from playing ball. Russell was his biggest fan. Charlie flashed that big grin of his with a thumbs-up sign, and I knew I could stop worrying about my safety. I relaxed and enjoyed the concert.

I never asked my white friend's father why he asked me to take his daughter and her friend to the concert. I wonder to this day. I never asked either of the girls out again. Interracial dating was not the popular thing to do in my town.

Years later, after my Moody Bible Institute experience, I flunked out of school at the end of the fall semester of my senior year. My emphasis on basketball, girls, work, and then studies, in that order of priority, finally caught up with me. Usually I flunked the midterm but aced the final. This system served me well until I forgot my exam schedule. There was not enough time to study, and I flunked out. My irresponsibility taught me some important lessons. (1) Your choices will always have consequences, so choose wisely. (2) God will forgive you, but you will still suffer the consequences of your sin. (3) Most of the "cool" people I hung out with really weren't my friends—we were just a clique. (4) The people I didn't have time for demonstrated that they truly were my friends. (5) God graciously brought to my attention my own prejudice, which had nothing to do with skin color.

With no money and no place to stay and too embarrassed to go home, I moved in with Johnny Washington, a black who had graduated from Moody the previous year. He worked at the Chicago Gospel Youth Center. Johnny introduced me to John and Joan Buell and Coco Jackson. Eventually they allowed me to live at the youth center, which was located on skid row. While I lived there, I worked with youth. More than one hundred kids came to the center each week. The staff was equally mixed racially. My role was one-on-one discipleship and coaching the boys' and girls' basketball teams.

I must admit that my experience at the center forced me to come face-to-face with my own racism. I was surprised to see whites working with black youths for low pay and sometimes even with their lives at risk. It was at the youth center that I met Mr. Erickson. His life challenged me. He was a white gentleman in his eighties—tall, bald, and a giant of a man. He taught the kids Scripture memorization and coached a group called the "Scripture Kids." The group traveled all over the Chicago area visiting churches demonstrating their amazing ability to recall and recite Bible verses forward and backward and from references. A young person had to memorize four hundred verses just to be put on the waiting list to join the group. The ages of the members ranged from five to twenty-three. They all loved this elderly white Christian gentleman.

Often the "Scripture Kids" were invited to minister to white churches. Many times they would not be met with smiles, but their knowledge of God's Word and their personalities usually won over the toughest crowds. Of course, Mr. Erickson knew they could and would.

In Chicago in the early seventies, especially on the weekends, there were certain places where even the police wouldn't go, but Mr. Erickson could go anywhere safely because he had earned the right. This was amazing to me because I was black and still couldn't do it when I first came to the youth center. But in time, I could. Remember Denny? Like him, I had to earn the right to minister in the inner city because I was an outsider.

I'm not sure what happened to Mr. Erickson, but his work demonstrated to inner-city kids and suburban churches that God is bigger than any culture or race.

Through my friendship with Dr. Gary Chapman, I eventually joined Calvary Baptist Church, a white Southern Baptist Church in Winston-Salem, North Carolina. The pastor, Dr. Mark Corts, liked to put former members who had been discipled at Calvary in positions of leadership whenever possible. Later, Calvary Baptist gave the money that made it possible for me to travel to Africa, Brazil, and Europe to play mission basketball.

What I'll never forget about Mark Corts is a statement he made to encourage me to go to seminary. "As long as I'm alive," he said, "I'll take care of you, but I want you to go to seminary, so if something happens to me, you can provide for yourself." He also promised me a job after I got my Master of Divinity. Sure enough, when it was time for me to graduate, Mark, being a man of integrity, offered me a job. I didn't take it because I thought a white guy could do the job just as well—and I *didn't* know how many white guys would be willing to work in the inner city. Here was another white man making a commitment to me and keeping his word. God was truly destroying some of the stereotypes by which I had lived.

I look at these white men—Gary Chapman, Mr. Erickson, and Mark Corts—and the Calvary Baptist Church staff and congregation as exceptions to the "rule" because all entered the game at great personal risk. What is the "rule"? *You can't trust white people!* God was beginning to make me sensitive to cross-cultural relationships.

## DOUBLE STANDARDS

When I decided to leave North Carolina and head to Chicago for college, I felt I needed to get away from home in order to spread my wings. I also knew my parents needed for me to get away, as they needed a rest. After eighteen years of parenting, I had worn them out!

To be honest, though, the first half of my first semester at Moody Bible Institute caused me tremendous depression. I had chosen to attend Moody because Gary graduated from that school. I thought if I could learn half as much as he knew about the Bible, God could use me for His purposes. From an academic and practical ministry perspective, Moody was the best institution I ever attended. I will always be indebted to Moody. It was there that I was given the opportunity to go to the mission fields of Africa and Europe and share the Gospel through playing basketball with Sports Ambassadors (the sports division of Overseas Crusade International). Those trips overseas forever changed my view of God.

But when I first arrived on campus, I noticed that the majority of the students—there were only twelve black students out of approximately 1,100—did not speak to me. Even though this attitude was not new to me, I had not expected to find racism on a Christian campus. (It turned out to be a situation I would face many more times in my schooling and career.)

I learned at Moody that prejudice is a sin like any other sin. Though it took me a long time to grasp this, I saw that racial prejudice was an area not easily dealt with by Christians. At first, I sincerely thought if you were prejudiced, then you were not—and could not be—a Christian. I remembered the words of 1 John 4:20–21:

> If anyone says, "I love God," yet hates his brother, he is a liar. For anyone who does not love his brother, whom he has seen, cannot love God, whom he has not seen. And he has given us this command: Whoever loves God must also love his brother.

It wasn't until basketball season started that students began to speak to me on a regular basis. I had often heard that "sports has the ability to take blacks from the outhouse to the penthouse," and now discovered the truth of that statement.

I was the first black ever to play basketball for Moody Bible Institute—and at Moody I was to see reverse discrimination for the second time in my life. At the tryouts during my freshman year, I was ready to work hard to earn my spot on the team. But to my surprise, the basketball coach told me to sit down without trying out. Then he made all the other players try out. Maybe he believed that blacks were naturally better athletes. Whatever the reason, without even trying out, I started every game my freshman year. I thought it was pretty funny. The other players didn't. They weren't mad at me. They felt they were being discriminated against by the coach—and that made them mad at him. It amused me that they were experiencing something I had felt my entire life. But I didn't tell them that.

Basketball opened the door for me socially. There were only three black girls at Moody my freshman year. Two already had boyfriends and one wanted a more serious relationship than I was ready or willing to commit to. Then a totally unexpected thing happened. A few white girls began to call asking me out for dates. Some even paid for the dates! I was amazed that some of the prettiest girls were often in their rooms on dating nights because no one asked them out.

I must admit, it was the friendship of these young Christian women at Moody that kept me from going crazy because of the paradox I was experiencing. They were easy to talk to. (Women in general seem to be more socially and culturally sensitive; guys are often more caught up in their egos and conquests.) Their sensitivity and support helped me to keep most things in perspective.

## MY "BROTHER" DAVID

After my college days, I basically bummed around for a few years. If I was in the area at the time of Calvary's church high school camp, I would go. The camp is in the mountains, which is always great for airing your head out so you can hear from God.

One summer, as camp was nearing a close, a white teenager,

David, asked me if I would spend the upcoming year (his senior year at Reynolds High School) in Winston-Salem. I had not planned to do so, but for some reason I told David yes.

David and I became inseparable. I had known him when he was much younger, because I had spent time with his older brother Richard. Richard was off in college. I became David's "other" older brother. David was the first white kid who would eat anything my mother put in front of him. He was at home when he came to my house. I had discipled some of the other guys in David's youth group, but they hadn't been at ease the way David was. My mother took real notice of this!

I was also at ease at David's home. His parents and Richard always made me feel a part of the family. I was not David's "black" friend. I was just his friend. There were times his parents would go out of town and ask me to stay over with David. I guess I discipled David somewhat informally. He would ask me millions of questions about the Lord and everything else, including girls. (He was quite the ladies' man.)

We were quite an odd couple! A twenty-four-year-old black boy/man and a white eighteen-year-old running around the city together. We often went shopping for his mother. When we got to the counter, just for fun, we would ask each other questions like "What else did Mom say to get?" You should have seen some of the looks on the faces of the cashiers when we did that. We couldn't wait to get out of the store to laugh!

David talked me into coaching the church's high school basketball team. I encouraged the guys to have a Bible study as well. (I do get myself into some crazy situations.) Picture this. I was coaching this all-white boys' basketball team in an all-white league. I got more than a few stares. The games were played in areas where you didn't see a lot of blacks. Whether we won or lost, we always prayed before and after the game.

David was a sensitive guy. I was not dating anyone (not by choice). Therefore, David more than once tried to set me up with a cheerleader at his high school. I didn't know how to drive a car with a stick. David had a Triumph Spitfire MG (we're talking *serious* car!). He took me up into the mountains and taught me how to drive it. Afterward he said, "Now whenever you want it, it's yours." God was using this kid to teach me how to be a servant and think of others first! Isaiah 11:6 says: "And a little child will lead them." David was leading me. We spent a lot of time praying for the youth group, thanking the Lord for their joys and taking their problems to Him in prayer.

The thing that set David apart from many other youths was his passion for God. David was not perfect. He was a normal teenager, though his passion for God seemed beyond his years. He reminded me of David in the Bible. Whenever he knew God wanted him to do something—apologize, encourage, serve—he did it. Maybe God was using David to disciple me.

Gary Chapman and Mark Corts stopped trying to get me to go to seminary, so in my usual contrary style, I decided to go. I chose to go to summer school, so in case I didn't do well, I would have only lost a summer. (Previously, I had not done well academically in college, and as a result my confidence was woefully low.) I entered Southwestern Baptist Theological Seminary in May. Just before my first major exam, I received a phone call from Steve Corts, the pastor's son. He was crying. He said that David, my "brother," had been killed in a car accident.

David was planning on going fishing. The day before he went, there had been an auto accident on the road he would take, leaving loose gravel everywhere. The road was never cleared. David, driving the speed limit (according to police reports), hit the loose gravel. The tires of his little open-top sports car couldn't get any traction on the curve of the road, and his car went into a spin. His head hit the bridge support, and he was killed instantly.

Steve Corts was calling on behalf of the youth group—they had collected enough money among themselves to purchase a plane ticket for me. I flew home, spoke at the funeral, and tried to answer some tough questions from the youth group. Since David and I had been so close, my presence seemed to comfort some of the kids.

It was after the funeral that something occurred that blew me away. The father of one of the players on the church basketball team invited me to their home. I had spent a lot of time with his son, daughter, and wife. Their house was close to the church, so I ate there every now and then. The father told me that he had really struggled with his own prejudice, but that he had taken note of the way I prayed with the team and the relationship between David and me. I was shocked that he said what he did because he had never acted like he ever had a problem with prejudice. His teenage daughter hugged me like family every Sunday in church, and he never said a word or acted like it even fazed him. He then gave me a large sum of money for seminary, saying, "I think David would want you to have this."

I realized then that I would never know how many people my relationship with David had touched. But I do know what it had done for me.

David's going to be with the Lord motivated me to study as an act of worship and praise. During my first full semester at seminary I made a 4.0 GPA.

David remains a part of my life. His parents gave me one of his pictures (he was quite an artist) that to this day hangs on my living room wall.

## MOVING ON

Since my seminary days, I have worked full-time in the ministry for a variety of Christian organizations and in a variety of places. I started the first technically African-American mission church for the Southern Baptists in Tulsa, Oklahoma. I say *technically* because the church was started with four blacks and two whites. Most recently, after leaving the pastorate, God led me to work for denominational and parachurch ministries. I now serve as a biblical diversity consultant for individuals, churches, Christian colleges, and other Christian institutions.

I have kept in touch with some of my friends from my youth, including the man who introduced me to Jesus. (I will always be grateful for Gary Chapman's influence.) I have worked with wonderful Christian men and women who seemed genuinely concerned that the body of Christ come together in unity.

I have also interacted with many men and women who claimed to know Christ but appeared to have little interest in solving the horrors of racism. Though from time to time people like that have discouraged me, they haven't stopped me, as God continues to teach me to die to self and live for Him.

In many of my experiences over the last thirty years, I was the first black to fill a position in a particular place.

This background has given me a sense of mission about cross-cultural relationships. Much of my time has been devoted to helping the white Christian community develop sensitivity to the black Christian community specifically and minorities in general. This has been and continues to be an extremely difficult task God has given me—but the rewards are phenomenal!

It is for His sake and the sake of the vision He has given me for racial unity that I offer this book to you.

*Winning the Race to Unity: Is Racial Reconciliation Really Working?* is written to analyze the racial reconciliation movement in the evangelical community at large and in churches and parachurch ministries. There are many one-on-one cross-cultural relationships today. This seems to be on the rise. But how is the Christian community as a whole doing in America? Racial reconciliation doesn't appear to be working as well today among the masses of Christians cross-culturally. My hope is that this book will explain why. I hope to provide biblical, practical steps that will improve relationships between the races if Christians of all races give racial understanding the same priority our Lord Jesus Christ does.

May our Lord Jesus Christ give His blessing to the individuals who read and choose to practice, by the indwelling power of the

Holy Spirit, the biblical principles given in this book. Without the Holy Spirit, this book will be just one more "try harder" volume.

*Dear Lord,*

*Thank You for showing us that even though we come from different worlds, we can become family through Your grace. But this will not happen automatically. All Christians need to actively seek to improve race relations in the body of Christ. We have so much to offer and teach each other. Thank You so much for giving David to me as my "little" brother. You taught me many things through him and touched many lives because of our friendship.*

*Amen.*

# 1

# Missing the Mark

## We Must Refocus Our Aim if We Are to Win the Race Game

*I have other sheep that are not of this sheep pen. I must bring them also. They too will listen to my voice, and there shall be one flock and one shepherd.*

—John 10:16

**G**od graciously endowed me with the ability to play basketball and gave me the opportunity to play both in college and overseas with missions basketball teams. My sports involvement has been a vehicle He has used to teach me lessons about race relationships. It was (and is) a natural open door for building cross-cultural friendships. I was the first black person many of my new white friends had ever known.

Without question, God used sports to give me a vision for unity in the body of Christ at large. I am convinced that whether we're on the court or in the pew, certain commitments and qualities—such as determination, diligence, and devotion—help to build an unbeatable combination of harmony and integrity. But victory is never easy. Sometimes it requires a flexibility that takes us beyond the familiar and the comfortable.

# WINNING THE RACE TO UNITY

## ANOTHER COURT

God continues to use sports in my life as an analogy for racial partnerships. For instance, as I've grown older, my ability to play basketball at a certain level has begun to diminish quite rapidly (amazing what happens with age!). As a result, I've decided to turn to tennis. The word spread that I wanted to learn this sport. The head coach of the University of Tulsa women's tennis team was referred to me. As this patient woman began to teach me how to play tennis, much of her instruction did not make sense. In fact, some of it seemed downright stupid. But I had a vested interest in her instruction because I was paying twenty-five dollars an hour to receive it (three lessons; she gave me the fourth for free), so I didn't give up.

To my surprise, when I followed her directions, the ball went where she said it would! Slowly I began to learn the game of tennis by faith as I did what I was told to do. With the instruction of the tennis coach and of Rudy Perkins (a former Southern Cal tennis player and one of my best friends) and Bill Funderburk, I experienced the joy of winning tennis tournaments. But before any tournaments were won, there were many more losses. Fortunately, I was able to learn from them.

The same is true in race relations. Step-by-step we learn by faith what we must do to bring about unity. My prayer is that each chapter of this book would be a step in the right direction for those of you who are serious about improving race relations, or a confirmation for those of you who are already active that you are moving in the right direction. Some of what I am saying may not ring true for you initially. This will not negate the truth of what has been written. This may simply be the first time you have heard some of these truths, or it may be the first time you have had the opportunity to view truth from a Christian African-American perspective. Please don't let yourself become defensive. Instead, ask God to help you to work through the tough issues. This is how spiritual growth takes place as we work through the tough issues by the power of the Holy

Spirit—as opposed to running away from our difficulties.

I hope you will be motivated to read this book from cover to cover because of your vested interest. For me, the vested interest in tennis was the twenty-five dollars an hour I had paid for instruction. For you as a Christian, hopefully, the motivation will come from such Scriptures as John 10:16, "I have other sheep that are not of this sheep pen. I must bring them also. They too will listen to my voice, and there shall be one flock and one shepherd," and John 17:21, "[I pray] that all of them may be one, Father, just as you are in me and I am in you. May they also be in us so that the world may believe that you have sent me."

There are other similar passages, such as 1 Corinthians 12:12–26 and 1 John 4:19–21, just to list a few. Our ability to glorify God and the integrity of the Gospel we preach is at stake.

One of my goals in writing this book is to deepen your relationship with our Lord and Savior and the hope that, as a result, your relationship with others will bring you spiritual joy and a better understanding of Christians from other cultures. Many of the truths in this book will make some people uncomfortable, but for those who persevere, the results will be worth the effort. We just need to keep in mind that what we are learning has eternal ramifications.

My wife, Brenda, and I conduct marriage seminars around the country. We have found that as we explain to husbands and wives how and why they are different, it gives them understanding and security. We have discovered that a basic understanding of differences reduces competition, alleviates fear, and produces patience. My hope is that this book will birth in you some of these same results in cross-cultural relationships. It is critical that we who are Christians learn to complement one another in the body of Christ. We need each other. The key is interdependency.

## THE WRONG QUESTION

The starting place to learn about anything is to ask questions. I asked my tennis coach how to serve the ball or hit a backhand in order to improve my game. The same is true when we begin to address the racial issue.

God is opening the door for me to consult with individuals, Christian colleges, churches, mission organizations, parachurch ministries, and general managers of Christian radio stations. All of the above who have hired me to consult with them have asked me the same question initially. It is intriguing to me that all these people from all these organizations ask the very same question. What is alarming is that they are all asking the wrong question. They are missing the mark.

Whenever I am asked this particular wrong question, a warning bell goes off in my head. This bell comes from the experience of thirty years of racial dialogue. It tells me that the individual (or organization) asking the question is probably not genuinely serious in his or her attempt to secure and practice information regarding Christian African Americans.

The authors of this question are usually looking for a way out. They are like those Christians who say to me, "I'm color-blind," or "I don't see color in my relationships." My response to such a statement is to tell them that's not true. Ask an individual the color of his car or his eyes and he will tell you they're blue or brown. So how come the color of someone's skin can't be assessed?

I usually engage the owner of this statement in a conversation that quickly reveals that he (or she) is not as "color-blind" as originally thought. The real issue is not the color of someone's skin, but how you treat him because of the color of his skin.

What is the wrong question? It reminds me of the question the rich young ruler asked Jesus about how to obtain eternal life. Jesus responded in Matthew 19:17–26 (NASB):

> [Jesus] said to him, "Why are you asking Me about what is good? There is only One who is good; but if you wish to enter into life, keep the commandments." Then he said to Him, "Which ones?" And Jesus said, "You shall not commit murder; You shall not commit adultery; You shall not steal; You shall not bear false wit-

ness; Honor your father and mother; and You shall love your neighbor as yourself." The young man said to Him, "All these things I have kept; what am I still lacking?" Jesus said to him, "If you wish to be complete, go and sell your possessions and give to the poor, and you will have treasure in heaven; and come, follow Me." But when the young man heard this statement, he went away grieving; for he was one who owned much property.

And Jesus said to His disciples, "Truly I say to you, it is hard for a rich man to enter the kingdom of heaven. Again I say to you, it is easier for a camel to go through the eye of a needle, than for a rich man to enter the kingdom of God." When the disciples heard this, they were very astonished and said, "Then who can be saved?" And looking at them Jesus said to them, "With people this is impossible, but with God all things are possible."

It seems the rich young ruler was asking the wrong question. He was asking, "Am I on the right track to get into heaven?" But Jesus, being Jesus, was and is in the stretching business. He was not about convenience but about a faith that requires risk and sacrifice. It is interesting that the rich young ruler knew that what he was doing was not good enough for him to gain entrance into heaven. What is frightening is that he was not willing to do what was necessary to spend eternity with Jesus. He was more than willing to rule but not willing to give up what he had and believe that Jesus could possibly give him even more.

It is easy to sit back and say that the rich young ruler was unspiritual. Yet many of us have the same response to cross-cultural relationships. Without a living, active faith in God, it will always be impossible to improve race relations even among Christians. Too many Christians have become comfortable and do not want to be stretched any more by God in any direction.

## SURPRISE, SURPRISE

When I think of the wrong question being asked so frequently these days about race, it also reminds me of the question and response in Luke 10:25–37 (NASB):

> And a lawyer stood up and put [Jesus] to the test, saying, "Teacher, what shall I do to inherit eternal life?" And He said to him, "What is written in the Law? How does it read to you?" And he answered, "You shall love the Lord your God with all your heart, and with all your soul, and with all your strength, and with all your mind; and your neighbor as yourself." And He said to him, "You have answered correctly; do this and you will live." But wishing to justify himself, he said to Jesus, "And who is my neighbor?" (vv. 25–29)

Jesus, of course, goes on to tell him the powerful parable of the Good Samaritan (vv. 30–37). The question should not have been, "*Who* is my neighbor?" but "How can I *serve* my neighbor?" Can you see the implications of this parable? The Jews hated the Samaritans and the Samaritans the Jews. Jesus was commanding the Jewish lawyer to serve everyone, even people who were not of his culture or race. And he said this at a time when Jewish tradition did not even allow Jews to walk through Samaria!

To everyone's surprise, Jesus held up the Samaritan as the model. Here the outcast of society accepted and aided his enemy. This principle is true in our society. Christian minorities are often more accepting of those in the Christian majority than those in the Christian majority are of them. In fact, like the Samaritan, Christian minorities will often go out of their way to help. They have to because they understand the pain of rejection. Not helping someone in need would make these Christian minorities just like the people they don't want to be like!

And so the wrong question many white evangelicals are asking when attempting to relate cross-culturally is this: "*How can I relate to the African American?*"

What is so wrong with this question? It seems harmless enough, but let's look at it closely. Why? Because the reality is that Christian African Americans see white America as controlling the economy and real estate, starting businesses and white parachurch ministries, even going overseas as missionaries—all without asking for any input from African Americans. But when these same white Christians go overseas as missionaries, they learn the language (many times from nationals) and the culture, study the history of the people they intend to serve, adapt to the food, and often wear the clothing of the country. Much of this is done before they ever step foot onto the mission field.

So when white evangelicals ask, "How can I relate to Christian African Americans?" Christian African Americans are shocked. We are shocked because even *asking* the question is confusing! We wonder why these same white evangelicals don't take the identical approach with African Americans here that they do with indigenous people around the world. Could it be that these same white evangelicals don't value knowing Christian African Americans as much as they do those people who have the same dark complexion but live overseas? Could it be that these same white evangelicals know that those people of a different complexion who live overseas are not coming to *their* America?

I know that question isn't a nice one. Nor is it easy to hear. But with no answers coming from the white evangelical community, inquiring minds want to know. Minds tend to wonder. With little explanation given by white evangelicals, their silence seems to say quite loudly that many white Christians don't really care about their Christian brothers and sisters who are of a different race and culture yet live right here in America.

## A WAY OUT

When white evangelicals ask this question, it looks to African Americans as though they are looking for a way out of developing a serious relationship with African-American Christians. We African-American Christians have a question of our own: "Do white evangelicals really *want* to relate?"

I believe that any white evangelicals who are *serious* about relating to African-American Christians will read the history of African Americans (written by African-American authors, Christian and non-Christian), study the culture, and understand that African Americans are more expert on themselves than whites are (later in this book, suggested readings will be given). The fact that many white evangelicals don't study African-American history and culture continues to assist in building the wall of racism between the two races. I know that your reading this book means you are doing just what I'm recommending, and I commend you. Please keep reading. There are many insightful and helpful books written by African Americans about the African-American experience and heritage, including contributions made by blacks not just to America, but to the world. Your reading books such as this one is a step toward breaking down the wall of racism. Later in this book, I'll discuss specific examples in history that will help in our understanding.

As a history major in college, I learned that historiography teaches that the more you learn about other peoples, the more you learn about yourself. So, even from a selfish perspective, all Christians should be motivated to learn about as many cultures as possible. This point makes it even more amazing that it seems few white candidates for missions work in Africa study African Americans. What a tremendous opportunity this would give them to learn about African culture by studying African Americans before going overseas to minister.

African-American Christians know that whites who are serious about developing a relationship with African-American Christians don't sit around asking *how,* but start doing *something.* They know that you can't learn how to swim if you never get into the water!

White evangelicals who are serious about cross-racial understanding will *go* (the Great Commission) where the African-American Christians are, just like the missionaries do. White missionaries have never asked the people of various countries to come to them.

How could white Christians ask people of different cultures here to come to them? But they do. How many times have I heard from white Christians, "We'd like to hire African Americans; we just don't know any. Besides, none have applied for the job." This is one of the major problems in bridging the race gap between white and black Christians.

## SERVANT VS. PATERNALISTIC ATTITUDES

Another way many white evangelicals—and here I'm speaking especially of churches, missions organizations, and parachurch ministries—miss the mark in their attempt to relate to the Christian African-American community lies in their policy of assimilation. This is the idea of absorbing the Christian African-American culture, history, and traditions into the white Christian community without the white Christian community having to make any basic adjustments.

This is not at all what the Bible has in mind. *All* cultures must make adjustments for the sake of Christ.

Matthew 9:16–17 states:

No one sews a patch of unshrunk cloth on an old garment, for the patch will pull away from the garment, making the tear worse. Neither do men pour new wine into old wineskins. If they do, the skins will burst, the wine will run out and the wineskins will be ruined. No, they pour new wine into new wineskins, and both are preserved.

Al Campanis, formerly of the Dodgers, and Jimmy the Greek, a former sports announcer for CBS television, both said that they did not believe that blacks were as intelligent as whites. Therefore, whites should not allow blacks to be placed in positions of authority or any decision-making positions. (Al Campanis and Jimmy the Greek faced the red eye of the TV camera: here pretense must be maintained. Both men were fired from their jobs. Their punishment was manifestly unfair.)[1]

I'm not sure their firing was right because they were simply expressing their own opinions and perspectives. They were fired for being honest. Yet, when you look at sports organizations in general, and blacks in decision-making positions in those organizations, you have to wonder if the administrators who fired these two men weren't hypocrites. What is sad to me is that this situation is comparable to that in the evangelical community.

Look at the lack of blacks in leadership in Christian churches and ministries that say they want to reach blacks. Look at those few blacks who are employed by those churches and organizations. Usually you will see that their budgets are significantly smaller than their white counterparts—and so with their lines of authority. You will probably not find much equality in the attention given to issues that make a difference in the Christian minority community. This is a shame, for if it made an effort, the white evangelical community could easily endear itself to the Christian minority community. So—does the evangelical community believe the same as Al Campanis and Jimmy the Greek? If you look at who is in the boardroom or at the top management levels of these organizations, you won't find many blacks in decision-making positions in the evangelical community.

Yet, doesn't 1 John 3:18 call us to love not simply with tongue or word, but with our actions and deeds as well?

## AFRICAN AMERICANS ARE NOT THE ENEMY

Let's take a hypothetical situation. Let's pretend a predominantly white Christian organization or church sincerely desires to minister to the African-American community. Someone has the idea to hire an African American to fulfill this vision. The following is a story of what usually happens:

A white Christian organization or church recruits and hires an African American named Jerome. Jerome is immediately told, "We don't know anything about your race and culture, but we want to do something. Will you please come join us and assist us in reaching your people? You will have the authority to do whatever you need to do to accomplish your goal!" Jerome can't help but be excited about this tremendous opportunity to serve the Lord and work with these unusually understanding white evangelicals.

But things seem to change once he starts to work. No contract is signed. He believes the verbal agreement is better than any contract because he is working with Christians. He begins to do what he was hired to do. He uses different approaches to reach a different race of people, and his strategies begin to be questioned with negative overtones. Without any hint of warning, the African American hears: "We don't do it that way!" The promised authority is never realized because it was never given in the first place. No matter how logical the minority's point of view as to how the actions of the organization or church will be viewed by the people he was hired to reach, his opinion is ignored. In fact, the organization or church begins to make decisions in the area of race relations without the input of the very person it hired to lead it. Meetings are actually held without Jerome being invited—he's not part of the inside planning. This attitude of controlled action reduces Jerome to a token.

What has happened? Unfortunately, the church or Christian organization has operated out of fear of change or fear of the unknown rather than out of faith that God brought Jerome to them. This fear has often become a stronger motivator than faith in God to do what has already been agreed upon.

The result of these good but shallow intentions is that Jerome now feels betrayed and hurt by people with whom he will spend eternity. He feels lonely and unsupported, a common by-product of this kind of working condition. The Christian African American discovers that he has been deceived (intentionally or unintentionally) by Christians who seemed to be more concerned with boards, constituents, trustees, and money than with God. And if Jerome doesn't quit first, he will probably be asked to leave somewhere between three to five years later. The organization may even put unwarranted charges of violation of company policy in his file because he stated his disappointment with the organization. Often, inside and outside the organization, he is asked how he is being treated by Christians (black and white) who are praying for the individual, church, or organization to be successful. If he tells the truth, he will get in trouble with the organization. If he lies, he will be in trouble with God. He may even be faced with the dilemma of taking this Christian organization or church to court because it has breached its contract or simply quietly walking away from the organization feeling like a failure, even though he tried to serve it to the best of his ability. He has to provide for his family, but the church or Christian organization may have damaged his reputation. All of this because he in good faith trusted his white Christian colleagues.

This happens all the time in the secular business world to people of all races. And unfortunately, it happens quite frequently to whites in Christian churches and/or ministries. The hurt is naturally greater when this happens in a ministry. But when this happens to blacks hired by churches or ministries that say they want to minister to blacks, the pain and ramifications are much more devastating. Correctly or incorrectly, the perception is racism.

When an African American is hired by a church or Christian organization for the purpose of assisting it in reaching the black community, it is usually for the knowledge and experience this person has in this area. Peter Drucker would identify such a person as a "knowledge" worker. Drucker describes in *The Effective Executive* how a knowledge worker should be allowed to function: "The knowledge worker cannot be supervised closely or in detail. He can only be helped. But he must direct himself, and he must direct himself toward performance and contribution, that is, toward effectiveness."[2]

If Drucker is right, then churches and ministries that desire to reach the black community by hiring a black must prepare themselves before the black ever sets foot in the institution for a different kind of working relationship. Due to the fact that this institution is attempting to do something it has never done before (or done well before), it must be willing to allow this "knowledge" worker to work in a different manner. The institution must allow time for this new approach and concentrate on the results. Thus the institution must not treat the new staff member the same as everyone else, not because of the color of the person's skin, but because of the dynamics of the task.

Drucker goes on to say, "Such a man (or woman) must make decisions; he cannot just carry out orders. He must take responsibility for his contribution. And he is supposed, by virtue of his knowledge, to be better equipped to make the right decision than anyone else. He may be overridden; he may be demoted or fired."[3] This may be where the majority of the problem is, not a personal racism (not ruling this out) so much as an institution that has not "counted the cost." Who these individuals report to will be critical. Institutions without a sacrificial mind-set are usually set up to fail—and usually do—in their attempts at cross-cultural ministry. Their negative behavior may not be intentional but may be perceived as such by blacks.

## PARTNERSHIP VS. PATERNALISM

I wish I could tell you that Jerome's story is only hypothetical, but unfortunately it is not. It has happened many times and continues to be done to many of our black Christian brothers and sisters by otherwise well-meaning, but tragically misinformed, white Christian brothers and sisters. As I have interviewed blacks in many Christian parachurch ministries, I have heard this story too often. It is all too true! An article in *Ministries Today* titled "Plain Vanilla Christianity" reveals the struggles of several African Americans in Christian parachurch ministries.[4] Somehow the mark is being missed!

What the white evangelical community needs to work toward is developing a partnership *with*—not *for*—African-American Christians. Developing such a partnership will require a radical change in thinking. That, in turn, will lead away from a mind-set of paternalism and into a powerful partnership that the world will be sure to take notice of. In other words, change *must come* in the traditional approach white Christians have taken in attempting to relate to the Christian African American.

What kind of changes in thinking? They are very simple. They are the changes in thinking that are motivated by the Holy Spirit in the hearts of humble, submissive Christians. Many white evangelicals must go beyond the rhetoric of saying that blacks and whites are equal before God to actually demonstrating it with consistent, progressive actions. This new perspective in thinking will alleviate the fears of those who are accustomed to having control by redirecting their faith where it should have always been—in God. If our faith is in God, then we will be more open to see God move in ways we have not seen Him move before. We will be more open to watching *God* be in control and not ourselves. Hebrews 11:1 says, "Faith is being sure of what we hope for and certain of what we do not see."

Building relationships with someone who is different demands faith and trust. It demands an attitude of hoping for the best. This attitude—motivated by the love of Christ through the power of the Holy Spirit—must move white evangelical leaders to attempt to understand what it is like to be a minority in the workplace or ministry where they are. It means understanding that whatever position the black has been hired for, he has multiple inherent responsibilities. One is to the job for which he or she has been hired. Another is as a bridge builder between two cultures and/or races. Another is serving as an in-house race relations consultant. Still another is exercising public relations skills: protecting the organization, often when it needs protection but doesn't realize it. Finally, he is a pioneer, taking the organization or church where it has never gone before. All of this will demand much understanding and support by the organization or the church. It will also require that the individual be part of the decision-making body of the particular organization or church.

This kind of understanding will make it easier for Christian love to be translated into action. It will affect budgets, ranges of authority, and the openness to listen to different ideas and perspectives. This attitude will also mean that people from all ethnic backgrounds will be hired in all types of positions for a variety of parachurch ministries and cross-cultural churches, not just for those that are black or minority related, or for music ministries.

Thus, if any predominantly white Christian organization or church wants to hit the mark in the area of relating to Christian African Americans, it must be willing to put these suggestions into practice by faith. And until Christians of *all* races can see one another as each other's neighbor—that is, until neighborly love is seen as an action and not a feeling—nothing is going to change dramatically. First John 3:16 says: "This is how we know what love is: Jesus Christ laid down his life for us. And we ought to lay down our lives for our brothers."

This verse challenges us as Christians to be willing to die for fellow believers. God is not asking all Christians to die for Him, but He is asking all Christians to live for Him, and thus for one another. When Christians treat each other as though they are willing to die for each other, then we will see a radical change in the relationship between Christians of different races. First John 3:18 (NASB) says: "Little children, let us not love with word or with tongue, but in deed and truth."

*Dear Father,*

*Help us to make sure that our actions match our confession. Help us not to become defensive as You may reveal areas in our lives which may not as of yet be submitted to You. Let us rely on Your Holy Spirit to produce through us actions that bring honor to Your Name.*

*Amen.*

## NOTES

1. Studs Terkel, *Race: How Blacks and Whites Think and Feel About the American Obsession* (New York: Free Press, 1992), 4.

2. Peter Drucker, *The Effective Executive* (New York: Harper Business, 1967; reprint 1993), 5.

3. Ibid., 6.

4. Jo Kadlecek, "Plain Vanilla Christianity," *Ministries Today*, November/December 1996, 34–41.

# 2

# Putting on God-Glasses

## A Biblical Perspective for Developing Cross-Cultural Relationships

*But the Lord said to Samuel, "Do not look at his appearance or at the height of his stature, because I have rejected him; for God sees not as man sees, for man looks at the outward appearance, but the Lord looks at the heart."*

—1 Samuel 16:7 (NASB)

Not long ago, I had a conversation with a white Christian friend. The topic turned toward racial issues, and as we talked, my friend suddenly stopped me and said, "Clarence, I know that racism is wrong, but I'm not sure why." I quickly got out my Bible. Together, we looked at several passages that addressed the prejudging of which racism is a product. These same passages also give us a blueprint for fostering cross-cultural relationships. As a result of our time together, my friend developed a biblical rationale for fighting racism or any form of prejudging.

Unfortunately, his situation is not uncommon. Many Christians are unaware of the rich and plentiful examples the Bible provides regarding the issues of prejudice, race, and culture. Specifically, they simply do not know or—sadly, in some cases, ignore—what God's Word says about how Christians are to treat others who might be different. Both the Old and New Testaments provide valuable insight into how we should respond to the issue of racism and to those people around us who might be different from us. The Holy Spirit convicts us that it is not right to prejudge others or to harbor racial prejudice in our hearts. Yet many Christians often cannot cite a biblical basis for this teaching.

That's why I believe it is critical to examine the Scriptures in light of this sensitive subject. Let's look at how God, Jesus, and the church responded to Christians in incidents of prejudging (sometimes even instances of prejudging other believers).

## IT CAN HAPPEN TO SPIRITUAL LEADERS TOO

A closer look at 1 Samuel 16:7 reveals that this great judge and prophet, Samuel, struggled with prejudging. Remember when God told Samuel to anoint a new king for Israel? Saul, Israel's first king, had been rejected by God because of his constant disobedience. Saul was quite the physical specimen (1 Samuel 9:2), so it might have been logical to expect that the new king would be or should be like him. Probably without intending to, Samuel got caught up in the "tradition" that all kings should be tall, dark, and handsome. Therefore, Samuel was already susceptible to perpetuating a stereotype for kings.

Yet God rejected Samuel's choice for the new king. We don't know if Samuel consulted with God for directions. It doesn't appear he did; instead, Samuel seems to have done what most of us have done at one time or another: he relied on tradition. The problem is that getting locked into tradition doesn't require faith (Matthew 15:3, 6; Mark 7:8–9, 13; Hebrews 4:2; 10:38) or thinking; nor is risk involved. Some traditions can create a false sense of security because of the control factor. And, of course, we all have a tendency to get comfortable with traditions, whether they be good or bad.

We must remember that getting to know someone's heart—as God requires—takes time. Christians' efforts to look at the hearts of people must not be stopped or limited by first impressions. It may take many more than a few casual encounters before a person can see that we are serious about wanting to get to know him. Then, and only then, will a person trust us enough to reveal his heart to us.

However, Samuel was a man of God. Therefore, he not only listened and heard God, but he also obeyed God and let go of his prejudgment. But that's not always easy, as we see in an example from Numbers 12:1: "Miriam and Aaron began to talk against Moses because of his Cushite wife, for he had married a Cushite." Moses, Miriam, and Aaron were in leadership positions in serving the Lord, yet a problem was created simply because Moses' wife was different. Possibly the difference was in skin complexion. Here, again, people who know God well are struggling with prejudging another person. The evidence is that God disapproved of this. In the case of Samuel, He intervened before a tradition in kingship was birthed. In the case of Miriam and Aaron and their intentional prejudging, God subjected them to consequences that were much more severe: He inflicted Miriam with leprosy.

In the same way, many Christians hear from God in regard to doing the "right thing" concerning prejudging and racism, but it is obvious that few act in accordance with what they have heard, thus the need for and rise of efforts like Promise Keepers and other race relationship movements. Through those movements, many men have been convicted by what they know they should have been doing all along. Hence the positive response of some Christians, particularly white Christians, to these race relations movements. The majority of minorities have not embraced these efforts yet.

An important lesson for all Christians to learn—maybe African Americans in particular—is not only forgiveness, but passionate prayer for those who prejudge them (Romans 12:14–21). I love Samuel's response to the Israelites when they disobeyed God and sought out a human king: "As for me, far be it from me that I should sin against the LORD by failing to pray for you. And I will teach you the way that is good and right" (1 Samuel 12:23). Moses also set us an example by interceding for Miriam (Numbers 12:13). This is the true measure of a mature Christian who has adopted a lifestyle that pleases God regardless of how racism has affected them.

## BRIDGE BUILDING: DOING IT JESUS' WAY

Just as the Old Testament lays a firm foundation for guiding us, so too does the New Testament. Perhaps the best biblical model for developing cross-cultural relationships is the encounter between Jesus Christ and the Samaritan woman found in John 4. In order to understand the racial dynamics of this encounter, let's look at the history of the relationship between the Jews and the Samaritans (who were half-Jews).

To begin to understand this relationship between the two groups, one must go back to the reign of Solomon. In 1 Kings 9:4–7 Solomon is told by the Lord that if he and his sons will walk in integrity, his throne would be established forever, but if he and his sons turned away from God, God would cut Israel off from the land. God had said that kings were not to intermarry with pagan worshipers, not to acquire a great number of horses or much silver or gold, and not to enslave their people (Deuteronomy 17:14–20; 24:7). Solomon violated all of these commands. So God informed Solomon (1 Kings 11:1–13) that He would tear the kingdom away from him, but not during his lifetime, for David his father's sake.

God was true to His word and took away the kingdom during the reign of Solomon's son Rehoboam. The kingdom was divided, with the tribes of Judah and Benjamin comprising the southern kingdom and the remaining tribes becoming the northern kingdom. The northern kingdom, which is sometimes called Israel or Samaria, was taken into captivity by Assyria in 722/721 B.C. The southern kingdom, which is sometimes called Judah, was taken into captivity by Babylon in 587/586 B.C.

After the fall of Samaria, those who were old and not of royalty who were left behind comprised the majority of the Samaritan population. (A thorough review of Assyrian records reveals their deportations were usually limited to the noble families.) After this deportation, "the king of Assyria brought people from Babylon, Cuthah, Avva, Hamath and Sepharvaim and settled them in the towns of Samaria to replace the Israelites" (2 Kings 17:24). These people did not worship the Lord, so He "sent lions among them" (v. 25). The king of Assyria sent a priest to teach the people to serve the Lord God. Eventually, however, though these people "worshiped the LORD," they "also served their own gods in accordance with the customs of the nations from which they had been brought" (v. 33). The Jews who were left behind in the deportation began to worship those gods and intermarry with those who did not worship the Lord.

As a result, intense hatred between the Jews and Samaritans developed. After the Jews were released from Babylon after seventy years of captivity, the Samaritans, described in Ezra 4:1 as "enemies of Judah and Benjamin," heard that the Jews were rebuilding the temple and asked if they could help (v. 2).The Samaritans were refused in no uncertain terms (v. 3). This response created a schism between the Jews and the Samaritans that remained through New Testament times.

In John 4, Jesus Christ makes an intentional journey through Samaria. Verse 4 of the chapter states that Jesus "had" to go through Samaria. Jesus had to go, not just because of a geographic need but mostly because of His greater mission to meet the woman at the well. Samaria did lie between Judea in the south and Galilee in the north. Thus a man who desired to go from Judea to Galilee directly would necessarily pass through Samaria, unless he opted for the long detour through the Transjordan, which had a largely Gentile population. We must understand that Jews were more than ready to make the long detour because of the schism between the Jews and the Samaritans.

We should also understand that a "good" Jew would not have anything to do with a Samaritan, just as a "good" Samaritan would have nothing to do with a Jew. Jewish traditional law forbade Jews to go through the land of Samaria. This is similar to what happened in Acts 11:2–3: "So when Peter went up to Jerusalem, the circumcised believers criticized him and said, 'You went into the house of uncircumcised men and ate with them.'" Here the Jews criticized Peter for even going into the house of Cornelius, a Gentile. To do so broke a Jewish traditional law. Not breaking traditional law was more important to the Jews than the fact that Cornelius had become a fellow believer. Jewish traditional law also said Samaritan women were always ceremonially unclean. (It seems to me that some evangelicals have the same problem.)

Jesus Christ had to break traditional laws of His race and culture in order to develop a cross-cultural relationship with the Samaritan woman. Jesus had to be willing to face rejection or at least questioning of His actions by His disciples, His own race.

It is unfortunate, but many Christians are not willing to reach out to people of a different race or culture if it might mean risking possible rejection or questioning by their own race, even though the Great Commission (Matthew 28:19–20) says to "go." What don't we Christians understand about "go"—the g or the o?

## FOLLOWING JESUS' STEPS

Let's look and see exactly what Jesus Christ does in order to develop a cross-cultural relationship with the Samaritan woman:

The first step Jesus takes is to break a traditional law (which had become greater than Scripture for the "religious right") by traveling into the country of Samaria. Second, Jesus goes to where the Samaritan woman lives. This is the Great Commission in action. Third, He meets her on her own turf (the well), knowing that she would feel more comfortable in those surroundings. Jesus also puts Himself on *her* time schedule, and not her on His schedule. Too many Christians today only want to minister to people if everything is on their own schedule and turf. Faith and risk are not on their agenda. The other person's concerns and needs are not an issue. Fourth, Jesus breaks another traditional law by actually speaking with a Samaritan woman, someone viewed by Jews as ceremonially "unclean."

Jesus sees her eternal future as worth the risk of being ostracized by His own race. We Christians today must be willing to risk the same type of rejection in order to build solid cross-cultural relationships.

Fifth, Jesus makes Himself vulnerable to the Samaritan woman by asking her for help. By asking for water, Jesus was meeting her "where she was." Her concerns and needs became His. Jesus' approach shows He was being observant. Too often, when we attempt to witness we are so focused on looking for an opportunity to turn the conversation to the point where we can share the Gospel that we aren't really listening to the person we desire to witness to or observing what is important to him or her.

By making Himself vulnerable to the Samaritan woman, Jesus provides her with the option of rejecting Him. Jesus gives a "rejected" woman a position of power in their relationship, something she may never have experienced before. This power is also an extremely high form of respect. To any oppressed or rejected person or people, respect is critical in developing a relationship of trust. Jesus empowers the Samaritan woman by allowing her to be in control of their situation.

This empowerment was a sign of equality as well as dignity. It was a radical act even for a godly man in His day, when women were viewed as little more than slaves. A woman's greatest asset during this period was her ability to produce a male heir. If a woman was pregnant and near her due date, the entire village would come and wait for the baby to be born. If the baby was a boy, the village celebrated the birth for three weeks. If it was a girl, everyone went home, and there was no celebration.

Sixth, Jesus demonstrates He has "staying power" because her initial rejection did not run Him away. Rejection is usually the first defense mechanism of an oppressed or frequently rejected people. This initial rejection is to protect the oppressed person from any more hurt. Today this initial rejection is also designed to evaluate the mental toughness of those who are coming into the black community. The ability to survive is what will earn respect and provide opportunities to develop relationships and thus minister. John 4:6–7 states: "Jacob's well was there, and Jesus, tired as he was from the journey, sat down by the well. It was about the sixth hour [12:00 noon]. When a Samaritan woman came to draw water, Jesus said to her, 'Will you give me a drink?'"

These verses show that she was rejected by the women of her town. She was drawing water at noon, which is the hottest part of the day. Usually, women drew water when it was cool, at the end of the day. Verses 17 and 18 of the chapter say: "'I have no husband,' she replied. Jesus said to her, 'You are right when you say you have no husband. The fact is, you have had five husbands, and the man you now have is not your husband. What you have just said is quite true.'" These verses demonstrate that she had been rejected numerous times by the men in her life.

Many white evangelicals say that they have made attempts to develop relationships with black Christians only to have their offers of friendship politely rejected. When these well-meaning white Christians ask me why, I remind them of (or in some cases, educate them about) the history of white evangelicals with black Christians. The relationship is similar to the relationship between the Native Americans and the U.S. government and its treaties. Few, if any, of more than three hundred treaties made in good faith between Native Americans and the U.S. government have been kept.

The track record of white evangelicals with black Christians is very similar. Therefore, white evangelicals should not be surprised by initial rejection. They must earn the right to be trusted by black Christians. But many white Christians refuse to put themselves in a relationship where they are not in control (no faith—Hebrews 11:6), which disallows God the opportunity to do His supernatural work.

Let's summarize the parallels between the interaction of Jesus and the Samaritan woman and the interaction of white and black Christians. First, Jesus relates to her on her terms (water is what she is concerned about right now!). White evangelicals need to become concerned about the issues that are important to black Christians, as well as attempt to see things from their perspective.

To fail to become concerned about issues important to blacks is to say very loudly and clearly that black Christians aren't important to evangelicals. It is to fail to understand 1 Corinthians 12:14–26. Let's look at verses 25 and 26 of that chapter, which state: "So that there should be no division in the body, but that its parts should have equal concern for each other. If one part suffers, every part suffers with it; if one part is honored, every part rejoices with it." To fail to do so is also to fail to understand 1 John 4:19–21 (with special emphasis on verse 20).

> We love because he first loved us. *If anyone says, "I love God," yet hates his brother, he is a liar. For anyone who does not love his brother, whom he has seen, cannot love God, whom he has not seen.* And he has given us this command: Whoever loves God must also love his brother.

Jesus sees and explains the "big picture" to the Samaritan woman. He doesn't condemn or condescend to her in John 4:17. He wants worshipers who can see beyond skin color, as in verse 24. He doesn't talk about "racial reconciliation" here, but about believers who can worship in spirit and in truth!

## CHANGING LIVES

The Bible teaches against prejudiced Christians (Aaron, Miriam, Peter, Jews and Gentiles). Why did Jesus treat the Samaritan woman with respect and equality? He had to. It was His nature.

An encounter with Jesus is life changing! It should not matter whether it is cross-cultural or cross-racial. The key isn't the color of someone's skin but "Can I trust you with my life?"

The Samaritan woman is used by Jesus Christ to improve race relations at the risk of suffering possible rejection. The Bible tells us that the people of her community followed her because she went to them and they could see the change in her. She demonstrated genuine love for them even though they had previously rejected her.

Changing lives is what fuels Jesus Christ (vv. 31–35). But what has happened to Christians, the parachurch ministries, and many churches today? Evangelism no longer seems to be a priority for the church and parachurch ministries in America, and changing lives no longer seems to drive the majority of Christians.

The Samaritans evaluated Jesus' motives (as they should have). Jesus had to earn the right to minister to them. This is a biblical principle many white evangelicals are either not aware of or have simply ignored. Jesus earned the right to speak by going where the Samaritans were, treating them with respect, not condescending to them, being consistent, and being sincere.

The reason few evangelicals do this in cross-cultural situations seems to be fear coupled with a lack of faith. In contrast, 1 John 4:18 says, "Perfect love drives out fear, because fear has to do with punishment."

## THE TRUTH ABOUT THE NEW TESTAMENT CHURCH, RACE, AND GRACE

We have seen how God and Jesus Christ responded to prejudging. Now let's see how the New Testament church dealt with prejudging.

Acts 10 describes a watershed event for the New Testament church. Up to that point, Jews did not accept Gentiles as equals, let alone as fellow believers.

*Preparation for the Mixing of Two Cultures*

In Acts 10, Cornelius, a Gentile, is seeking God. He is a God-fearer, which doesn't mean that he was a Christian but that he was monotheistic (believed in one God). In Acts 2:5, there are God-fearing Jews. After Peter preached, three thousand of these God-fearing Jews accepted Jesus Christ as their Lord and Savior. Therefore, the term *God-fearing* doesn't necessarily mean Christian. Just because you are in church doesn't mean the church is in you!

### It Is Hard to Change What Has Been Ingrained

In Acts 10:9–16, Peter goes up to the roof to pray. While he is praying, he becomes hungry. God deals with what is on people's minds. Therefore, God gives Peter a vision that relates to food. The vision is to let Peter know that now Gentiles can become Christians. Peter, being Peter, takes a little convincing. It is hard to change the way we have been trained! Of course, it is not our initial response but the end result with which God is most concerned (see God's dealings with Sarah and Abraham). God doesn't quit. He repeats the event three times (v. 16).

### Your Relationship with God Will Reveal Your Heart

What is exciting is to see how Peter changes and accepts the Gentiles (vv. 19–23). He goes to Cornelius's home and explains to him what the Gospel message is (vv. 39–41). Then he tells Cornelius how to become a Christian (v. 43). The Jewish believers who had gone with Peter to Cornelius's home are "astonished" (shocked, freaked out, minds were blown) that the gift of the Holy Spirit had been given "even" to the Gentiles (v. 45).

### Breaking Down Racial Barriers Won't Necessarily Make You a Hero with Christians

One would think that any group of Christians would be excited to hear that unbelievers have now accepted Jesus Christ as their Lord and Savior. Reading Acts 11:1–3 may surprise you. When the rest of the apostles (leaders of the church) and other Jews hear that Peter has led Cornelius and other Gentiles to salvation in Christ, they criticize Peter for his actions instead of rejoicing with him. In response, Peter quotes the Lord and explains that he had to be obedient to God (11:15–18). After all of the objections of the Jews are answered, they praise God that now God has granted the Gentiles repentance unto life. Be ready for rejection by Christians when you begin to cross racial barriers. Dr. T. B. Maston, former professor of Christian ethics at Southwestern Seminary, wrote a book, *Bible and*

*Race,*[1] published in 1959, that said that blacks and whites were equal. Dr. Maston told me he received quite a lot of hate mail from white Christians on account of what he said.

## THE RACIAL STRUGGLE OF THE NEW TESTAMENT CHURCH

The Jews were now willing to accept Gentiles as Christians if the Gentiles would add Jewish tradition to their salvation (15:1). The Council of Jerusalem intervened so that Gentiles could accept Christ without all of the Jewish baggage (vv. 23–29). The key was the leadership of James the brother of Jesus, who was viewed as the chief leader of the church. In order to improve race relations among Christians, key white leaders must make sure it happens from the top down. Excuses such as "I don't know anything about blacks" are no longer acceptable. Make time to read and learn.

This is one of the complaints of minorities who work in predominantly white churches or ministries. Just like the Gentiles in the previous paragraph, minorities feel pressured to reject their own culture and assimilate into the predominant culture. Time has not changed the tendency of some Christians to want everyone to be just like them.

## WHICH WILL YOU CHOOSE: CHRIST OR CULTURE?

The church in Rome was *cross-cultural,* as were many of the New Testament churches. The church at Rome was predominantly Gentile, with a Jewish minority.

The term *cross-cultural* is preferred as opposed to the term *multicultural. Multicultural* simply means that several different cultures or races are present together, but it does not imply any interaction —which is often the case. Thus no learning is exchanged by those present. One culture runs the show. *Cross-cultural* implies interaction from all and thus learning from all the cultures or races that are present.

One of the problems the church in Rome struggled with was Jews refusing to give up their observance of certain requirements of the law. The issues of contention in Romans 14 were observance of dietary restrictions and special days (vv. 1–6).

What did God lead Paul to tell the church in Rome about these issues? At the outset, Paul told the church at Rome not to condemn one another over debatable issues (v. 1). Then he informed the believers about those things that *do* have a positive impact on others: "For the kingdom of God is not a matter of eating and drinking, but of righteousness, peace and joy in the Holy Spirit, because anyone who serves Christ in this way is pleasing to God and approved by men" (vv. 17–18).

The heart of the matter is that members of the church should not cause fellow believers to fall by placing a stumbling block in their path (vv. 7–8; 13–16; 19–21). Rather, on debatable issues over matters of tradition, where doctrine is not at stake, believers should "make every effort to do what leads to peace and to mutual edification. . . . So whatever you believe about these [debatable] things keep between yourself and God" (vv. 19, 22).

We must try to put ourselves in the place of these Jewish believers. Remember the story of Daniel and his fellow captives, who were blessed by God as they ate according to the dietary commands given by God Himself? The Jewish believers in the church had been taught from childhood about this event. Paul was now saying that all the things that Mom and Dad and Grandma and Granddad had taught them in regard to what they ate were no longer valid. Moreover, he was saying that this part of their history was a detriment to the other believers in the church, who were Gentiles. This instruction had to be a shock to the Jews.

We must also understand that Mom, Dad, Grandma, and Granddad may all have been still very much alive. They might not have been Christians, or they may have been believers but still practicing Old Testament dietary laws. To reject those dietary regulations could be viewed by the family as a rejection of *them*. Some of the families may even have seen the rejection of the dietary laws as choosing Gentiles over them, which would be the ultimate rejection. Think about the possible hurt that would accompany such rejection. Much more was at risk than simply "not eating your vegetables."

The Jewish Christians in the church at Rome had to choose between their culture and past (much of which had been part of their religion, honored by God, for God chose the Jews) and Jesus Christ.

Jesus Christ's incarnation, sinless life, death, burial, and resurrection made things God honored in the past no longer necessary. Jewish believers no longer needed to follow the Old Testament sacrificial law, go to the temple for worship, or have an earthly high priest, for Christ was the eternal High Priest. It is often difficult for us to separate our culture and Christianity.

Let's bring this Christ and culture question home to "where we live." Suppose you teach your children all their lives that God is love and that we are to love all people. Then your children become Christians. They remember your teaching, which affects the way they treat people. In high school, college, or on the job, one of them is attracted to someone of the opposite sex. Your only question as a loving Christian parent is: "Is the person a Christian?" Your child answers "Yes."

Eventually, your child begins to date this person seriously. It is at this point that you discover your child's significant other is of a different culture or race. All of a sudden, you are more concerned about the past and future of our race, rather than seeking to determine if this new "Christian" couple is in God's will. *What will people say? What will the rest of the family say?* This was actually a problem in a church with which I was asked to consult. The church was what I would call a multicultural church, not a cross-cultural one.

Here again, as Christians we may find ourselves in situations where we must choose Christ over our culture. If this situation arises, we will have to take a stand against our very own culture. Needless to say, this will not make us popular with our culture or race. One of the results of this kind of stand will be loneliness due to rejection.

Of course, more important than favor with man is favor with God (Psalm 118:8–9). Standing with God produces the peace of God (Galatians 5:22–23; Philippians 4:6–7). Making this stand does not mean that we are rejecting our past or are ashamed of it. In many cases, we should be proud of our past and relatives. The issue is living in the present. It means understanding that the past, no matter how great it may have been, cannot be allowed to override our present life as a Christian in a way that doesn't honor Christ.

Therefore, if you are serious about improving race relations among Christians in America, this effort will cost you. Are you willing to pay the price? Has your relationship with God reached the point where you can live without the praise of men? Are you willing to have the new friends God will give you who will be of a different culture or race?

Please understand that this call is not limited to white Christians. They may have the most work to do at this point in time, simply because of the dynamics of belonging to the majority race in America, but God is also looking for African Americans, Asians, Hispanics, Native Americans—for all Christians of any culture or race—to make this stand.

This partnership will produce a "new man," referred to in Ephesians 2:15. This new man will require all of us to willingly lose some of our racial identity for Christ's sake, even though America is the "melting pot" where nobody wants to melt.

Can God count on you? Are you ready for your faith to be stretched?

If the answer is yes, then reading the rest of this book may reveal areas that may require prayer to determine how God wants to use you to make a difference. Soul-searching will take place on this journey.

Remember 1 John 4:20–21:

If anyone says, "I love God," yet hates his brother, he is a liar. For anyone who does not love his brother, whom he has seen, cannot love God, whom he has not seen. And he has given us this command: Whoever loves God must also love his brother.

## PRACTICING WHAT HE PREACHES

Last fall, I had lunch with a fellow faculty member, Dr. Jay Butler of New Geneva Theological Seminary in Colorado Springs. The purpose of this lunch was just to get to know each other. We discovered that we had a mutual friend in Dr. Malcolm Newton, then a professor at Denver Seminary. Jay began to tell how Malcolm had impacted his life.

Jay described himself as a white, middle-class male in his forties. He wanted to give me some biographical information about himself in order for me to have a better understanding of what he was about to say. He grew up in a predominantly white, middle-class environment in the southwestern part of the United States. He attended public schools, which were racially mixed—whites were the minority. Jay's parents taught him to consider all people equal and treat them with respect.

The conversation became a little more serious when Jay said, "I never considered myself to be racist in any sense of the word. As an adult, I was offended when lumped into any group that was characterized as racist." Jay believes there are many people in this country with a background similar to his.

I didn't know what to expect next. Jay confessed, "Less than a year ago, God began to open my eyes to a perspective on race relations I had never had. It was as though He took scales from my eyes."

He said the first scale that dropped for him was a huge one. He had served as chief operating officer of a Christian ministry, where he was responsible for all employment policies and hiring practices. He thought he had always tried to be color-blind, not discriminating for or against any individual because of the color of his skin or ethnic background. One day, while he was reading his organization's ministry statement, the fact that his staff was overwhelmingly white and middle-class and that a majority of the people his organization actually ministered to were also white and middle-class suddenly caught his attention as never before. Jay said, "I realized that the overwhelming majority of people God had *called* us to minister to were *not white*. For the first time, I made the connection that we could never fulfill our mission with the current racial complexion of our staff [and board]." Jay knew that he had to become intentional in recruiting minority staff members or the organization could not fulfill its mission.

It was not long after that revelation that Jay attended a seminar on racial reconciliation. To Jay's amazement, one of the panel members, Dr. Malcolm Newton, said that everyone in the audience was in some way racist. This angered Jay tremendously. (What impresses me about Jay is that he talked to this panelist after the program. Many Christians, when angered, do not do the biblical thing and confront the person, but go away mad and often gossip about the situation. This adds fuel to the fire, especially in the area of racial prejudice.)

Jay and Malcolm agreed to meet to talk again. That was another turning point in Jay's life in his understanding of racial issues. Jay said, "God made me realize that I needed to see life through Malcolm's eyes, and that I could only do that by listening—not judging. Whether I *agreed* with his perspective was actually irrelevant. I simply needed to *understand* his perspective. In doing that, I was slowly able to see things through his eyes, and I realized the world looked very different from that perspective."

Jay also said something I will never forget. It is something I believe many white evangelicals struggle with. Jay's statement may give them some freedom from this struggle. Here is what he said: "I realized that although I had never actively been racist, neither had I ever actively done anything to change racism that did exist. It never bothered me when I attended conferences, meetings, seminars, schools that were all white. I never asked, 'Why are there no (or few) minorities here? Should I try to do something about it?' It never bothered me that most of the positive stories in history and other textbooks were white and that minorities were frequently characterized in negative ways. It never bothered me that the few minorities who worked with me were almost never in real decision-making positions where they could have an influence on the perspective and direction of the organization."

*Wow!* So often, when whites hear about the pain of slavery or present injustices, their response goes like this: "I didn't own slaves and I didn't make this present system." Jay's statement wipes away all excuses and forces all of us to examine ourselves to see what we have done or are doing proactively to make things better. Everyone has a responsibility!

Jay realized his passive response to clear injustices was really "passive racism" (Jay's term). He went on to say, "In that moment, I realized I, too, had to stand up and confess to being racist. Not because it was the 'in' thing to do in some circles, but because it was true. I also realized that if I was going to change, I would have to become intentional about it. I had to seek out and work to develop relationships with people of color. I had to listen to how our culture appeared to them. I had to work hard to attract minorities to our ministry—to executive and decision-making positions. I had to stand up and say something when I was in any environment that was even passively racist."

This is now Jay's commitment. He says he still has a lot to learn about things he has only recently realized were important. His prayer from here on is that his life and ministry will be characterized as one that actively works toward healing the wounds that have separated blacks and whites and other minorities.

It is quite evident God has touched Jay's heart. Jay's testimony has been used by God to touch *our* hearts. God has given Jay tremendous insight for improving race relations. It all started when Jay had the courage to reexamine what he and his organization were doing in their employment practices and to seek out counsel about racism and recognize the sin of racism in his own heart. In turn, Malcolm had the faith to challenge his audience regarding racism and later to speak directly with Jay and explain what he was doing that made him guilty of the sin of racism (Matthew 18:15). Instead of walking away angry and possibly stereotyping a race when he first heard Malcolm, Jay made a friend. God touched his life and made it shine brighter by providing him with a more biblical perspective on culture and race. God is using Jay to touch other lives. The result is that Jay is richer and freer now than he has ever been in his life.

> *Dear Lord,*
>
> *Help all of us who struggle with prejudice and some of us who don't know it, or don't want to admit it, to become free of the shackles of racism, which keep us from getting closer to You and each other within the body of Christ and the struggling society which surrounds us.*
>
> *Amen.*

## NOTE

1. T. B. Maston, *Bible and Race* (Nashville: Broadman, 1959).

# 3

# Did You Know This History?

## How a More Accurate Understanding of History May Change Present Misconceptions

*The more you learn about other cultures and races, the more you learn about yourself.*

—Dr. Voskil, Covenant
College Historiography 101

In the first chapter of this book we talked about missing the mark in relating to African Americans. One of the first steps to take in hitting the mark with African Americans is to study African-American history. My hope is that this chapter will give the reader a better understanding of African-American culture, history, and perspectives.

History is selective. People write about the history important to them. In America, the majority of people are of European descent, and so historians have written primarily from a European perspective. This is simply a dynamic of the majority/minority system. Unfortunately, in such a system much of the history of minorities is often omitted. This chapter will introduce to some and refresh for others the contributions African Americans have made to Christianity and to America.

# WINNING THE RACE TO UNITY

## AFRICAN-AMERICAN CONTRIBUTIONS TO CHRISTIANITY

*Missionaries and Pastors*

God has used Christian African Americans to assist Him in kingdom building. As I have met missionaries from time to time, most of the white ones express concern that so few African Americans participate in missions today. The following paragraphs reveal the leadership role African ex-slaves and African Americans played in foreign missions and provide insight into the factors that have resulted in African Americans not being as involved in foreign missions as they once were.

- In 1773, Rev. George Liele became one of the first American missionaries overseas. Rev. Liele, a freed slave and Baptist pastor, joined a British merchant going to Jamaica. In 1784, Liele planted the first Baptist church in that country. He planted a church of three thousand and founded the Jamaican missionary society.[1]

- In 1782, David George pastored the first black Baptist church in America. He also preached in Nova Scotia. In 1792, Rev. George was recruited to settle in Sierra Leone and organize a Baptist church.[2]

- Betsy Stockton was the first American single person to travel overseas as a missionary. She went to Liberia. Originally, she was a slave of Dr. Green, then president of Princeton University, which was at the time a strong Christian college.

- Peter Claver entered the Jesuit Novitiate at Tarragona. He took his final vows in 1604. In 1610, he landed at Cartagena (modern Colombia), the principal slave market of the New World, where a thousand slaves were landed every month. After his ordination in 1616, he dedicated himself by special vow to the service of Negro slaves—a work that was to last thirty-three years. He baptized more than three hundred thousand slaves. He prevailed on their masters to treat them kindly.[3]

80

- In 1735, Christian Protten, a black from Denmark, went to the Gold Coast (Ghana) and teamed up with Gold Coast missionary Phillip Quaquoe, who became the primary missionary to his own people. He started schools that are still functioning today.

- In 1807, Paul Cuffee, a successful Quaker shipowner of African-American and Native-American ancestry, advocated settling freed American slaves in Africa. He gained support from the British government, free black leaders in the United States, and members of Congress for a plan to take emigrants to the British colony of Sierra Leone. Cuffee intended to make one voyage a year, taking settlers to Africa and bringing back valuable cargoes. In 1816, at his own expense, Captain Cuffee took thirty-eight American blacks to Freetown, Sierra Leone, but his death in 1817 ended further ventures.[4]

- In 1807, Lott Carey bought his freedom and pastored a church of more than eight hundred in Richmond, Virginia. In 1815, Rev. Carey helped to organize the Richmond African Baptist Missionary Society. Carey and Rev. Colin Teague sailed for Sierra Leone. Arriving in 1821, they were the first U.S. missionaries to that country. In 1822, the Missionary Society sponsored Carey and twenty-eight other colonists on a journey to Liberia.[5]

- In 1815, John Steward, of the Sandusky, Ohio, area, preached and served as a missionary to the Wyandott Native American Indians through a black interpreter.

- In 1821, Richard Allen—teacher, pastor, and doctor—went to Liberia as a missionary and founded a church.

- Bishop William Paul Quinn, born in Calcutta, India, of black and Hindu parentage, planted forty-seven churches among the slaves in the central valley of the Mississippi. In 1816, he was present at the organization of the African Methodist Episcopal Church. He pastored in New Jersey, Pennsylvania, and

Illinois. When he submitted his report on the forty-seven churches he established, the General Conference at Pittsburgh, Pennsylvania, elected him a bishop on May 19, 1844. He became senior bishop on May 9, 1849.[6]

- In 1831, many black ministers who preached a missionary vision for Africa were trained as ship captains so that they could take the Gospel not just to Africa, but all over the world.

- In 1843, Sojouner Truth left New York and began abolitionist work. She was one of the first black women abolitionist lecturers.[7]

- In 1847, Theodore Wright entered Princeton Theological Seminary. He was the first black graduate of a theological seminary.

- In 1890, William Henry Shepard went to the Congo with medical aid. He became the first black leader of the African Presbyterian Mission.

- In 1882, six black missionaries started a business in West Africa that flourished so much in six months that they were able to use their profits to support other missionaries.

- Samuel Adjai Crowther was born in a West African village. He was captured and sold as a slave and later dramatically rescued. He became a Christian and founded many mission stations. He translated the Bible into Yoruba and became the first black Anglican bishop. He also served as a missionary to Niger. He said, "The time has come for Niger."[8]

- Montrose Waite Crover continued in missions abroad when blacks were not allowed to go on missions anymore by colonial governments.

There were many other black missionaries to Africa. Here are just a few of them: Alexander Crummell, Kelly Kemp, Nancy Jones, F. M. Allan, Sarah Gorah, Lulu Fleming, Edward Wilmot, J. J. Fuller, Joe Bryan, and Emma Delany.

Black missionaries did not go just to Africa. They went to Asia, South America, Russia, India, Burma, Thailand, and China. In 1951, Darius Swann went to China. He said, "The Negro distress has prepared [me] to witness to the hurting world."

### Decline of Blacks in Missions

The decline in blacks participating in foreign missions took place for four reasons. (1) Colonial governments in Africa and Asia prevented black missionaries from entering their territories. (2) Beginning in the 1850s, white mission agencies refused black candidates to their mission organizations. (3) Blacks faced segregation in American society and were often the victims of terrorism, sometimes at the hand of organized groups, such as the Ku Klux Klan, sometimes at the hand of ad hoc groups with a particular agenda. (4) Crop failure on plantations in some post–Civil War years made the black community focus on itself for survival. Plantation owners and sharecrop owners threatened blacks if a certain amount of crops were not produced. All of this resistance to blacks caused them to concentrate their energies on dealing with their own situation in America just to survive.

## AFRICAN CONTRIBUTIONS TO CHRISTIANITY

Some of the early church Fathers, such as Augustine, who greatly influenced John Calvin, and Tertullian, Origen, and Athanasius, were from Africa. These church leaders were our African brothers. Without them, we would be struggling theologically today.[9]

## AFRICAN-AMERICAN CONTRIBUTIONS TO AMERICA

### African-American Inventors

African Americans have made numerous significant inventions that benefit all Americans. Table 3.1 lists just a few of those inventions. One African American, Otis F. Boykin, was granted more than twenty-six patents, some of which are listed in table 3.2. Henry Blair was the first black inventor in America to be patented, those patents coming for his revolutionary corn-planting (1834) and cotton-planting (1836) machines. Some other early patent-holding blacks are listed in table 3.3. Black history is being made every day.

## Table 3.1
### INVENTIONS BY AFRICAN AMERICANS AND AFRICANS

| PRODUCT | INVENTOR | DATE |
| --- | --- | --- |
| air conditioning | Frederick M. Jones | July 12, 1949 |
| almanac | Benjamin Banneker | approx. 1791 |
| auto cutoff switch | Granville T. Woods | January 1, 1839 |
| auto fishing device | G. Cook | May 30, 1899 |
| automatic gear shift | Richard Spikes | February 28, 1932 |
| baby buggy | W. H. Richardson | June 18, 1899 |
| bicycle frame | L. R. Johnson | October 10, 1899 |
| biscuit cutter | A. P. Ashbourne | November 30, 1875 |
| blood plasma | Charles Drew | |
| blood plasma bag | Charles Drew | approx. 1945 |
| cellular phone | Henry T. Sampson | July 6, 1971 |
| chess | Egypt, India, Persia, Iraq, France, Spain | |
| clothes dryer | G. T. Sampson | June 6, 1862 |
| disposable syringe | Phil Brooks | |
| dust pan | Lawrence P. Ray | August 3, 1897 |
| egg beater | Willie Johnson | February 5, 1884 |
| electric lamp bulb | Lewis Latimer | March 21, 1882 |
| elevator | Alexander Miles | October 11, 1867 |
| eye protector | P. Johnson | November 2, 1880 |
| fire escape ladder | J. W. Winters | May 7, 1878 |
| fire extinguisher | T. Marshall | October 26, 1872 |
| fireplace damper | Virgie M. Ammons | September 30, 1975 (U.S. patent 3,908,633) |
| folding bed | L. C. Bailey | July 18, 1899 |
| folding chair | Brody and Surgwar | June 11, 1889 |
| fountain pen | W. B. Purvis | January 7, 1890 |
| gas mask | Garrett Morgan | October 13, 1914 |
| golf tee | T. Grant | December 12, 1899 |

| | | |
|---|---|---|
| guided missile | Otis Boykin | |
| hand stamp | Walter B. Purvis | February 27, 1883 |
| heating furnace | Alice H. Parker | December 23, 1919 |
| | | (U.S. patent 1,325,905) |
| ice cream scooper | A. L. Cralle | February 2, 1897 |
| improved sugar making | Robert Rillieux | December 10, 1846 |
| insect-destroyer gun | A. C. Richard | February 26, 1899 |
| ironing board | Sarah Boone | December 30, 1887 |
| lawn mower | L. A. Burr | May 19, 1889 |
| lawn sprinkler | J. W. Smith | May 4, 1897 |
| lemon squeezer | J. Thomas White | December 8, 1893 |
| lunch pail | James Robinson | 1887 |
| mailbox | Paul L. Downing | October 27, 1891 |
| paper (papyrus) | Africans | |
| peanut butter | George Washington Carver | 1896 |
| pencil sharpener | J. L. Love | November 23, 1897 |
| photo print wash | Clatonia J. Dorticus | April 16, 1895 |
| | | (U.S. patent 537, 442) |
| programmable remote control | Joseph N. Jackson | |
| record player arm | Joseph Hunger Dickenson | January 8, 1819 |
| refrigerator | J. Standard | June 14, 1895 |
| rolling pin | John W. Reed | 1864 |
| rotary engine | Andrew J. Beard | July 5, 1892 |
| | | (U.S. patent 478,271) |
| spark plug | Edmond Berger | February 2, 1839 |
| stethoscope | Imhotep | Ancient Egypt |
| stove | T. A. Carrington | July 25, 1876 |
| straightening comb | Madam C. J. Walker | approx. 1905 |
| street sweeper | Charles B. Brooks | March 17, 1890 |
| telephone transmitter | Granville T. Woods | December 2, 1884 |
| thermostat control | Frederick M. Jones | February 23, 1960 |
| traffic light | Garrett Morgan | November 20, 1923 |
| tricycle | M. A. Cherry | May 6, 1886 |
| typewriter | Burridge and Marshman | April 7, 1885 |

SOURCE: *An African-American Bibliography, New York State Library*

*Series (The University of the State of New York: The State Education Department, The New York State Library: Albany, New York, 12230), January 1991.*

## Table 3.2
### PARTIAL LIST OF PATENTS ATTRIBUTED TO OTIS F. BOYKIN

| PATENT # | INVENTION | DATE |
| --- | --- | --- |
| U.S. 2,891,227 | wire type precision resistor | June 16, 1959 |
| U.S. 2,972,726 | electrical resistor | February 21, 1961 |
| U.S. 4,267,074 | self-supporting electrical resistor composed of glass, refractory materials, and noble metal oxide | May 12, 1981 |

SOURCES: *U.S. Department of Energy (Washington, D.C.: Office of Public Affairs), 1979, p. 20, and Louisiana State University Libraries, Chemistry Library, Baton Rouge, Louisiana, 1996.*

## Table 3.3
### PARTIAL LIST OF PATENTS ISSUED TO BLACKS IN THE 1800'S

| INVENTOR | INVENTION | DATE |
| --- | --- | --- |
| J. Hawkins | metal oven rack | 1845 |
| J. Lee | dough-kneading machine | 1894 |
| T. Elkins and J. Standard | improved refrigerators | 1879, 1891 |
| S. R. Scotton | curtain rod | 1892 |
| J. L. Love | crank handle pencil sharpener | 1897 |
| H. H. Reynolds | drawbridge safety gates | 1890 |
| H. Grenon | razor strop | 1896 |
| A. L. Rickman | rubber overshoes | 1898 |
| Jones and Long | bottle cap | 1898 |

SOURCES: *James Williams, "At Last, Recognition in America" (Vol. 1, Chicago, 1978); Augustus Low and Virgil A. Clift, Encyclopedia of Black*

*America (New York, 1981), pp. 1102–14. An African-American Bibliography, New York State Library Series (The University of the State of New York: The State Education Department, The New York State Library: Albany, New York, 12230), February 1991.*

## The Revolutionary War

Many people know that Crispus Attucks, an ex-slave killed in the Boston Massacre of 1770, was among the first martyrs to the cause of American independence from Great Britain. Some five thousand black soldiers and sailors fought on the American side during the Revolutionary War. After the war, some slaves, especially soldiers, were freed, and the Northern states abolished slavery. This was done state by state and not by federal law.

In 1782, Deborah (Robert) Gannet, a black Christian woman who disguised herself as a man, served in the Fourth Massachusetts Regiment for seventeen months and was later cited for bravery for her military service. She did not lose her virginity. It was not known that she was a woman until she was wounded. She fought because of her love for her country. She is the first woman ever to serve in the armed forces of America.[10]

## Slavery

The ratification of the Constitution in 1788 further cemented slavery in the South. The Constitution viewed a slave as only three-fifths of a person for the purposes of taxation and representation in Congress. The ramifications of the Constitution extended the African slave trade for another twenty years. The African slave trade "officially" ended in 1808. The result of this cessation was an increase in domestic slave trading, with a tremendous emphasis placed on slave breeding as never before. Women slaves were forced to conceive as early as thirteen years of age and have babies as often as possible. In order to save her child from a life of slavery, it was not uncommon for a slave mother to kill her newborn baby. This early form of abortion was indirectly caused by those who promoted slavery.

Family stability was not a part of slave life. There was little if any privacy. It was against the law for slaves to learn to read or write. A social class system on the plantation kept the slaves divided and fighting against each other. In the first class were the house servants; second, were the skilled artisans; and third, the majority, were the field hands, who had the most difficult life.

Blacks made attempts at freedom. The history books I had in school called these attempts by slaves to gain their freedom "revolts" or "massacres." (It is interesting that when slaves or Native Americans won battles against whites, those battles were called "massacres," but when whites won them, they were called "great victories.") A slave named Cato led a revolt in Stono, South Carolina, in 1739, where thirty white lives were lost. Gabriel Prosser and Denmark Vesey led revolts. The most famous leader was Nat Turner. His fight for freedom resulted in the deaths of about sixty whites.

Freedom fights took on various forms: running away from slave owners, poisoning slave owners, destroying machinery and crops, arson, and malingering. In 1807, two boatloads of enslaved Africans arriving in Charleston, South Carolina, starved themselves to death rather than submit to slavery. This extreme form of resistance could not be denied its immediate effectiveness, but it did not stop slavery.

## A Hunger for Education

Contrary to the stereotype that blacks were lazy, blacks demonstrated an insatiable appetite for learning. Just look at the number of black institutions of higher learning established to feed this voracious appetite:

- Alabama A&M University was founded in 1865.
- Alcorn State University in Mississippi was founded in 1871.
- Delaware State University was founded in 1891.
- Florida A&M University was founded in 1887.
- Fort Valley State College of Georgia was founded in 1895.

- Kentucky State University was founded in 1886.
- Langston University of Oklahoma was founded in 1897.
- Lincoln University of Missouri was founded in 1866.
- North Carolina A&T was founded in 1891.
- Prairie View A&M University of Texas was founded in 1876.
- South Carolina State was founded in 1896.
- Southern University of Louisiana was founded in 1880.
- Tennessee State University was founded in 1912.
- Tuskegee University of Alabama was founded in 1881.
- The University of Arkansas, Pine Bluff, was founded in 1873.
- The University of Maryland, Eastern Shore, was founded in 1886.
- Virginia State University was founded in 1882.

Mary McLeod Bethune (1875–1955) was the first African American to enroll in Moody Bible Institute. The training school she and Nannie Helen Burroughs ran produced the most women missionaries of any school in the country.[11]

## Civil War Contributions

The African-American contribution to the Union effort in the Civil War was enormous. The historian and linguist W. E. B. Du Bois observed that "Negro military labor [was] indispensable to the Union armies" and quoted Gerald Williams on this subject:

Negroes built most of the fortifications and earth-works for General Grant in front of Vicksburg. The works in and about Nashville were cast up by the strong arm and willing hand of the loyal Blacks. Dutch Gap was dug by Negroes, and miles of earth-works, fortifications, and corduroy-roads were made by Negroes. They did fatigue duty in every department of the Union army. Wherever a Negro appeared with a shovel in his hand, a white soldier took his gun and returned to the ranks. There were 200,000 Negroes in the camps and employ of the Union armies, as servants, teamsters, cooks, and laborers.[12]

Yet, amazingly, Du Bois reports, "the South was for a long time convinced that the Negro could not and would not fight. The idea of [blacks] doing any serious fighting against white men is simply ridiculous,' said an editorial in the Savannah Republican, March 25, 1863."[13] General Lee was hesitant to use slaves as soldiers—a move he would later regret!

Union Army General Morgan observed that

"[h]istory has not yet done justice to the share borne by colored soldiers in the war for the Union. Their conduct during that eventful period, has been a silent, but most potent factor in influencing public sentiment, shaping legislation, and fixing the status of colored people in America. If the records of their achievements could be put into shape that they could be accessible to the thousands of colored youth in the South, they would kindle in their young minds an enthusiastic devotion to manhood and liberty."

Black men were repeatedly and deliberately used as shock troops, when there was little or no hope of success. In February, 1863, Colonel Thomas Wentworth Higginson led black troops into Florida, and declared: "It would have been madness to attempt with the bravest white troops what [was] successfully accomplished with black ones."[14]

Black soldiers say this trend still exists today. In Vietnam, 41 percent of the casualties of U.S. forces were African Americans.

Du Bois observes:

In April [1863], there were three white companies from Maine and seven Negro companies on Ship Island, the key to New

Orleans. The black troops with black officers were attacked by Confederates who outnumbered them five to one. The Negroes retreated so as to give the Federal gunboat *Jackson* a chance to shell their pursuers. But the [*Jackson's*] white crew disliked the Negro soldiers, and opened fire directly upon the black troops while they were fighting the Confederates. Major Dumas, the Negro officer in command, rescued the black men; repulsed the Confederates, and brought the men out safely. The commander called attention to these colored officers: "[They] were constantly in the thickest of the fight, and by their unflinching bravery, and admirable handling of their commands, contributed to the success of the attack, and reflected great honor upon the flag."[15]

During the siege of Petersburg, a Union officer

reported that the "black corps was fittest for the perilous services," but Meade objected to colored troops leading the assault. Burnside insisted. The matter was referred to Grant, and he agreed with Meade. A white division led the assault and failed. The battle of Crater followed. Captain McCabe says: "It was now eight o'clock in the morning. The rest of Potter's (Federal) division moved out slowly, when Ferrero's Negro division . . . burst from the advanced lines, cheering vehemently, passed at a double quick over a crest under a heavy fire, and rushed with scarcely a check over the heads of white troops in the crater, spread to their right, and captured more than two hundred prisoners and one stand of colors."

General Grant afterward said: "General Burnside wanted to put his colored troops in front. I believe if he had done so, it would have been a success."[16]

When black soldiers were captured, they did not receive treatment appropriate for a prisoner of war. Following a Union defeat at Fort Pillow, when the Union soldiers had surrendered,

[the] black troops were shot down in their tracks; pinioned to the ground with bayonet and saber. Some were clubbed to death while dying of wounds; others were made to get down upon their knees, in which condition they were shot to death. Some were burned alive, having been fastened inside the buildings, while still others were nailed against the houses, tortured, and then burned to a crisp.[17]

As the war progressed, "the dilemma of the South [in] the matter of the Negro grew more perplexing," Du Bois notes. "Negroes made good soldiers; that the Northern experience had proved beyond peradventure."[18] Various plans for enrolling blacks in the Southern army were put forth, but were delayed by resistance to the idea of blacks as superior soldiers. Finally the matter came to a head.

[Confederate President] Jefferson Davis discussed the matter with the Governor of Virginia, [declaring that] enlisting Negroes would be freely accepted. March 17, [1865] it was said: "We shall have a Negro army. Letters are pouring into the departments from men of military skill and character asking authority to raise companies, battalions, and regiments of Negro troops."

Thus on recommendation from General Lee and Governor Smith of Virginia, and with the approval of President Davis, an act was passed by the Confederate Congress, March 13, 1865, enrolling slaves in the Confederate army [but it] was too late now, and on April 9, 1865, Lee surrendered.[19]

John C. Underwood, a longtime Virginia resident, said of black troops in his testimony before the Committee on Reconstruction:

I had a conversation with one of the leading men in [the South], and he said to me that *the enlistment of Negro troops by the United States (the Northern Army) was the turning-point of the rebellion*

*(Civil War)*; that it was the heaviest blow they ever received. He remarked that when the Negroes deserted their masters, and showed a general disposition to do so and join the forces of the United States, intelligent men everywhere saw that the matter was ended. I have often heard a similar expression of opinion from others, and I am satisfied that the origin of this bitterness towards the Negro is this belief among the leading men that their weight thrown into the scale decided the contest against them. However the fact may be, I think that such is a pretty well settled conclusion among leading Rebels in Virginia.[20]

Although "the whole number [of] enlisted [blacks] will never be accurately known, since the Department of the Gulf and elsewhere, there was a practice of putting a living Negro soldier in a dead one's place under the same name," the number of blacks directly involved in the Northern effort was considerable:

Official figures say that there were in all 186,017 Negro troops, of whom 123,156 were still in service, July 16, 1865; and that the losses during the war were 68,178. They took part in 198 battles and skirmishes. Without doubt, including servants, laborers, and spies, between three and four hundred thousand Negroes helped as regular soldiers or laborers in winning the Civil War.[21]

Blacks served as commissioned officers as well in the ranks. There were lieutenant colonels, majors, captains, lieutenants, and medical officers, including surgeons.[22]

Blacks were not the only ones to suffer on account of race during the war. White officers who dared command all-black troops paid a severe price for this association. To a Confederate soldier, being "killed by a Negro was a shameful death. To be shot by the Irish and Germans from Northern city slums was humiliating, but for masters to face armed bodies of their former slaves was inconceivable."[23] Consequently, "the officers in command of black troops were branded as outlaws. If captured, they were to be treated as common felons."[24] Jefferson Davis, the president of the Confederacy, saw such officers as "criminals engaged in exciting [the] insurrection" of blacks.[25]

Colonel Shaw, who was white, commanded an all-black regiment. When his regiment suffered 50 percent losses (killed or wounded), and he himself was killed, and "a request was made for [his] body, a Confederate Major said: 'We have buried him with his niggers.'"[26]

The united service of blacks and whites was memorialized on an inscription on St. Gaudens' Shaw Monument in Boston Common written by Harvard President Charles William Eliot:

### THE WHITE OFFICERS

Taking Life and Honor in their Hands—Cast their lot with Men of a Despised Race Unproven in War—and Risked Death as Inciters of a Servile Insurrection if Taken Prisoners, Besides Encountering all the Perils of Camp, March, and Battle.

### THE BLACK RANK AND FILE

Volunteered when Disaster Clouded the Union Cause—Served without Pay for Eighteen Months till Given that of White Troops— Faced Threatened Enslavement if Captured—Were Brave in Action —Patient under Dangerous and Heavy Labors and Cheerful amid Hardships and Privations.

### TOGETHER

They Gave to the Nation Undying Proof that Americans of African Descent Possess the Pride, Courage, and Devotion of the Patriot Soldier—One Hundred and Eighty Thousand Such Americans Enlisted under the Union Flag in MDCCCLXIII-MDCCCLXV.[27]

The concluding days of the Civil War were ones of deep emotion and great optimism for blacks. Following the Confederate surrender to the Union Army in April 1865, Abraham Lincoln visited the Confederate capital at Richmond, Virginia, and addressed the Connecticut colored troops, known as the 29th Colored Regiment.

> In reference to you, colored people, let me say God has made you free. Although you have been deprived of your God-given rights by your so-called masters, you are now as free as I am, and if those that claim to be your superiors do not know that you are free, take the sword and bayonet and teach them that you are—for God created all men free, giving to each the same rights of life, liberty and the pursuit of happiness.[28]

"The mass of slaves," Du Bois reports,

> were in religious and hysterical fervor. This was the coming of the Lord. This was the fulfillment of prophecy and legend. It was the Golden Dawn, after chains of a thousand years. It was everything miraculous and perfect and promising. For the first time in their life, they could travel; they could see; they could . . . sit at sundown and in moonlight, listening and imparting won-der-tales. They could hunt in the swamps, and fish in the rivers. And above all, they could stand up and assert themselves. They need not fear patrol; they need not even cringe before a white face, and touch their hats.[29]

This euphoria lasted for but a brief time before other measures, such as the Black Codes, imposed a new kind of slavery, but it was a taste of freedom.

### Post–Civil War Contributions

With the decline of Reconstruction, the National Army dwindled in numbers, but African Americans continued to serve in the U.S. Army and took an active part in the Indian wars in the West. Sta-tioned at such outposts as Fort Snelling, Minnesota, in the 1880s, the 25th Infantry escorted western migrants, protected mail and stage routes, and fought in attacks on the Apaches, Kiowas, Cheyennes, Comanches, and Arapahos. The 10th Cavalry played an even more dramatic role. It was credited with capturing the feared Indian leader Geronimo in 1885. With fewer desertions than white counterparts and greater devotion to the army, the "Buffalo Soldiers," as the Indians named them, distinguished themselves and received fourteen Congressional Medals of Honor for their efforts.[30]

African Americans were the heroes of the Spanish-American War. At Las Guasimas, Cuba, on June 23, 1898, the all-black 10th Cavalry, with more experience from the Indian wars and better guns (machine guns), *led* the rest of the American forces and overwhelmed the Spanish. Afterward, Roosevelt remarked: "No troops could behave better than the colored soldiers."[31] During the battle of El Caney, Teddy was even more grateful: The 9th and 10th Cavalries rescued his Rough Riders when they were pinned down by a heavily fortified garrison.[32]

### Barney L. Ford

Barney L. Ford, a runaway slave, was noted for his ability to influence the election of several senators in such a way that Colorado did not become a state until its Constitution provided voting rights for Negroes.

He arrived in Denver in 1860, served as an agent for the Underground Railroad, and was the first Negro to serve on a U.S. Grand Jury in Colorado. A giant in the business world, he was nominated for the Territorial Legislature in 1873.

Colorado became a state in 1876 and enacted its first civil rights law in 1885, S.B. 161, "An Act to Protect All Citizens in Their Civil Rights." Voting for the bill from Colorado Springs were Senator Irving Howbert of the Eighth District and Representative John Campbell in the House. Barney Ford died in 1902. In January 1992, he was posthumously inducted into the Colorado Business Hall of

Fame, becoming its first minority member.[33]

## George Henry White's Valedictory Speech

George Henry White was a former slave who became a Congressman, serving in the House of Representatives as a Republican. Freed at the age of ten, he went to school intermittently as he helped his family with farming and cask making.

In 1873, he entered the study of medicine at Howard University, but soon transferred to study law in North Carolina. He was admitted to the North Carolina bar in 1879. The next year, he won the Eighth District seat to the state house of representatives. In 1884, he was elected to the state senate. In 1896, White won the Republican nomination for Congress from the Second District.

George Henry White was the sole black representative to take the oath of office when the Fifty-fifth Congress met on March 15, 1897. He was a member of the Committee on Agriculture. He introduced an unprecedented bill to make lynching a federal crime punishable by death. The bill expired in the Judiciary Committee.

During his two terms in the House, White sought in vain to secure financial relief for Civil War hero and former Congressman Robert Smalls and former Louisiana Governor P. B. S. Pinchback. After a large group of white men murdered the black postmaster of Lake City, South Carolina, and his baby son, in February 1898, White presented a resolution for the relief of the victim's wife and five surviving children, all of whom had been wounded. Representative Charles Barlett of Georgia objected to White's request and no action was taken.

One has to wonder if any Christians were serving at this time in the Fifty-fifth Congress.

White did not run for a third term because of the scurrility of the congressional campaign and widespread efforts to drive blacks from public life in North Carolina.

It is in his celebrated "valedictory" speech of January 29, 1901, White noted that his departure would leave Congress without any black representatives. He also made mention of the progress of the ex-slave:

> If the gentleman to whom I have referred will pardon me, I would like to advance the statement that the musty records of 1868, filed away in the archives of Southern capitols, as to what the negro was thirty-two years ago, is not a proper standard by which the negro living on the threshold of the twentieth century should be measured. Since that time we have reduced the illiteracy of the race at least 45 percent. We have written and published nearly 500 books. We have nearly 300 newspapers, 3 of which are dailies. We have now in practice over 2,000 lawyers and a corresponding number of doctors. We have accumulated over $12,000,000 worth of school property and about $40,000,000 worth of church property. We have about 140,000 farms and homes, valued at in the neighborhood of $750,000,000, and personal property valued at about $170,000,000. We have raised about $11,000,000 for educational purposes, and the property per capita for every colored man, woman, and child in the United States is estimated at $75.
>
> We are operating successfully several banks, commercial enterprises among our people in the Southland, including 1 silk mill and 1 cotton factory. We have 32,000 teachers in the schools of the country; we have built, with the aid of our friends, about 20,000 churches, and support 7 colleges, 17 academies, 50 high schools, 5 law schools, 5 medical schools, and 25 theological seminaries. We have over 600,000 acres of land in the South alone. The cotton produced, mainly by black labor, has increased from 4,669,770 bales in 1860 to 11,235,000 in 1899. All this we have done under the most adverse circumstances. We have done it in the face of lynching, burning at the stake, with the humiliation of "Jim Crow" cars, the disfranchisement of our male citizens, slander and degradation of our women, with the factories closed against us, no negro permitted

to be conductor on the railway cars, whether run through the streets of our cities or across the prairies of our great country, no negro permitted to run as engineer on a locomotive, most of the mines closed against us. Labor unions—carpenters, painters, brick masons, machinists, hackmen, and those supplying nearly every conceivable avocation for livelihood have banded themselves together to better their condition, but, with few exceptions, the black face has been left out. The negroes are seldom employed in our mercantile stores. At this we do not wonder. Some day we hope to have them employed in our own stores. With all these odds against us, we are forging our way ahead, slowly, perhaps, but surely. You may tie us and then taunt us for a lack of bravery, but one day we will break the bonds. You may use our labor for two and a half centuries and then taunt us for our poverty, but let me remind you we will not always remain poor. You may withhold even the knowledge of how to read God's Word and learn the way from earth to glory and then taunt us for our ignorance, but we would remind you that there is plenty of room at the top, and we are climbing.[34]

## A BRIEF OVERVIEW OF AFRICAN-AMERICAN HISTORY

In 1865, slavery was "officially ended." Many thought that blacks would die here in America because of disease and destitution—meaning their supposed inability to function in white society. Just the opposite occurred. The black population doubled from 1861, just before the Civil War, to reach 4 million by the time World War I began.

A study by Barbara Agresti showed that blacks in 1885 were living in family groups more than in 1870 and that the percentage of one-parent families was lower the latter year. Also, many more children were living with both parents.

A study by Herbert Gutman showed that between 1855 and 1880, 70–90 percent of households were considered "husband present."[35]

In 1870, Senator Charles Sumner introduced a civil rights bill to Congress to grant equal accommodations to blacks and whites in public settings—including schools, churches, stores, and transportation. It became law but failed in practice because federal courts didn't enforce it. In 1881, the Tennessee law referred to as the "Jim Crow Law" directed railroad companies to provide separate cars or portions of cars for first-class Negro passengers instead of relegating them to second-class accommodations, as had been the custom. Jim Crow laws segregated blacks in all public areas.

In 1890, the *Plessy v. Ferguson* court judgment resulted in the standard "separate but equal."

By 1900, 90 percent of all blacks still lived in the South. By the time of World War I, blacks were streaming into northern cities by the tens of thousands.

In 1910, the NAACP (National Association for Advancement of Colored People) was founded. This was one of many groups formed to fight for equality for blacks. The YMCA and YWCA had been established in the 1800s partly for the same reason.

The 1920s saw the emergence of the "New Negro." The need for farm laborers had declined, so blacks moved to the city to be in the job force. Yet the rural black family was better able than an urban family to preserve the family. Worse still, instead of work, blacks found further discrimination and chronic unemployment.

In 1932, Franklin D. Roosevelt appointed Negroes and other minorities to office positions. New acts and laws were passed to prevent rioting and segregation. Yet despite these laws, segregation was still widespread and blacks formed their own communities. The church remained the most powerful institution in the black community.

The 1954 *Brown v. Board of Education* decision seemed to be the breakthrough to end segregation in public schools. Looking back, it was not the blessing blacks perceived it to be. Government involvement would be necessary if things were going to improve for the Negro. Except for some liberals, whites across the board, including the majority of the white evangelicals, were still the enemy!

In the 1950s and 1960s the Civil Rights Movement was underway. This movement was characterized by black non-violent protests of racial injustice. In 1968, Dr. Martin Luther King Jr. was assassinated.

By 1974, there were blacks sitting in forty-five state legislatures, and the number of blacks in Congress had increased to sixteen in the House, including four women.

## SO WHAT DOES ALL THIS MEAN?

There should be some excitement to see the contributions made to America by blacks—Christian as well as non-Christian. There should also be some sadness because of the pain inflicted unjustly on blacks because of the color of their skin and on the whites who dared to help them.

These facts are just a drop in the bucket. As an African American and a history major, it was not easy to stop writing down these facts! African Americans have turned wars around, owned banks, fought and lived with Native Americans. They are the inventors behind scores of products and processes.

We must understand that the historical facts in this chapter are not just African-American history—they are *American* history.

That means that if you are white and want to "reconcile" with your black Christian brother or sister, you must understand that this history is the heritage (good and bad) he or she will bring into the relationship. The issue is not that you necessarily agree with the interpretation or perspective of that history, but that you at least try to understand it.

A person's past can't help but impact who he or she is today. If you are white and say to a black person, "I *know* how you feel," he knows that "feeling" for you may be impossible. If you are white and believe blacks should "just get over it," then you are not ready to develop a cross-cultural relationship. The black heritage is part of who we are. To reject this heritage is to reject the person. Such an attitude is motivated by selfishness. Biblical relationships are based on serving without demanding anything in return. If you don't understand people, how do you expect to minister to them effectively? This doesn't mean you need to know everything about them, but that you do care about who they are.

The more one understands American history, the more one understands that throughout American history there has never been a consistently good relationship between blacks and whites to which blacks would want to return or have restored. So can there really be any such thing as racial *reconciliation?*

## THE MOYNIHAN REPORT

Senator Daniel Patrick Moynihan's report, "The Negro Family: The Case for National Action," submitted in 1965 to President Lyndon B. Johnson, gave America the impression that blacks were lazy. Yet the contribution of African-American Christians to missions, inventions, and the American economy—in spite of intense opposition by non-Christians and Christians alike—is amazing. It also, importantly, demonstrates that the work ethic of the vast majority of African Americans is one of creativity and productivity, not one of laziness.

Therefore, when African Americans cry out for affirmative action, they are not trying to take the place of someone of a different color or to make a quota. They are calling for an equal opportunity in an unequal society, Christian and non-Christian alike. If we are honest, we must admit that in practice, there seems to be little difference in the way Christian and non-Christian whites in America deal with race. Thus, those Christians who oppose issues important to African Americans in regard to opportunities for a better life must rethink their positions if they are truly serious about practical ways to improve race relations, since history more than substantiates that the majority of African Americans have a strong and creative work ethic. The majority of African Americans aren't lazy—just the opposite is true!

The issue is creating an honest, *truly level* playing field. This will cost those who are serious about equality! There must be input from minorities for this to happen. Jim Crow laws, historic discrimination in housing and employment, and continued instances of racism even today have proved that, for whatever reason, it is extremely difficult if not impossible for many whites in authority to keep their commitments to minorities. This track record of historical failure makes it difficult for blacks to begin or continue to trust white Christians.

There must be positive, consistent actions to dispel misperceptions. History can be enlightening.

*Dear Lord,*

*Thank You for teaching some of us history we may have never known before. It is exciting and encouraging to know the role played by African-American Christians in world missions and in the building of America. At the same time, Father, help us to learn from the painful lessons of history that all men are equal before You.*

*Amen.*

## NOTES

1. Sharon Harley, *The Timetables of African-American History: A Chronology of the Most Important People and Events in African-American History* (New York: Simon & Schuster, 1995), 74.

2. Ibid., 52.

3. Berchman's Bittle, O. F. M. Cap., *A Saint a Day* (Milwaukee, Wis.: Bruce, 1958).

4. Paul Cuffee, *Memoirs of Captain Paul Cuffee, a Man of Colour: The Epistle of the Society of Sierra Leone in African & etc.* (New York: W. Alexander, 1812–1817).

5. Harley, *Timetables of African-American History,* 74.

6. Bishop William Paul Quinn, African Methodist Episcopal Church, Home page, (AMEC-NET.ORG) web2.airmail.net/quinnchp/.

7. Harley, *Timetables of African-American History,* 76.

8. John Milsome, *From Slave Boy to Bishop* (n.p., n.d.).

9. Carl F. Ellis, "The Gospel, the Black Man and Slavery," *Body of Christ* 9, no. 3 (November

1997) (Denver): 3.

10. Harley, *Timetables of African-American History*, 114.

11. Glenn Usry and Craig S. Keener, *Black Man's Religion: Can Christianity Be Afrocentric?* (Downers Grove, Ill.: InterVarsity, 1996), 18.

12. W. E. B. Du Bois, *Black Reconstruction in America: [An Essay Toward a History of the Part Which Black Folk Played in the Attempt to Reconstruct Democracy in America, 1860–1880]* (1935; reprint, with an introduction by David Levering Lewis, New York: Atheneum, 1992), 106; Gerald Williams, *History of the Negro Race in America from 1619 to 1880*, vol. 2, 1800–1880, *American Negro: His History and Literature*, no. 1 (1883; Philadelphia: Ayer, 1968), 262.

13. Du Bois, *Black Reconstruction in America*, 106.

14. Ibid., 106–7. For Morgan, Du Bois is quoting Joseph T. Wilson, *History of the Black Phalanx* (Hartford, Conn.: 1890; New York: Da Capo, 1994), 305. For Higginson, Du Bois is quoting Williams, *History of the Negro Race*, 2:314.

15. Ibid., 107. For the interior quote, Du Bois cites Wilson, *Black Phalanx*, 211.

16. Ibid., 111. For General Grant, Du Bois cites "Testimony Before Congressional Committee," in Wilson, *Black Phalanx*, 428.

17. Ibid., Du Bois, 114–15.

18. Ibid., 115.

19. Ibid., 119. The interior quote is from Wilson, *Black Phalanx*, 494.

20. Ibid., 120, italics added. For Underwood, Du Bois is quoting Report of the Joint Committee on Reconstruction, 1866, 8.

21. Ibid., 112.

22. Ibid., 113. Cf. Wilson, *Black Phalanx*, chap. 4, and Williams, *History of the Negro Race in America*, 2:299–301.

23. Ibid.

24. Ibid.

25. Ibid., 114.

26. Ibid., 109. For the Confederate major, Du Bois is quoting Wilson, *Black Phalanx*, 256.

27. Ibid., 112–13.

28. Ibid., 112, quoting Hill, "Sketch of the 29th Regiment of Connecticut Colored Troops," *The Hartford Courant*, 26–27. The account of Lincoln's visit to the troops was recorded by a member of that regiment.

29. Ibid., 122.

30. Jeffery C. Stewart, *1001 Things Everyone Should Know About African American History* (New York: Doubleday, 1996), 204.

31. Ibid.

32. Ibid.

33. Negro Historical Association of Colorado Springs 13, no. 12 (December 1995): 6.

34. Congressional Record of the Fifty-Fifth–Fifty-Sixth Congress, 29 January 1901.

35. George H. Gutman, *The Black Family in Slavery and Freedom, 1750–1925* (New York: Pantheon, 1976).

**4**

# What Honest Abe Really Believed and Why It Matters

---

## Lessons We Could Learn from History

*Those who cannot remember the past are condemned to repeat it.*

—George Santayana

Any attempt to solve the race problem or at least gain a better understanding of it will benefit from a look into history to see how many white evangelicals dealt with this issue in the past. Instead of examining all of the failures, let's take a close look at a white, conservative, Christian Republican whose actions had and continue to have a profound effect on millions of African Americans in America.

The man whose actions I would like to examine more closely is Abraham Lincoln. At first glance this might seem like an unusual choice. Lincoln was president of the country throughout the Civil War, and what he did during and immediately before that conflict made him one of America's most revered chief executives. His name is almost synonymous with freedom for blacks. At a time when slavery was permitted in the South and blacks were constitutionally recognized as being only three-fifths of a person for the purpose of the census and to determine taxation and congressional representation, he argued that slavery should be banned throughout the territory of the Louisiana Purchase. His debates with Stephen Douglas over this issue made him and his views on the subject nationally known, so much so that immediately after his election in November 1860, Southern states began pulling away from the Union, knowing that he was not sympathetic to their cause. It was also he who drafted and then signed the Emancipation Proclamation. It was he who worked behind the scenes for ratification of the Thirteenth Amendment, which constitutionally outlawed slavery. It was also he who authorized the enlistment of blacks as regular, paid soldiers in the Union Army. And it was he who led the country through a war fought in part to achieve one national standard: that blacks should be free from the evil of slavery throughout the entire United States (although the reintroduction of the Black Codes in the South following the Reconstruction era imposed restrictions on blacks not much better than those they had endured under slavery).

We must remember that this war, like most wars, was not fought over slavery. It was the industrial North against the agricultural South, and the business of slavery figured prominently.

So why do I wish to examine his actions? This is not an attempt to degrade Mr. Lincoln as a person, but to show that, in significant ways, his views and politics parallel attitudes and actions among many white Christians today that translate into negative results for African Americans. What is amazing is that these attitudes and actions have not changed in more than one hundred years.

## WHAT REALLY HAPPENED?

Most people know that President Abraham Lincoln signed the Emancipation Proclamation on January 1, 1863, although slaves were not freed immediately. (This was because the document declared emancipation only for those blacks in Confederate territory. The war had not yet been won; therefore, the terms of the proclamation could not be enforced at the time it was signed; neither did the slave owners inform their slaves of their new freedom.) The signing of this document for freedom for the slaves was a "good" action taken by President Lincoln. But what most people do not know much about is the how, why, and when behind Lincoln's work on this historic document.

According to the historians Philip Kunhardt Jr., Philip Kunhardt III, and Peter Kunhardt, in their book *Lincoln: An Illustrated Biography*, it was in August of 1861 that the black abolitionist Frederick Douglass began a "passionate campaign to *convince* President Lincoln to employ black soldiers in the Union Army" (italics added),[1] which Douglass saw as intertwined with the goal of freedom for the slaves.

> Why does the Government reject the negro? Is he not a man? Can he not wield a sword, fire a gun, march and countermarch, and obey orders like any other? . . . If persons so humble as we can be allowed to speak to the President of the United States we . . . would tell him that this is no time to fight with one hand, when both are needed; that this is no time to fight with only your white hand, and allow your black hand to remain tied. . . . While the Government continues to refuse the aid of colored men, thus alienating them from the national cause, and giving the rebels the advantage of them, it will not deserve better fortunes [than] it has thus far experienced—Men in earnest don't fight with one hand, when they might fight with two, and a man drowning would not refuse to be saved even by a colored hand.[2]

After the fall of Fort Sumter, President Lincoln issued an appeal for volunteers. Blacks all over the North responded. Dr. G. P. Miller, a black physician in Battle Creek, Michigan, asked the War Department for authority to raise "5,000–10,000 free men to report in sixty days to take any position that may be assigned to us (sharpshooters preferred)."[3] The Lincoln administration thanked the black volunteers and sent them home with an understanding that the war was a "white man's war."[4] It is a matter of record that the Lincoln administration continued "the course thus far pursued," barring blacks from the army and returning fugitive slaves to rebel masters.[5] Congressional liberals, abolitionists, black leaders, and "hard-war" Unionists asked Lincoln to stop the "military slave hunt and hit the South where it would hurt the most: free the slaves and give them guns. What kind of war was the president fighting anyway? What was he trying to do? Lincoln said he was trying to save the Union. What then was to be done with slaves who abandoned their masters in droves and flocked to the Union lines? Lincoln said his policy was to have no policy."[6] When Gen. John C. Freemont issued a proclamation freeing the slaves of Missouri rebels, Lincoln revoked the proclamation and kicked up a storm of abuse.[7] Congressional liberals, abolitionists, black leaders, and "hard-war" Unionists said he was vacillating.[8] They also had other less complimentary descriptions.

For almost two years Lincoln held close to this course, appeasing the slaveholding Border States.

President Lincoln spoke often of freeing the slaves during his presidential campaign. As president, however, it was Douglass's ability to debate that moved Lincoln to action.

Bill Pollard, chairman of The ServiceMaster Company, says in his book *The Soul of the Firm* that "leaders must fulfill their campaign promises."[9]

In our society today, when a president doesn't fulfill his campaign promises, it is not unusual for him to be a one-term president. The Watergate incident lowered our country's trust in its leaders. Today many African Americans are studying their history. As they discover that President Lincoln made these campaign promises and it appears that Douglass was the catalyst for his actions, Lincoln is seen as not fulfilling his campaign promises.

Conservative Christians tend to give Lincoln *all* the credit and glory for freeing the slaves without at least mentioning Douglass, and it has given many Americans a distorted view of what actually happened. But this is only the beginning of an unraveling of this distorted picture of history. As stated earlier, this is not an attempt to slight President Lincoln but to accurately reveal all the facts, which for some reason or other have been overlooked previously.

The Kunhardts document that Lincoln was blaming the black presence for America's problems. Does this sound a little familiar? At an August 1862 meeting at the White House with black leaders Lincoln stated, "Our white men [are] cutting one another's throats . . . [and] but for your race among us there could not be war. . . . It is better for us both, therefore, to be separated."[10] This same evening, Lincoln went on to say,

> You and we are different races. We have between us a broader difference than exists between almost any other two races. Whether it is right or wrong I need not discuss, but this physical difference is a great disadvantage to us both, as I think your race suffer[s] very greatly, many of them by living among us, while our[s] suffers from your presence.[11]

Lincoln did not seek the opinion of his visitors.[12]

We must remember the slaves did not bring themselves to America, nor did they want to be here in a foreign land with a foreign language and in chains. It is quite amazing that in Lincoln's day, as today, many white Christians were not sure how they should relate to blacks.

## IS SEGREGATION GOD ORDAINED?

Lincoln's separatism was like that of some in our modern Bible colleges and seminaries, both in what they have said and in what they have failed to do.

In 1960, Bob Jones III stated, "A Negro is best when he serves at the table . . . when he does that, he's doing what he knows how to do best. And the Negroes who have ascended to positions in government, in education, this sort of thing, I think you'll find, by and large, have a strong strain of white blood in them."[13]

A statement such as this should have brought so much criticism from the evangelical community that Bob Jones, Sr. would have had to come out and retract it. But the evangelical community by and large did not speak out against this kind of reasoning. A few years later, Bob Jones Jr. made this statement:

The fact that we do not accept blacks as students here does not mean that we are against the Negro race, that we do not love the Negro, or that we are not concerned about his spiritual welfare. I wish there was an institution like Bob Jones University established exclusively for Negroes; however, with the present emphasis in this country, Negroes would not accept a school established solely for blacks because the whole emphasis today is on a breaking down of racial barriers which God has set up.[14]

Bob Jones III made a similar statement in 1975.

Bob Jones University later changed its position and accepted blacks as students. There was tremendous pressure brought against the institution to do this, not by the evangelical community, but by the federal government, and Bob Jones University wanted to keep its nonprofit status.

To Bob Jones University's credit, it has published a book honoring black Christians.

I realize that many Christian colleges and seminaries did not publicly share Bob Jones University's perspective on race, but their silence made a loud sound in the black Christian community.

This is still happening today. At one of the most prestigious Christian colleges in America, a former felon, who became a Christian while in prison, was accepted at this institution on his own merit. After being accepted, a school official interviewed him. Then he called the school's president and the president reversed the acceptance.

In this case, white Christians came to the rescue. This young man is completing his third year with a 3.2 GPA.

Blacks in many cases, though, have not been able to depend on many of their white Christian brothers for help in areas of injustice. In most cases, blacks have had to depend on the government for help in the area of injustice. Sometimes, it was the white Christian brothers who were the source of the injustices.

The young man mentioned above came out of one of the only post-prison ministries in America. This ministry had to sue the county in order to establish a halfway house in the area. Initially, many white Christians in the area were against it. This has changed, as the Christian community has since seen how effective this ministry is.

As late as 1981, a seminary of one of the largest denominations in the United States had a missions class that promoted what is known as the *homogeneous church*. According to Donald McGavran, quoted in *Understanding Church Growth,* "People like to become Christians without crossing racial, linguistic or class barriers."[15] This is the thinking behind the concept of the homogeneous church.

Quite a few Christian evangelical Bible colleges and seminaries have promoted the homogeneous church theory. Yet *homogeneous church* is another term for *separation*. Although it is not certain that all New Testament churches were what we would call cross-cultural, it is clear that in a great many of them various ethnic, cultural, and class barriers were broken down. Throughout Acts and the Epistles, it is clear that God "integrated" His church by bringing Jews and Gentiles together into common worship, fellowship, and church government (although there were frequent disagreements brought about by the union of the two groups). In Acts 10, the Holy Spirit falls on Cornelius and his household, showing Peter and the group with him that salvation had been granted to the Gentiles as well as the Jews. In Acts 6:1–7, it is clear that the church included Aramaic-speaking Jews as well as Greek-speaking Jews. In Acts 15, the apostles and elders at Jerusalem convene to determine how to deal with Gentile believers already part of the church, and a similar meeting occurs in Acts 21. Also in Acts 21, a riot occurred in Jerusalem because people assumed that Trophimus, a Greek Christian they had seen with Paul, had been brought with him to the temple precincts. The epistle to Philemon implies that slaves and masters were in the same congregation, and it asserts that a slave, Onesimus, was held in such high repute that he was a valuable assistant to the apostle Paul. James 2:1–4 assumes that rich and poor worship in the same house churches (and that the church was having trouble dealing with this correctly). The epistle to the Galatians asserts that Gentile believers are a full-fledged part of the church. Jews and Gentiles are to eat together, and Jews are not to require Gentiles to follow Jewish customs or to become circumcised (Galatians 2:11–14).

The homogeneous church theory seems to be inconsistent with the Great Commission as well as being responsible for promoting indirect racism. The theory teaches very subtly that the races should worship God separately. This makes genuine integration in the body of Christ much more difficult. It also makes it harder for the races to see each other as equals and, more important, as brothers and sisters in Christ.

Even without the name, the concept of the homogeneous church has existed from the days of American slavery and has perpetuated the division between black and white Christians. This gap is probably greater than most whites realize. It is also why the masses of black Christians do not trust white Christians and basically don't attend events that would be considered evangelical.

Cross-cultural churches are special, maybe because God intended for us to be one. Having belonged to predominantly black and white churches, and pastoring a cross-cultural one, I have found diversity has many problems—but the rewards of such a church or fellowship are incredible!

The parents of many white Christians today followed Bob

Jones's and Donald McGavran's philosophy. So while many white Christians today will say they have never owned slaves nor said the things that some white Christians have said, blacks will ask white Christians, "What did *you* do to *help* our cause as Christians?" One of the greatest problems most white evangelicals have today in their understanding of the racial problem is the tendency to concentrate only on the *effects* of a situation (various problems in the country, for example) and totally divorce themselves from the possible causes. Of course, there is a good reason for divorcing themselves from the causes. If they do not do so, they may have to admit that they are at least partially responsible for the produced effects. Accepting this fact would force these evangelicals to the biblical conclusion that restitution and restoration are part of their responsibility. But if they only concentrate on the effects, then they feel no responsibility to make restitution for a situation they may have created or at least helped to create. Most obviously didn't own slaves, but neither did they take active steps to redress the condition of blacks.

Often it seems those Christians who are labeled "liberals" theologically have fewer problems accepting blacks because they have a more inclusive mind-set. Unfortunately, "liberal" also usually means "anything goes," so that is part of the negative baggage of liberalism. But "conservative" usually means "You've got to be just like me." Therefore, you can see why it may be easier for liberals to accept people who are different from themselves than it is for conservatives to do so. You can observe this same pattern in politics as well.

Lincoln's blaming blacks for America's problems is parallel to the tendency many evangelical whites today have to blame blacks for welfare programs and affirmative action. Review Christian magazines and tapes concerning welfare; you will see that the discussions and pictures are usually about blacks. This is interesting when, in fact, there are more whites on welfare than there are blacks. Whites also forget the historical repression of blacks in all areas of life—including reduced educational opportunities and the means of making a living—that requires restitution to repair and atone for the damage. In this complaining about welfare and affirmative action, there is a denial of white greed (past and present) at the expense of blacks. Is there also the refusal to do justice because justice would result in *sharing the power,* which, it appears, some people in power just can't bring themselves to do (even if they are Christians)?

Things aren't necessarily getting better. Why don't you do a little research to find out who was the president recently, who was considered a conservative and even a Christian. He changed college grants into loans so the government would be repaid, which was a great idea. The only problem was that parents of minority college candidates had a difficult time being approved for these loans. The amount of the loans was determined by the net worth of the family's income. At this particular time in history, the net worth of a white household was ten times greater than that of blacks. Guess who got the loans? Intentionally or unintentionally, the percentage of blacks who would have entered college to receive an education that would affect the kind of job they could obtain was lowered. Thus, the "level playing field" was not being lowered, but actually being tilted higher.

Again, there was no outcry from the Christian community with an alternative plan for inclusion.

Maybe this is just another example of whites not thinking how certain actions affect minorities. It is difficult for blacks to see white leaders, Christian or non-Christian, as not being intelligent; thus often these unthinking actions that lead to exclusion and not inclusion tend to be viewed as racist by some blacks.

These unthinking acts may be the result of not studying issues and/or their consequences from a minority perspective. If a person doesn't educate himself or herself in the area of race/racism, he or she may be unconsciously racist in his or her thinking and subsequent actions. There is a tremendous need for many more servant-leaders in positions of leadership in the evangelical community and government.

## A RESPONSE TO A SEPARATIST ATTITUDE

At the same meeting where Lincoln's comments blaming blacks for the war took place, Lincoln also discussed a plan to free and then deport blacks to Africa. The response from black leaders was swift and furious.

"The tone of frankness and benevolence which he assumes in his speech," exploded black abolitionist Frederick Douglass in New York, "is too thin a mask not to be seen through. The genuine spark of humanity is missing in it" [the concern of many black Christians with the Christian conservative right]. And Isaiah Wears, the black Philadelphia leader, added, "To be asked, after so many years of oppression and wrong . . . to pull up stakes . . . and go . . . is unreasonable and anti-Christian. . . . It is not the negro race that is the cause of the war; it is the unwillingness on the part of the American people to do the race simple justice."[16]

It was only after President Lincoln was faced with this response that he began to seek the will of God concerning this issue. It seems that black Christians today also have to confront (challenge) many white evangelicals about their own injustice. Then and only then do these evangelicals begin to seek the "will of God." Why doesn't the Holy Spirit move these individuals who profess to believe in the Lord to seek His will *before* they are confronted with the racial injustice they have either committed, tolerated, ignored, or perpetuated? Minority Christians want their white brothers to answer this question. For example, when white Christian churches or organizations continue to exclude minorities from their decision-making bodies, and the white Christian says that he or she must seek the "will of God" as to how to respond to racial injustice, we blacks wonder what Bible is being read (read the essay "Plain Vanilla Christianity," mentioned in chapter 1).

## FREEDOM IS NOT WHERE YOU ARE, BUT WHO YOU ARE

When President Lincoln finally signed the Emancipation Proclamation in 1863, the slaves were now "officially" free. There was a celebration party of Lincoln's cabinet at Secretary Chase's house. According to John Hay, "All seemed to feel a sort of new and exhilarated life; they breathed freer; The President's Proclamation had *freed* them as well as the slaves" (italics added).[17] Phil Williams, who conducts seminars revealing the role of over five thousand African Americans (many of whom were Christians) in the Revolutionary War, often says, "You see, no one is free unless everyone is free." Some of the blacks in the Revolutionary War served as foot soldiers, sailors, and spies. Let me encourage you to do some research to find more of their contributions.

All people, especially Christians, need to understand that freedom is not where or how you are, but who you are! Our freedom as Christians is found in Christ and not in the circumstances, as Paul explains in Philippians 4:11–13:

> I am not saying this because I am in need, for I have learned to be content whatever the circumstances. I know what it is to be in need, and I know what it is to have plenty. I have learned the secret of being content in any and every situation, whether well fed or hungry, whether living in plenty or in want. I can do everything through him who gives me strength.

Lincoln's cabinet could breathe freer because the integrity of their character, which had been compromised by slavery, was no longer being compromised. Imagine—if some of these men were Christians (and some were)—the Holy Spirit would have been convicting the daylights out of them. The black slaves were bound by physical chains, while these members of Lincoln's cabinet were bound by moral chains. Freedom is not *where* we are, but *who* and *whose* we are! In the same way, it seems that many white evangelicals, churches, and parachurch ministries are enslaved. This is why

Promise Keepers has been so well accepted by the white Christian community. God is using Coach Bill McCartney to free many of these white Christian evangelical males who have in one way or another compromised the integrity of lives in the areas of marriage and family relationships. However, now the Holy Spirit is also convicting Christian males of their sin in the area of race.

## NO OTHER OPTION

Douglass's observation, quoted at the beginning of this chapter, that the North was losing the war, has been documented by Civil War historians. The Union *was* losing the war. That Lincoln's policy was changed at all is due not to humanitarianism but to Rebel battlefield brilliance—the South knew what it was fighting for—and the daring and hope of fugitive slaves.[18]

It came to Lincoln in the summer of 1862 that the Union could not escape history. "Things," he explained later, "had gone from bad to worse, until I felt that we had reached the end of our rope on the plan of operations we had been pursuing; that we had about played our last card."[19] On Tuesday, July 22, Lincoln called his cabinet together and put his "last card" on the table. It was a good one, a draft of a preliminary Emancipation Proclamation.[20] "[He] had . . . come to the conclusion that it was a *military necessity* absolutely essential for the salvation of the Union," Secretary of the Navy Gideon Wells recorded in his diary (italics added).[21] Secretary of State William Seward, however, "at a later cabinet meeting, urged caution, arguing that the government should wait for a military victory before proceeding, lest the proclamation be misinterpreted as a sign of defeat. Reluctantly, Lincoln agreed."[22] Image maintenance appears to have been a priority, even with people who would have described themselves as Christians.

In their discussion of the meeting Lincoln had with black leaders in August 1862, the Kunhardts report:

With his great plan postponed, and the war going poorly for the

Union, Lincoln seemed to lose his resolve in the matter of [emancipation]. During this long dismal summer of 1862, he turned once again to his idea of colonization. Realizing that what prejudiced Northern whites feared most was for blacks to "swarm northward" and "intermingle," competing for jobs [this is similar to people supporting missions because they want better conditions for people overseas—they just do not want them in America; some Northern whites opposed slavery, but didn't want blacks in the North], Lincoln had long advocated black emigration, for freed blacks to be willingly colonized to places such as Liberia, Haiti, or Central America. Like his hero Henry Clay before him, Lincoln believed blacks would be eager to return to the lands from which their ancestors had been stolen, or, at the very least, to make their escape out of white supremacist America. Insisting that such colonization be "voluntary and without expense" to the emigrés, Lincoln felt that if he could convince even a small number of them to go, it would help him immensely to accomplish the political miracle of emancipation. On August 14 [1862], he addressed a delegation of free Negroes, invited to the White House to hear his ideas.[23]

The president must be applauded for asking blacks what they thought about his idea. But the negative feature is that Lincoln was still thinking about deporting the slaves. The Kunhardts report that "it was partly through Douglass's influence that Lincoln had finally given up his ideas about colonization and begun to believe in Negro suffrage, in particular for soldiers."[24]

And, as we have seen, there was the valor of the black soldiers.

In July 1863 the all black 54th Massachusetts Regiment fought a heroic and historic battle at Fort Wagner, South Carolina, spearheading a desperate charge and proving itself equal to the bravest of white troops. Frederick Douglass's son Lewis, present at the attack, wrote, "How I got out of that fight alive I cannot tell. . . . I wish we had a hundred thousand Colored troops." Contemplating the heroism of these men, Lincoln was forever changed. He spoke less and less (and finally not at all) about colonization, and more and more about the black man's earned place in America.[25]

## MEETING THE STANDARD

What an amazing statement the previous quote is! The suffering of slaves as they helped build this great country of America with backbreaking work did not prove to be sufficient in Lincoln's eyes to earn blacks a place in America. Only when these blacks provided a service that benefited Lincoln's people's more urgent need did he feel that these blacks, upon whom he had once blamed the war, now had earned a place in America. The blacks had finally met Lincoln's standard.

It is sad to say, but many evangelicals use this same principle in relating to black Christians. There is a tremendous desire to keep the races separate. Thus, you have strong preaching supporting the "homogeneous" and "language affinity" churches. Many white evangelicals, like Lincoln, also have a standard for blacks. They must go to the "right" school and have the "right" white Christian friends. Then, and only then, can these black Christians be trusted. The phrase one often hears when certain people aren't listening is "They're just like us." The idea is that if these blacks are just like whites, then whites don't have to change or sacrifice. History can be justified, and thus the things that are presently being done. If blacks can't accept this, they are just not enlightened. If at least one or two blacks can be found who agree with all the majority race is doing, everything is cool. This attitude seems to be motivated by many white Christians' fears, which are unfounded and a result of a lack of faith in God (1 John 4:20–21).

## IT "JUST TAKES TIME" TO RIGHT A WRONG

What is amazing is that after Lincoln was convinced that blacks had earned a place in America, he still did not seem to believe that blacks and whites were equal. "Douglass had been skeptical about Lincoln's slowness to attack slavery, but he had been more supportive of the President since the issuance of the Emancipation Proclamation," the Kunhardts say. "Still, Douglass was particularly angered that black troops received *less pay* than whites of comparable rank" (italics added).[26] Lincoln's actions said, whether he wanted them to or not, that a white life was more valuable to him than a black life! Lincoln attempted to excuse the fault. "Lincoln pointed out that the enlisting of blacks in the army at all was a substantial achievement, considering white opposition in the North," the Kunhardts report. "But he assured Douglass that 'in the end [black soldiers] shall have the same pay as white soldiers.'"[27]

Basically, blacks have heard and continue to hear this point of view, which is, "It just takes time, be patient." How long are black Christians to be patient? What is taking the white evangelical community so long to begin putting the biblical principle of love into practice with Christians of different cultures and races?

This attitude, which fuels many actions, continues to build the impetus for blacks to follow Minister Farrakhan, the leader of the Nation of Islam. Many of the blacks who follow Farrakhan are Christians who reject the theology of the Nation of Islam but want to be in a place where they can be accepted. Farrakhan is scratching where black men are itching.

> By the year's end, Lincoln had deemed his efforts a success. The Emancipation Proclamation had won him Europe's approval of the Union cause, and it had done so without any of the predicted social chaos. "It is the central act of my administration," Lincoln liked to say. It is the "one thing that will make people remember I ever lived."[28]

Remember, President Lincoln was not actively working to free the slaves during the war until Frederick Douglass and others talked him into it. Remember, this president also blamed the black presence as the cause for the war. Now, something that was not his idea, something he was forced to do in order to win the war becomes his *crowning glory* as president. He does not give Douglass the credit he deserved for the role he played in this crowning act of his presidency.

It seems that everyone has a dream. Before Dr. Martin Luther King Jr.'s "I Have a Dream" speech, Frederick Douglass's dream was that America have a great interracial future.

## LINCOLN WAS A TEACHABLE LEADER

President Lincoln wanted Douglass to be an agent to stir slaves across Union lines, and Douglass offered suggestions to Lincoln on various matters.[29] Lincoln must be commended for listening to Douglass. Lincoln listened to the *expert* on his people. The failure to listen to and act upon the advice of minorities as to how to relate to their own race seems to be the number one problem in improving the racial situation in the evangelical community today. It appears many whites have a difficult time listening to and acting on the advice from blacks as to how to minister to blacks. The issue seems to be control and doing something that is safe and requires no faith. Faith requires risk because you have to believe in what you cannot see. As it turned out, "sudden Union victories [in the autumn of 1864] rendered Douglass's new role obsolete, and he ended up playing only a limited role in Lincoln's [1864] presidential campaign, *effectively muzzled by Republican leaders* eager to avoid being branded as the 'Nigger Party'" (italics added).[30] Image maintenance was still critical. It seems that the possible risk of suffering for the sake of someone else was out of the question. Yet 1 John 3:11–20 says:

> This is the message you heard from the beginning: We should love one another. Do not be like Cain, who belonged to the evil one and murdered his brother. And why did he murder him? Because his own actions were evil and his brother's were righteous. Do not be surprised, my brothers, if the world hates you.

We know that we have passed from death to life, because we love our brothers. Anyone who does not love remains in death. Anyone who hates his brother is a murderer, and you know that no murderer has eternal life in him.

This is how we know what love is: Jesus Christ laid down his life for us. And we ought to lay down our lives for our brothers. If anyone has material possessions and sees his brother in need but has no pity on him, how can the love of God be in him? Dear children, let us not love *with words or tongue but with actions and in truth.* This then is how we know that we belong to the truth, and how we set our hearts at rest in his presence whenever our hearts condemn us. For God is greater than our hearts, and he knows *everything.* (Italics added.)

Today the evangelical community still struggles with putting this principle of biblical love into practice in writing budgets that give black interests support, in giving blacks genuine authority to carry out the programs they have been hired to lead, and in just plain equality across the board.

## WORKING THROUGH DIFFICULTIES BUILDS LASTING RELATIONSHIPS

The experience of having to work together brought about a mutual love and respect of Douglass and Lincoln for each other.

Although Frederick Douglass later described Lincoln as a "white man's president," with black Americans at best his "stepchildren," he himself became an important adviser. "There is no man in the country whose opinion I value more than yours," Lincoln said in asking for Douglass's reaction to the second inaugural address. "Mr. Lincoln," the *black* orator responded, "that was a sacred effort." (Italics added.)[31]

I would love to see the day when this kind of trust can be experienced cross-culturally within Christianity on a regular basis. Until this happens, I don't think revival will come. It will also help in defusing the drawing power of the Nation of Islam. "I dream of racial unity. God will not bless this nation spiritually until we can love each other sincerely as brothers and sisters in Christ."[32]

We need to learn from history, for we seem to be repeating, in the name of Christianity, some of the same mistakes made by those who came before us.

## WHAT CAN WE LEARN FROM THIS HISTORY?

First, Lincoln did do the right thing. Some people know the right thing to do and never do it. Remember, Jesus told doubting Thomas that he was blessed because he saw and believed. Jesus told Thomas that many saw and didn't believe.

Second, doing the right thing, especially in the area of race, will not make you popular and will usually cost you more than you originally planned to give. There were many white abolitionists who lost everything—and some even gave their lives for the freedom of blacks.

Third, exercising faith is not easy to do because faith is about obedience, not results.

Fourth, working together provides a vehicle for people of different races to learn how much we all need each other. It is OK to disagree as Douglass and Lincoln did; but note that somehow that did not affect their respect for each other. In fact, their respect for each other increased!

Fifth, those in leadership must be teachable for the sake of themselves and the masses.

These are just a few of the practical things we can learn from history. Let us not continue to repeat the same mistakes today.

*Dear Lord,*

*This was a very hard chapter to write, and I can only imagine how extremely difficult it may be for some of my brothers and sisters in Christ—black and white—to read. Father, help us to keep in mind that we want to make race relations better, and that in order for race relations among Christians to get better, we must all yield to the Holy Spirit and be willing to change for Your sake and for the sake of those we desire to serve for Your glory. Help us to realize that we may also need to change in order for us to get closer to You.*

*Amen.*

## NOTES

1. Philip B. Kunhardt Jr., Philip B. Kunhardt III, and Peter W. Kunhardt, *Lincoln: An Illustrated Biography* (New York: Knopf, 1994), 157.

2. Ibid.

3. Lerone Bennett Jr., *Before the Mayflower: A History of Black America* (New York: Penguin, 1988), 190.

4. Ibid., 191.

5. Ibid.

6. Ibid.

7. Ibid.

8. Ibid.

9. C. William Pollard, *The Soul of the Firm: ServiceMaster's Religious Pursuit of Excellence* (New York and Grand Rapids: HarperBusiness and Zondervan, 1996), 142.

10. Philip B. Kunhardt Jr. et al., *Lincoln,* 197.

11. Lerone Bennett Jr., *Before the Mayflower,* 192.

12. Ibid.

13. Bob Jones III, in Bob Jones Sr., *Is Segregation Scriptural?* (1960).

14. Bob Jones Jr., in *Is Segregation Scriptural?*

15. Donald McGavran, *Understanding Church Growth,* quoted in C. Peter Wagner, *Your Church Can Grow* (California: Gospel Light, Regal Books, 1980), 110.

16. Philip B. Kunhardt et al., *Lincoln,* 197.

17. Ibid.

18. Lerone Bennett Jr., *Before the Mayflower,* 196.

19. Ibid.

20. Ibid.

21. Philip B. Kunhardt et al., *Lincoln*, 196.

22. Ibid.

23. Ibid.

24. Ibid., 256.

25. Ibid., 227.

26. Ibid., 216.

27. Ibid.

28. Ibid., 227.

29. Ibid., 256–57.

30. Ibid., 257.

31. Ibid., 256–57.

32. H. B. London Jr., "Sanctuary," *Pastor's Family* 1, no. 3 (February/ March 1997): 32.

# 5

# Is Racial Reconciliation Really Working?

## (The Way Everyone Wants It To!)

*Your high independence only reveals the immeasurable distance between us. The blessings in which you, this day, rejoice, are not enjoyed in common. The rich inheritance of justice, liberty, prosperity and independence, bequeathed by your fathers, is shared by you, not by me. The sunlight that brought life and healing to you, has brought stripes and death to me. This Fourth [of] July is yours, not mine.*

—Frederick Douglass, at the request of
President Lincoln, addressing leaders on the
Fourth of July, 1862, Rochester, New York

The title of this book and of this chapter is not an attack on, nor an attempt to undermine the ministries of Promise Keepers, Reconcilers Fellowship, Mission Mississippi, or any other groups dedicated to improving race relations among Christians.

I am indebted to many Promise Keepers, especially to those in the national office in Denver. Chuck Lane, one of the founders, is being used by God to mentor me. Alvin Simpkins, the national manager of the Prayer Department, is mentoring me in the area of prayer. Corwin Anthony and Steve Shanklin are prayer partners. Tom Fortson has become a good friend. And Coach Bill McCartney has prayed for Brenda and me by name every day for the last six years. Brenda and I can never repay our debt to these godly men.

This book's purpose is to build on the foundation Promise Keepers and other ministries have already laid and, with them, to go on to the next logical step. Therefore, we are on the same page—maybe working at improving race relations from different perspectives—but with the same goal in mind.

In writing this chapter, I feel like the man driving out demons who was not one of the disciples. This disturbed them, and they ran back and told Jesus. The account is found in Mark 9:38–40:

> "Teacher," said John, "we saw a man driving out demons in your name and we told him to stop, because he was not one of us."
> "Do not stop him," Jesus said. "No one who does a miracle in my name can in the next moment say anything bad about me, for whoever is not against us is for us."

I am certainly not doing miracles, but I believe I am working *with* Promise Keepers, not against them. We may have different terminology and methods, but we are on the same team and desire the same results—improving race relations among Christians.

*Racial reconciliation* has become an extremely popular term. In fact, it is the Christian "politically correct" term to refer to a harmonious relationship between blacks and whites. Already, many whites and blacks have embraced it. But if so many Christians have accepted the term, why is it that some Christians—particularly many black Christians—still struggle with it?

## WHAT IS RACIAL RECONCILIATION AND DOES IT DIFFER FROM BIBLICAL RECONCILIATION?

Let's attempt to define the term *racial reconciliation* before any further discussion. First, the word *reconciliation*. The prefix, *re,* implies a previous "good" relationship. Thus, the word *reconciliation* carries the idea of being restored to a previously good relationship. *Webster's Collegiate,* Tenth Edition, says, "To make friendly *again;* or to bring *back* to harmony" (italics added).

130

In *biblical* reconciliation, God and man started out in a perfect relationship. Man sinned, thus becoming an enemy of God. God's grace, mercy, and love provided the perfect atonement for man's sin in the person of Jesus Christ. Through the death, burial, and resurrection of Jesus Christ, man now can be in fellowship with God again. Basically, there was a good relationship that was damaged and has now been restored.

Second Corinthians 5:17–21 is often used as a proof text for using the term *racial reconciliation.* But this text is talking about *spiritual* reconciliation, bringing man back to God. It is about sin and salvation, not race relations. Similarly, Ephesians 2:16, which says, "And in this one body to reconcile both of them to God through the cross, by which he put to death their hostility," speaks about reconciling the Jews and Gentiles not to each other, but to *God*, through the Cross. The emphasis is on spiritual reconciliation. We shouldn't try to make the Bible say something it isn't saying.

When people use the phrase *racial reconciliation,* analytical black Christians are naturally reminded of the biblical context of spiritual reconciliation. And they remember that, in the context of American history, blacks and whites in this country have not had a previously good, consistent relationship to which most blacks would want to be restored.

## A SECULAR HISTORICAL REVIEW

A brief overview of the secular historical relationship will explain why.

There were a few free blacks who came to America in 1619. Most of these blacks came, like many whites, as indentured servants. An indentured servant was a person who had signed a contract to work for another person, usually for seven years. Those seven years were a repayment of the price one would pay to come to the New World, which the master paid up front. At the end of the seven years, the indentured servant was free to go and begin life as a free person in the New World.[1]

This arrangement worked well, but only for a short time. A problem began in 1660, when white indentured servants started to escape on a regular basis. They were virtually impossible to recapture, because they could easily assimilate into the dominant culture of the society because of the color of their skin. Many of these indentured servants had the choice of prison in England or servitude in America. (Which raises the question whether America actually was founded entirely by God-fearing people—a question we may need to reexamine, especially since the state of Georgia was first settled by criminals. We must always clarify things within their context.)

This problem of white indentured servants running away before completing the term of their contract caused ship owners, sea captains, and the people who employed indentured servants to lose money. Businessmen being businessmen, they had to discover a way to stop losing money and make some money. Obviously, the black indentured servants could not assimilate into the dominant culture at all. So by 1701, the blacks who came to this country were brought here as permanent slaves, not as indentured servants who had freely chosen to begin a new life in the colonies.[2]

In order to justify slavery of other human beings, someone determined that blacks were not fully human. Once Europeans convinced themselves of that idea, slavery was in business as never before. Therefore, slavery was accepted.

## MANY CHRISTIAN AFRICAN AMERICANS STRUGGLE WITH THE FOUNDING FATHERS

One point of contention between black Christians and white Christians is the celebration of the Founding Fathers by so many white evangelicals. Many white conservative evangelicals revere the Founding Fathers and hold them up as godly men whose example all should follow. These conservative evangelicals will tell you that the Founding Fathers were great Christians—and great men in general.

No one doubts that the system of government set up by the Founding Fathers has many benefits. But blacks know that most of the Founding Fathers were not only Deists (people who do not believe in a personal relationship with Jesus Christ for salvation), but people who promoted slavery. Slavery was even described as Christian. Ephesians 6:5–8 was usually quoted to slaves to convince even Christian slaves that slavery was God's will.

When the Founding Fathers said, "All men are created equal," they were not referring to nonwhites. Black slaves were considered as property, and *no* blacks—slave or free—were accorded the civil rights enjoyed by whites. No blacks could vote, and for census purposes to determine taxation and congressional representation, slaves were counted as three-fifths of a person. The hypocrisy of the Founding Fathers is seen most clearly in Patrick Henry's speech protesting England's demand of taxation without representation. Patrick Henry cried, "Give me liberty or give me death!" Yet he had no problem serving as governor of a slave state. It was he who said, "Who would believe that I, too, own slaves." It is difficult to believe that the Founding Fathers could be so passionate about their own freedom, for which they would eventually go to war, yet be so insensitive to blacks' desire for freedom—just like the Founding Fathers felt England behaved toward them.

George Washington owned more than three hundred slaves. Washington struggled with this issue but didn't do anything about it. In his will, he authorized the emancipation of his slaves upon the death of his wife.[3] Jefferson's adulterous affairs with his female slaves are well chronicled.

The clergy of the day were not much better. In eighteenth-century New England, and throughout the country, scores of ministers owned slaves. Notables who owned slaves include such venerables as Jonathan Edwards, whose famous sermon, "Sinners in the Hands of an Angry God," is still in print and read by scores of people today. The Reverends Cotton Mather, Peter Fontaine, and Bishop Joseph Butler were slave owners. Much of the preaching by white ministers was pointedly designed to reinforce the attitudes of Englishmen toward Africans, and to instill in the slaves a contentment with their "God-appointed lot" in this life. Churches and churchmen in provincial America were heavily involved in maintaining a system of slavery.[4]

Yet the only criticism some conservative evangelicals make of the Founding Fathers is that they just made a "mistake" in the area of slavery.

Blacks question how anyone can be called "good" who was involved in something as terrible as slavery. Slavery was about money, and the Founding Fathers supported this brutal system.

Blacks *and whites* know how brutal slavery was. This "mistake" of slavery included kidnapping, rape, promotion of sexual immorality for profit, destruction of the family (biblical and family values), dehumanizing of a race, torture, and murder—many times in the name of God. A book could be written on the brutality of slavery. Blacks know that children of six years of age had ropes put around their necks. Things were put inside slaves orally and through the rectum to keep them from appearing sick in order to sell them for a profit.[5] Slave girls were forced to have sex when they were thirteen. (I think about my own girls. I can't imagine them having babies now.)

Does this sound like the work of Christian men? Do these men even sound like "good" men? Exodus 21:16 says: "Anyone who kidnaps another and either sells him or still has him when he is caught must be put to death."

Some African-American Christians wonder, if the Founding Fathers were Christians, why were they not hearing the convicting voice of the Holy Spirit? There is slavery in the Bible, and the Bible doesn't do away with slavery, but there is a difference between the slavery in the Bible and the slavery practiced in America. There are specific laws in the Old Testament outlining the rights of a slave and the procedures Israelites should follow in granting freedom to slaves in their possession. In the New Testament era, slaves were employed throughout the Roman Empire and slaveholders could legally exercise extreme brutality toward their slaves, though a mechanism also existed for slaves to buy their freedom. Slaves often served as tutors for the children of their masters. A few slaves in America could buy their freedom, and some did, but they could not own property or even be taught to read and write, except on a very informal basis, and then not legally. Consequently, many African Americans have difficulty embracing the Founding Fathers—some even find it impossible to do so. If we are honest, some African-American Christians even have a difficult time embracing white Christians who embrace the Founding Fathers. And when an African American embraces the Founding Fathers, many African Americans wonder if this person is really black.

Blacks played a significant role in the Revolutionary War and other wars involving the United States. Many of the contributions of African Americans to America, which you read about earlier in this book, have been omitted from many (not all) history books used in our public schools. This is part of America's problem—fear of the unknown. If more whites had been taught in school about the heroic exploits of African Americans in our wars, as inventors, and in government service, this knowledge would make it more difficult to justify racism. (Well, that is another chapter.)

Therefore, most black communities don't celebrate the Fourth of July with the same fervor as many whites do. In 1862, the black abolitionist Frederick Douglass was asked to address President Lincoln and others in Rochester, New York, celebrating the Fourth of July. Douglass went to great lengths to recount the struggle of the colonials in their journey for freedom from England. He then characterized the spirit of the colonial.

They were men of peace; but they preferred revolution to peaceful submission to bondage [so Nat Turner didn't do anything any self-respecting Christian colonial wouldn't do]. They were quiet men; but they did not shrink from agitating against oppression. They showed forbearance; but that they knew its limits. They believed in order; but not in the order of tyranny. With them, nothing was "settled" that was not right. With them, justice, liberty and humanity were "final"; not slavery and oppression. You may well cherish the memory of such men. They were great in their day and generation. Their solid manhood stands out the more as we contrast it with these degenerate times.[6]

Then Douglass said:

Fellow-citizens, pardon me, allow me to ask, why am I called upon to speak here to-day? What have I, or those I represent, to do with your national independence? Are the great principles of political freedom and of natural justice, embodied in that Declaration of Independence, extended to us? and am I, therefore, called upon to bring our humble offering to the national altar, and to confess the benefits and express devout gratitude for the blessings resulting from your independence to us?[7]

Finally, Douglass revealed his heart, and the heart of many slaves and present-day blacks, Christian and non-Christian:

But, such is not the state of the case. I say it with a sad sense of the disparity between us. I am not included within the pale of this glorious anniversary! Your high independence only reveals the immeasurable distance between us. The blessings in which you, this day, rejoice, are not enjoyed in common. The rich inheritance of justice, liberty, prosperity and independence, bequeathed by your fathers, is shared by you, not by me. The sunlight that brought life and healing to you, has brought stripes and death to me. This Fourth [of] July is yours, not mine. You may rejoice, I must mourn. To drag a man in fetters into this grand illuminated temple of liberty, and call upon him to join you in joyous anthems, were inhuman mockery and sacrilegious irony. Do you mean, citizens, to mock me, by asking me to speak to-day? If so, there is a parallel to your conduct. And let me warn you that it is dangerous to copy the example of a nation whose crimes, towering up to heaven, were thrown down by the breath of the Almighty, burying that nation in irrecoverable ruin! I can to-day take up the plaintive lament of a peeled and woe-smitten people![8]

In no uncertain terms Douglass informed his audience of the sins and the hypocrisy of the Founding Fathers and those who would celebrate the Fourth of July and yet allow slavery to continue.

## DOES HISTORY REPEAT ITSELF?

After the Civil War, there was a period called *Reconstruction*. During this time, there was an air of excitement for ex-slaves. Frederick Douglass said,

I seem to myself to be living in a new world. The sun does not shine as it used to. . . . [N]ot only the slave emancipated but a personal liberty bill, a civil rights bill . . . given the right to vote, eligible not only to Congress, but the Presidential chair—and all for a class stigmatized but a little while ago as worthless goods and chattel.[9]

Wendell Phillips said, "We have not only abolished slavery, but we have abolished the Negro. We have actually washed color out of the Constitution."[10] (I'm glad he didn't live to see today.) In the 1860s and 1870s there were black sheriffs and mayors in the South. By the 1870s, there was a black man in the Senate and a black governor in Louisiana.

As ex-slaves prospered, many white people felt that government had gone too far. It seems unbelievable that anyone could think that the government had gone *far enough!* How could any person or government repay a race of people for being enslaved, taken from their land, many not surviving the voyage across the ocean, standing (oftentimes nude) on auction blocks, watching their family sold (many times to different slave masters—and seldom were these families ever united), having heritage and culture irreversibly altered?

As these ex-slaves strove for equality, their former masters, the white males, believed that they were being discriminated against. They created a slogan, "Emancipate the Whites."[11] It was OK to enslave blacks for hundreds of years, but twelve years of blacks striving for equality versus more than two hundred years of slavery caused white males to panic. Today, it is called reverse discrimination. In fact, in the Saturday, July 16, 1997, edition of the *Denver Rocky Mountain News,* the headline read: "White male 'disadvantaged.'" The subtitle stated: "Springs man qualifies for affirmative action because it was used against him, judge rules." History may be repeating itself in our lifetime.

## AMERICA GOES BACKWARD

The outgrowth of the panic mentioned earlier was manifested in February 1877. Representatives of the white South and white North made an agreement: "Home Rule" for the South and the presidency for the Republican, Rutherford B. Hayes. The result was a de facto suspension of constitutional rights of blacks in the South. On April 10, 1877, federal troops were withdrawn from Columbia, South Carolina, and the white minority took over the South Carolina state government. Less than two weeks later, the guard changed in Louisiana. The Supreme Court ruled in 1883 that the Civil Rights Act of 1875 was unconstitutional.[12]

These events led to incredible acts of violence against blacks in the 1880s and 1890s. Lynchings increased as well as assaults by the Ku Klux Klan. Neither the white church, the white academy (the schools), nor the white Supreme Court opposed it.[13]

Next, blacks had to fight for the Civil Rights Act of 1964. The March on Washington (D.C.) was led by Dr. Martin Luther King Jr.

All along, the white evangelical church was strangely silent. Or, when it did speak, it defended racism and segregation.

These are just a few of the things that demonstrate the ongoing relationship between blacks and whites in America. It is obvious to see that it has been neither a good nor an equal relationship.

## TRYING TO RIGHT A WRONG

On January 15, 1997, several African Americans received the long-denied Congressional Medal of Honor. The citation for second lieutenant Vernon J. Baker described his exploits:

In 1945, serving with the 92nd Infantry Division in April, during a two-day action near Viareggio, Italy, he single-handedly wiped out two German machine gun nests, led successful attacks on two others, drew fire on himself to permit the evacuation of his wounded comrades, and then led a battalion advance through enemy minefields.[14]

Edward Allen Carter Jr., of Los Angeles, was a staff sergeant with the 12th Armored Division. When his tank was destroyed in action near Speyer, Germany, in March 1945, he led three men through extraordinary gunfire that left two of them dead, the third wounded, and himself wounded five times. When eight enemy riflemen attempted to capture him, he killed six of them, captured the other two and, using his prisoners as a shield, recrossed the exposed field to safety. The prisoners provided valuable information. Mr. Carter died in 1963.[15]

John Robert Fox, of Cincinnati, was a first lieutenant with the 92nd Infantry Division when he was killed in action in December 1944 near Sommocolonia, Italy. Fox voluntarily remained behind as an artillery spotter during his unit's withdrawal from a position being overrun by a superior German force. Despite the reluctance of the gun crews with which he was in contact, he ordered artillery strikes closer and closer to his own position, finally insisting that all firepower be directed at his position as the only way to defeat the enemy. His body was eventually found amid those of more than one hundred enemy soldiers.[16]

Willy F. James Jr., a private first class with the 104th Infantry Division in April 1945; Ruben Rivers, a staff sergeant with the 761st Tank Battalion; Charles L. Thomas, a major with the 103rd Infantry Division; and George Watson, a private in the 29th Quartermaster Regiment were all honored with the Congressional Medal of Honor. Only Mr. Baker is still living.[17]

Although 1.2 million African Americans served in the military during World War II, not a single black received one of the 433 Medals of Honor awarded during the conflict. A full-scale probe was launched in 1993. The result of the probe was the honoring of these deserving soldiers.[18]

## AFRICAN AMERICANS ARE STILL FIGHTING FOR EQUALITY

Another reason it is difficult for racial reconciliation—or whatever you want to call it—to take place is the fact that things are not equal now. Blacks are still fighting for equality. I'm sure if there were equality today, many blacks would be able to overlook the past much easier. The problem is that the past is *today* for most blacks, whether they be Christian or non-Christian.

## THINK ABOUT IT

I hope this overview makes it easier for whites to understand why many black Christians question or often reject the term *racial reconciliation.* I knew I didn't feel comfortable with this term, but didn't know why, until I heard Rev. Jerald January, former U.S.A. Director of Compassion and now CEO of Jerald January Ministries and the Urban Block Party, comment on it. He was the first person I ever heard articulate the problems with the term *racial reconciliation.* He made his statements at a cross-cultural Christian meeting in Colorado Springs whose purpose was to determine ways to improve race relations. He also made similar comments in 1997 at the Roundtable Discussion on Racial Reconciliation sponsored by Gary Bauer, president of the Family Research Council. To my amazement, those who had once advocated the term agreed with Jerald when they heard his explanation. Everyone agreed that Jerald's perspective made perfect sense. In fact, most people who have heard his explanation for not using the term *racial reconciliation* agree that it is not the logical term to use.

Jerald was not being negative, but simply being historical, logical, and practical. History demonstrates that there has never been a good, consistent relationship between blacks and whites in America, Christian or non-Christian. Thus there is nothing to reconcile. Blacks do not want to be "restored" to the racial conditions of the past.

## MORE REASONS SOME BLACKS ARE HESITANT TO RECONCILE

In an article entitled "Been There, Done That," Barbara Williams Skinner, the widow of the late evangelist Tom Skinner, states that there is no excuse for allowing racial barriers to stand.[19] She also explains why many African-American Christians struggle with reconciliation, listing four reasons many African-American Christians aren't excited about "reconciling."

***Reason #1:*** *Although there is much talk about diversity, multiculturalism, and racial reconciliation, actual understanding between the races is at an all-time low.* African Americans see it as no coincidence that while the prison industry explodes, affirmative action—which most blacks believe has helped many reach the middle class while hindering very few whites—is being rolled back. The vast majority of black Christians who identify themselves as Democrats watch as millions of white Christian activists drive their Republican bandwagon head-on against homosexuality and abortion but jump into reverse when it comes to fighting poverty and racism. All of this appears as solid proof that the white community—including white Christians—really does not care about the plight of the black community.[20]

*Reason #2: Racial reconciliation sounds a lot like the failed integration of the 1960s.* For too many African-American Christians over age forty, racial reconciliation brings to mind the worst aspects of integration. African Americans were required to give up too much of what is rich and beautiful about their own African-American culture, while whites did not give up anything. Many blacks were taught that getting the right education, speaking properly, and mastering all aspects of white American culture would make them more accepted by whites. They "Europeanized" themselves only to discover a painful reality—in the end they were no more socially acceptable to white Americans and were left alienated from many in the African-American community. Blacks have grown tired of always being the ones who have to do the changing in order to make peace, and, even then, meeting opposition.[21]

*Reason #3: Blacks fear losing the last truly African-American institution—their churches.* The black church is one of the few institutions totally owned and controlled by African Americans. An estimated sixty-five thousand churches—reaching 16 million people each week—are some of the few places African Americans can witness strong and dynamic black leadership at all levels, build social and leadership skills, advance their political and public policy interests, improve their communities, and reach inner-city youth and those needing financial help to attend college. At the same time, like nowhere else, they receive spiritual encouragement for the struggles of life. Indeed, the church is our last and most important refuge of empowerment.[22]

In the face of the serious moral crisis of black family breakdown, drugs, and crime, reconciliation seems like a strange diversion of precious energy and resources to a cause with little chance of success. Surely reconciliation is a higher calling than separation—but not if the definition of reconciliation sacrifices the empowerment of African Americans. In the name of integration, blacks lost many of the institutions that addressed their needs: businesses, self-help organizations, and schools. Can they trust the new form of reconciliation to address their needs and give room for black leadership? Past experience answers a resounding no.[23]

*Reason #4: There is as much racial separation inside as outside the church.* The black church we know today is a result of racism. The phenomenon of Christian racial separation was initiated by whites during slavery and continued after slavery when white religious bodies excluded African Americans or—with a few exceptions—treated them as second-class members. Today, even with the end of Jim Crow segregation, and with no legal barriers to working, living, worshiping, or playing together, African Americans and whites operate in two almost totally and voluntarily separate worlds. *While blacks feel they tried the racial harmony game, whites have not demonstrated a willingness to come onto blacks' turf.* We rarely get to know one another in our family and social settings. Only a handful of the more than three hundred thousand white American ministers can count a friend among the sixty-five thousand African-American ministers. Truly integrated churches, with different races sharing the leadership, worship, singing, study of God's Word, and prayer are still a rarity. In addition, many white Christians believe that a lack of personal prejudice is sufficient for reconciliation. They are unwilling or unmotivated to join with their black brothers and sisters in the fight against *institutionalized racism.* By remaining silent, they allow injustice to continue in the social, political, economic, and criminal justice realms of America.[24]

Please understand that Barbara Williams Skinner is not bitter. She is very aware of the numbers of white Christians who are sympathetic to the black cause and the role they play in improving race relations in this country among Christians. There are many one-on-one cross-cultural relationships, but she is examining the Christian community at large in America.

Barbara Williams Skinner goes on to state that in spite of these obstacles, there is a new breed of Christian who desires to improve and is improving race relations among Christians. She mentions many of them in her article—blacks, whites, Democrats, and Republicans.

Barbara's article, like this book, is for those who are serious about improving race relations among Christians and who are willing to take a critical look at themselves to see if they are either part of the problem or part of the solution. There is no middle ground!

## BUILDING RELATIONSHIPS IS ESSENTIAL

Aside from the historical perspective, let's explore some basic principles regarding relationships. No one talks about *dating reconciliation.* Can you imagine walking up to a prospective marriage partner and saying, "I want to be socially reconciled to you." In this country, most people date before they get married. The purpose of dating in our culture is to learn about a person to determine if you want to begin and/or continue a relationship. In the dating process, people normally learn about each other's past. This knowledge is invaluable in understanding why a prospective mate acts in a particular manner. It also provides insight that can be useful in attempting to minister to your potential mate.

These principles are essential in developing cross-cultural relationships if we intend to have a *meaningful* and *lasting* cross-cultural relationship. People who believe we do not need to know the background of the people with whom we want to develop relationships are not being realistic. Most foreign missionaries, for example, have to learn the culture and the language of the people to whom they plan to minister.

## GOING THE EXTRA MILE

As I consult with individuals, churches, parachurch ministries, and organizations as to how to develop a positive cross-cultural environment, I hear some white evangelicals say, "I don't want to treat anyone *special.*" The late Spencer Perkins, writing in *Reconcilers Fellowship,* responded: "Because of the key role that white America played in creating the problem, it also must take the major responsibility by partnering with black leadership who are working toward solutions."[25] Matthew 5:7 states: "Blessed are the merciful, for they will be shown mercy."

Matthew 5:39–41 says: "If someone strikes you on the right cheek, turn to him the other also. And if someone wants to sue you and take your tunic, let him have your cloak as well. If someone forces you to go one mile, go with him two miles."

We may need to reexamine what God says about serving our brothers and sisters in Christ. Galatians 6:9–10 says: "Let us not become weary in doing good, for at the proper time we will reap a harvest if we do not give up. Therefore, as we have opportunity, let us do good to all people, especially to those who belong to the family of believers."

In 1 Corinthians 9:19–23, Paul speaks of becoming "all things to all men" in order to win some. He tells believers to attempt to serve others in the context of the national's culture. The question is, why don't we do this in America when attempting to minister to blacks, Hispanics, Asians, or Native Americans? Minorities have all had to learn the white culture because it is the dominant one (for now), and thus survival has depended on mastering this culture.

Not to learn about the culture of the people we are attempting to serve is sin expressed in the form of arrogance, prejudice, or an air of believing we are superior.

Many people are willing to do something to help as long as it does not cost them anything. This attitude will make these people virtually ineffective in ministry, because ministry always requires sacrifice and faith (Hebrews 11:6: "Without faith it is impossible to please God"). These kinds of people usually end up doing more damage than good. Nationals see through their conditioned efforts.

Do we want lasting cross-cultural results? If the answer is yes, we must learn about the other cultures—from *their* perspective and not from our own preconceived ideas.

If the term *racial reconciliation* is offensive to the masses of blacks, are we willing to change the term? People complained for years that they could not understand or read the King James Version. No one is saying that the King James Version is not the Word of God, but people began to produce different versions so that more people would read the Bible, which was the point to begin with. Why are we so opposed to doing this in order to establish lasting cross-cultural relationships?

## THERE'S BEEN ENOUGH TALK; WE NEED ACTION

In doing my research for this book, I discovered an article in the Dallas Theological Seminary publication *Kethiv Qere* that had much to say that was useful. The title of the article was "The Ministry of Whites in a Black Community."[26] It was published on October 14, 1977. (Much of what was discussed in this *Kethiv Qere* article will be dealt with in more detail in a later chapter of this book. It surprised me to see that this article and my chapter on this subject have so much in common.) The following are some statements from this article.

Dr. Walter Banks, a professor at Moody Bible Institute at the time of this article, said: "Motives must be genuine and serious, so that the right attitude . . . of respect for black culture, tradition, etc., coupled with love, humility, and real burden will alleviate many obstacles." He also said: "Suffering, suspicion, and slow progress must be expected."

Jim Westgate, a graduate of Dallas Theological Seminary and at the time of this article a member of the staff of Circle Church in Chicago (a cross-cultural church), said: "Any ministry of whites to blacks must be preceded by adequate exposure to black culture, history, [and] tradition."

Does it amaze you that twenty years later Christians are still saying the same things? Could the reason be that very little substantially has been done in the evangelical community in the last twenty years? This lack of progress in this area has frustrated many a black Christian.

Romans 5:8 states: "But God demonstrates his own love for us in this: While we were still sinners, Christ died for us." *Love* is an action word in the Bible. When black Christians evaluate what appears to be a lack of action on the part of their white Christian brothers for at least the last twenty years, correctly or incorrectly it is interpreted as a lack of love for them. That makes trust much more difficult to secure.

I wonder if this lack of action, interpreted as a lack of love, has been seen by non-Christians? John 13:34–35 says: "A new command I give you: Love one another. As I have loved you, so you must love one another. By this all men will know that you are my disciples, if you love one another."

If black non-Christians are viewing this appearance of a lack of love, could the evangelical community unknowingly and unintentionally be assisting in the building of Farrakhan's platform?

This is just something to think about.

Journalist Andrés T. Tapia, in an article in *Christianity Today,* "After the Hugs, What?" says:

> I believe the road to true reconciliation will involve whites coming on our turf, eating our food, listening to our music, and being uncomfortable as they experience faith, history, and culture through our eyes. It is not enough to come in as a tourist who returns home with souvenirs and a pen pal but rather as someone who has come to be among us.[27]

The first chapter of the gospel of John shows how Jesus came as one of us, not as an outsider. Mr. Tapia observes: "Racial reconciliation does not mean that evangelical whites have to vote for a certain party or candidate, but it does demand that they assess and speak out about how the issues and positions of candidates affect minority communities."[28] For example, there is the issue of a disproportionately large number of fourth-grade black boys being put in special education classes as a solution for discipline problems. Whites can speak out against this practice, asking that other solutions be found and questioning the thinking behind such an approach.

Before the 1996 presidential election, one political leader was invited by the black leaders to meet with them and discuss their issues. He chose not to do so. When interviewed by a white journalist on a TV show as to why he chose not to meet with the leaders, his response was, "I knew I couldn't get their votes." The white journalist asked some pointed questions, similar to these: "If you become president of the country, would you not be president of all the people? Wouldn't it be prudent to know the concerns of all the people? Wouldn't it have been wise to develop a relationship or respect and trust even though you might not have received their votes?" There was only a boyish smile as a response.

Mr. Tapia has this to say about the value of racial reconciliation for whites:

Whites need to recognize that racial reconciliation is not just the right thing to do; it is good for whites as well. During the [Promise Keepers'] pastors conference at the Georgia Dome last February, a Latino pastor commented, "They can pat me on the back and clap for me, but I think this is helping whites more than it is helping me right now," as white pastors wept in repentance for their racism. I suspect that whites are subconsciously recognizing their need for their brother and sisters of color.[29]

Mr. Tapia discusses two more areas that need to be examined:

[The] glass ceiling must be shattered. As long as people of color are not in decision-making positions in churches, parachurch organizations, seminaries, and Christian publications, true reconciliation cannot be complete. This, more than any other issue, has undermined racial progress in the evangelical movement. "They talk the talk, but when it came to sharing the power there was a brick wall," says Bill Pannell, formerly of Fuller Theological Seminary. Shared power would be proof of the dominant culture truly treating us as equals. . . .

Minorities have long been learning from white Christians. We have learned their hymns, read their books, practiced their theories. But it is time for whites to recognize they can benefit from minority perspectives on life and faith. If whites do learn from minority Christians, this will enrich, embolden, and strengthen the whole church. The shift from whites saying, "What can I do for you?" to "I need you" would signal that perhaps words and deeds are starting to come together.[30]

Pastor Eugene Rivers, an inner-city pastor with credentials from Harvard and Yale, makes some statements regarding racial reconciliation that may be difficult to read but must be read if Christians are to improve race relations within the body. Pastor Rivers does not major in tact. (This is not an apology as much as it is a warning. Please remember it has been at least twenty years since this dialogue began, and some people are getting tired of saying the same things over and over with no response.) Rivers was interviewed by the journal *Reconcilers.*

"I had a meeting with the editorial board of *Christianity Today,*" says Rivers,

> and they made an interesting observation, that Blacks are apparently not interested in racial reconciliation. I agree with that assessment. Black people want freedom. The kinds of emotional reconciliation sessions, where we receive apologies and extend forgiveness, are mostly just temporary purgings. Reconciliation minus *justice* is of cathartic value, but it doesn't go much beyond that.
>
> My sense is that white evangelicals want racial reconciliation because it implies peace, but in most cases, not justice. There's a "peace at any cost" mentality running through white evangelical motivations toward reconciliation. Peace for most well-intentioned folks means an absence of conflict.

White evangelicals never broke their necks to bring Blacks into fellowship with them, and so now they wonder why Blacks are not anxious to be reconciled? They are still looking for Blacks to make it easy for them, but if they can't find Blacks who aren't going to hurt their feelings by telling them the truth, then they'd just as soon not make the effort reconciliation requires. If Whites are serious about reconciliation, then they need to come ready to have some real conversation without playing around.[31]

Rivers is a "show me the money" type of statesman. He says, "If Whites are serious about racial reconciliation, they will demonstrate it by giving up power and control of material resources." Rivers insists that reconciliation should be *measurable.* "We talk numbers when we want to look at quarterly reports and profit margins; we talk Jesus, but in a very unmeasurable way, when it comes to our Christianity."[32]

Steve Barr, a white Harvard undergraduate student in the mid-1980s and a member of the Harvard-Radcliffe Christian Fellowship (HRCF), the InterVarsity group, and the largest Christian organization on campus at the time, attended a year-long seminar taught by Rivers on biblical faith, justice, and social responsibility. "During the course," says Barr, "many of us white students became convicted about not taking race and justice very seriously."[33] When the leadership of the predominantly white Christian fellowship seemed unresponsive, most of the black students and several white students left.

According to Barr, this mass exodus left the HRCF reduced in size and wounded in spirit. Those who left were bitter; many of those who remained were shocked, angry, or in pain over the rift. And, as a group, HRCF may have been left a little gun-shy. "I think it really set back the clock for HRCF for dealing with race," says Barr, "and it created a wariness and weariness over the issue that took a long time to heal."[34]

This same scenario is often played out in evangelical ministries and denominations. A few years ago, a large denomination made the news with its "declaration of repentance." That was great, but at the same time, it was going through a reorganization. In this particular denomination, the Anglo membership is in decline. It is the minority membership that is providing all the growth. But when a reorganization committee was initially appointed, the committee was composed of seven white males, all from a certain area of the country. One had been relocated out of the area, but his origin and much of his ministry was from the same area of the country as the others. When one of the committee members was questioned about this, his comment was, "We are all male and very pale." Later, the committee was enlarged, with one Hispanic and one Anglo female added.

Another denomination requested that I review the president's report to his board. In his report, he stated, "The minorities are the fastest growth group in our denomination, but unfortunately, the denomination doesn't have enough money to hire a minority to head this much needed position." A little research revealed that the Anglo group in this denomination was also in decline. I shared with this president that if he were in a business to make money, he would go out of business with the present philosophy of his denomination. I told him that he and his board needed to rethink their priorities.

He needed to take money out of the budget where churches were declining and put it where they were growing (remember the parable of the talents?). Fortunately, I knew the president well enough to talk candidly with him, and he was mature enough in his faith not to be intimidated by me (this was refreshing).

These two situations have brought outcries of frustration and anger from both of the denominations' black constituents. These denominations, justly or unjustly, have been accused of attempting to go back to the fifties. Blacks are concerned about this desire to move back in time, for, in the fifties, Jim Crow laws existed for blacks.

The idea of returning back to the fifties politically concerns blacks, who feel that if things aren't equal now, they will only get worse if we go back in time with present attitudes and practices.

Conservative evangelicals need to consider this when they attempt to relate to the black community. The Jim-Crow-laws experience is very real to those blacks who experienced it.

Pastor Rivers says, "Real, genuine reconciliation would mean that Whites would start a war with Whites to make sure that black people got what they needed in terms of justice."[35] I am excited to say that through the grace of our Lord, I have seen white Christian brothers and sisters do—and continue to do—this for me, but I believe this is the exception, not the rule.

## POLITICAL SENSITIVITY

This is the area where angels fear to go, and I don't blame them. I am in no way trying to tell anyone how to vote, but I am concerned that a political party has become the new religion of many Christians. The allegiance to this party is so great that if a Christian doesn't vote for the right party, he or she is viewed as being in sin or an outcast. What has sadly become quite obvious is the need for some of my Christian friends to express their political opinions in Christian settings when it isn't necessary or relevant, and it often detracts from what is being discussed. The saddest aspect of this new gospel is that my friends often degrade certain politicians unnecessarily, yet often close their eyes to the same shortcomings in their own politicians. Some of my Christian friends are behaving so unlike Christ! Several have told me they hate certain politicians. They are doing the opposite of Ephesians 4:29, which is speaking words that are edifying. Gloating about leaders' sins and speaking hatefully about them doesn't qualify as edifying. In fact, the biblical injunction is to pray for our government leaders (1 Timothy 2:1–2). Whether we like a leader or not, the Bible tells us that even bad leaders are God given and worthy of respect (Romans 13:1).

In the last presidential election, people of color overwhelmingly voted differently than their white counterparts according to numerous sources. I believe at least two things should be considered here: (1) there are Christians on both sides, and (2) the majority culture tend to have an agenda and people of color often a different agenda. Some people consider mostly one issue, and some consider more than one issue while voting.

Maybe if we can *calmly* discuss different perspectives, we could learn a lot from each other. Again, it doesn't mean that you will agree, but at least you will understand.

Remember the Rodney King beating? At the time, I was pastoring a cross-cultural church in Tulsa. We had one of the best Bible studies ever as people discussed their feelings. There were blacks, whites, one Native American, a former Black Panther, Democrats and Republicans. I'm not sure anyone changed his or her political persuasion, but we heard, some of us for the first time, a different perspective regarding the political parties. Our votes carried a heavier significance to us, because we learned that no political party helps all people. In fact, while a political party can help one group of people, it can actually hurt another group of people. One party favors one group of people economically and the other party, another group. This is why there is more than one political party. We may need to ask ourselves some questions: "Is there something about their situation that I may not understand?" "Am I willing to try to learn, which doesn't always mean I change my opinion, but to learn because I want to better understand my brother or sister in Christ?"

The issue is not persuading people to vote the same way you do, but trying to understand why people hold different views than you do. Understanding the difference can create intimacy if people are willing to work at it. We must remember God is sovereign. And we must continue to share the Gospel. As God changes hearts, then the votes will follow. Legislation doesn't change hearts. God does.

If we are honest with ourselves, we must admit that no political party is Christian. It is a concern of many black Christians that one group of Christians seems to think that one political party is Christian—and the only way for the country to return to God. It seems that salvation is now to be found in this political party instead of in the Gospel.

One of the former Republican freshmen told me before he became a Congressman, "I believe we, as Christians, are spending too much money fighting abortion. Understand me, I oppose abortion more than I ever did, but I don't think legislation is going to change things. I think we need to put more effort and more money into evangelism. When God changes someone's heart, He will change his lifestyle as well." We as the body of Christ have got to get back to the basics of Christianity.

I must comment on the issue of affirmative action, which may be tied with welfare as the two issues that are keeping Christians divided. I am in no way attempting to promote one side or the other, but I do want to give you the perspective of some black Christians.

First, when some black Christians hear their white brothers and sisters in Christ criticize affirmative action, blacks know that whites have benefited by the color of their skin, which is affirmative action, if you think about it. Secondly, when the statement is made that affirmative action is "rewarding for race," or "race obsessed," instead of a "color-blind" society, blacks know that race has *always* been an issue in America. It may be easier to ignore if you are in the majority, but the problem still exists.

Those who believe in a color-blind society remind me of the Introduction to Philosophy course I taught at a local college when I was in Tulsa, Oklahoma. The philosophers I was discussing believed in the "goodness of man." This is in direct opposition to the Word of God (Romans 1:18–32; 3:10–20, 23). There seems to be an unspoken assumption among many whites that all members of the majority race will treat all minorities fairly when it comes to school admissions, hiring for positions of leadership, and setting appropriate titles and salaries in corporate America and in Christian ministries.

There is also the assumption that the demise of affirmative action will create a level playing field. The question is, who will determine if this playing field is "level"? If things stay as they are, it will not be the minorities. The question blacks want answered is, what is motivating some white Christians to believe that things will change once affirmative action is eliminated? Christians are in the minority in this country. What is going to make non-Christians all of a sudden begin acting like Christians when they do not have the indwelling Holy Spirit to enable them "to do the right thing"?

We must remember the story of Zacchaeus (Luke 19:2–9). Before Zacchaeus could develop a relationship with those he had wronged, he had to make restitution. He was not forced to do this. It was something he did *gladly*. In fact, Jesus said that Zacchaeus's attitude was a sign of his salvation, a *changed heart!*

Many black Christians and non-Christians are looking and waiting for a positive agenda that reaches out to all Americans. (I'm not sure any political party can do this.) But so far, some political agendas seem to contribute more to racial division than they do to building bridges.

## CAN THE EVANGELICAL GOSPEL MINISTER TO MINORITIES?

In mid-October 1997, two weeks after Stand in the Gap, Rev. Carl Ellis, president of Project Joseph (a ministry designed to bring Muslims to Christ), spoke at Denver Seminary. His lecture compared the Million Man March to Stand in the Gap.

Rev. Ellis attended the Million Man March. He said, "Sixty percent of the attendees were Christians!" He also said, "There were a million black men at the March." Out of one hundred men interviewed by Rev. Ellis at the rally, not one was a follower of Farrakhan.

Rev. Ellis said the Bible can handle any situation, but he is not sure the "evangelical gospel" can. He said that when the white Christian community split over the "social gospel" around the turn of the century, the "evangelical gospel" immediately became incapable of ministering to minorities because it *did not* address the needs of minorities. The emphasis was on personal holiness, and it *did not* address people holistically. Jesus Christ usually dealt with the entire person. He met them where they were—remember the Samaritan woman?

Rev. Ellis says that the "evangelical gospel" doesn't address the six basic needs of black males, which is why many of these males may turn to the Nation of Islam. These six basic needs are *dignity, identity, significance, pain, rage,* and *the need for remasculation.*

Maybe this is why, for the last twenty years, the body of Christ has been talking about improving race relations but has been unable to do anything about it. It is as though we are preaching outstanding sermons about the Good Samaritan but unable to put the principles of the Good Samaritan into practical application. The evangelical community has talked long enough the last twenty years. It is time to take some action! We have got to practice what we are preaching.

The evangelical community must ask itself a very important question: Do we want to have a legacy of glorifying God regardless of the race that might inherit it, or do we want to say we have had a good run? In the future, by the middle of this century, those who are the minority now will become the majority. This shift in racial population is often referred to as the "browning" of America. This means that the grandchildren, and certainly the great grandchildren, of those in the majority now may well experience racial prejudice at the hands of the relatives of former minorities.

South Africa has set a tremendous example for America. When the minority whites in South Africa voted to give blacks the right to vote, they knew the consequences of that meant that they would never again be in control of the government because they were and are the racial minority. What integrity they demonstrated!

## COUNTING THE COST

Maybe the most important reason for eliminating the term *racial reconciliation* is that so many young non-Christian African

Americans are examining and comparing the claims of Christianity and the Nation of Islam. If Christians are in error with the term *racial reconciliation,* these nonbelievers may think Christians are wrong about Christianity as well. This is what many young black males are saying as I meet with them in traveling across the country.

After I spoke to a Christian business group in Denver last fall, a board member of a Christian organization approached me to talk. He said, "I agree with what you said, but we have millions invested in this term." My response: "You have a decision to make. How much is a soul worth?"

Now, we are getting to the real issue. It is going to "cost" anyone—any church or organization that is serious about and committed to improving race relations among Christians today. This cost will always be more than we anticipate because that is the faith aspect of it. An attitude of flexibility, teachability, and patience must be developed by those of the majority race who desire cross-cultural relationships with minorities. This is something they can learn to do. After all, in order to survive in any culture, minority children must master the system of the majority race without losing their own identity.

Another reason not to use the term *racial reconciliation* is that it doesn't point to anything or have any direction. It is a state of being. It also makes it easy to skip over the past. Often the past is painful for minorities, but it must be understood if a relationship is to be formed. The goal cannot be just to have one friend of another culture or race so we can say we have done our job. The goal must become a lifestyle!

## RACIAL PARTNERSHIP IS THE TICKET

Ninety-nine percent of the time when I explain my perspective on the term *racial reconciliation,* I am asked, What term would I recommend? My response is usually, Why do we need a name for it? Why don't we just do the right thing? Still, I realize that one culture seems to feel much more secure if it has a name for everything.

Therefore, I would propose that the term *racial partnership* symbolizes what most Christians want to see in the area of race relations.

The strength of the term *racial partnership* is that, first of all, it implies that equal parties are involved. This is something *racial reconciliation* doesn't necessarily do. Second, *partnership* implies a working together for a desired goal or result. This is hard work because you are forming something out of nothing! Partners starting a business very often have to work through their differences if they are going to be successful. Many times partners don't know each other as well as they think they do.

If we are honest, most partnerships are formed because the goal can't be achieved by one person or company. If it could, then there wouldn't be a need for the partnership. The same is true of us in the areas of culture, race, and even spiritual gifts in some of our own churches. We all need each other—we just pretend we don't because we are often afraid of what we may lose personally (control, for example) and what the finished product may look like.

Successful partners know the desired goal is worth some personal sacrifices. It is working through differences that build strong, close relationships. These principles are true in Christianity as well as cross-cultural relationships.

Often people are forced to become partners because they cannot take on a particular venture on their own. They need someone to help them. Similarly, as Christians, we need each other. I believe there is work God wants the body of Christ to do together so that we can learn how much we need each other and benefit from working with each other. None of us, even as Christians, has it all together, but together in Christ, we have it all!

Now let us work together to build some partnerships of which the world will take notice!

*O Lord,*

*My heart goes out to those who have worked through this chapter, but even more to those who stopped reading this book at this* point because the pain was too great. They could not or would not allow themselves to hear pain from the other side. Lord, please use another method to reach them because we need them too, just like they need us and may not know it. Lord, help them to see that this chapter is not condemning so much as it is assessing. It seems like it is condemning because the circumstances are so bad.

As I was writing this chapter, before I could even finish writing it, I sensed the need from You to stop and pray. I pray for those who were wounded maybe for the first time as they read this chapter. Father, I pray for those who had old wounds reopened again. Lord, I sensed the pain, but with no pain, I wonder if anything is gained. Father, may this chapter be one of Your many tools to finally get the body of Christ to go beyond talking to action, so that the healing that can only come from You through the power of the Holy Spirit may begin.

Father, I also pray that as the body of Christ begins to heal itself and truly become one, that the non-Christians will see Your love in action through us and be drawn to the You in us that they see. And may You be glorified as we, as Christians, prove to be Your disciples!

Amen.

## NOTES

1. Tom Skinner, *Black History: Training Seminar for Campus Crusade for Christ,* 15 August 1971.

2. Ibid.

3. Henry Louis Gates Jr. and Nellie Y. McKay, eds., *The Norton Anthology: African American Literature* (New York: Norton, 1997), 385.

4. Robert J. Cameron, *The Last Pew on the Left: America's Lost Potential* (Lafayette, La.: Prescott, 1995), 82.

5. Dr. Alexander Falconbridge, *An Account of the Slave Trade on the Coast of Africa* (London: 1788). *A Narrative of the Life and Adventure of Venture, A Native of Africa* (New London, Conn., 1798; expanded ed., Hamden, Conn., 1896).

6. Frederick Douglass, in Henry Louis Gates Jr. and Nellie Y. McKay, eds., *The Norton Anthology: African American Literature,* 383.

7. Ibid., 385.

8. Ibid., 386.

9. Frederick Douglass, in Lerone Bennett Jr., "Second Time Around: Will History Repeat Itself and Rob Blacks of the Gains of the 1960's?" *Ebony: Incorporating Black World Magazine,* September 1995, 88.

10. Wendell Phillips, in Lerone Bennett Jr., "Second Time Around," 88.

11. Lerone Bennett Jr., "Second Time Around," 90.

12. Ibid., 90.

13. Ibid., 88.

14. Ken Ringle, "For Black Soldiers, an Overdue Honor," *The Washington Post,* 14 January 1997, sec. A, 1, 6.

15. Ibid., A6.

16. Ibid.

17. Ibid.

18. Ibid.

19. Barbara Williams Skinner, "Been There, Done That," *The Reconciler* (Jackson, Miss.), Winter 1996, 4.

20. Ibid.

21. Ibid.

22. Ibid., 5.

23. Ibid.

24. Ibid.

25. Spencer Perkins, *Reconcilers Fellowship: Reconciliation Wednesday for Leaders* 1, no. 14 (15 October 1997)

26. Ruben S. Conner, "The Ministry of Whites in a Black Community," *Kethiv Qere,* 14 October, 1977.

27. Andrés T. Tapia, "After the Hugs, What?" *Christianity Today,* 3 February 1997, 55.

28. Ibid.

29. Ibid.

30. Ibid.

31. Eugene Rivers, Interview, *Reconcilers,* summer 1997, 4–6.

32. Ibid.

33. Steve Barr, Interview, *Reconcilers,* summer 1997, 4–6.

34. Ibid.

35. Eugene Rivers, Interview, *Reconcilers,* summer 1997, 4–6.

# 6

# The White
# Christian Problem
# in America

## The White Christian Community Cannot Continue to
## Do Ministry as Usual in Its Approach to Minorities

*No one tears a patch from a new garment and sews it on an old one.
If he does, he will have torn the new garment, and the patch from the
new will not match the old. And no one pours new wine into old
wineskins. If he does, the new wine will burst the skins, the wine will
run out and the wineskins will be ruined. No, new wine must be
poured into new wineskins.*

—Luke 5:36–38

Early in 1997 I attended the strategy meeting of a new Christian
organization. This new organization's purpose was to reach everyone in America with the Gospel by the year 2001. What a great goal!
I was excited about it!

While at this strategy meeting, I was determined not to get
involved in any racial discussions. This would not be possible. I was
minding my own business, doing my best to stay unnoticed. In fact,
I was in the rest room, powdering my nose, when a white Christian
man, whose conference I hosted a few years ago at Focus on the
Family, asked me what I thought about the lack of African-American
leadership in the new Christian organization. (I can't even go to the
rest room without getting into a discussion about the relationship
between black and white Christians!) My response: "This is the typical evangelical method in starting a new movement or organization."

The man I was talking to already knew this because he had developed quality relationships with several black pastors in his hometown. This white guy was so passionate about this subject that he got the head of the new organization to talk with me. The head of the organization said he had a black guy who was going to get more blacks involved. I had never heard of this black guy. Neither had the head of this organization heard of any of the blacks who are actually effective in the black community. For me, the saddest part of the meeting was when a Hispanic brother said that the Hispanic population is growing faster than any other group in America. He asked if this organization was producing Spanish literature for this group. He got the typical evangelical response: No.

So does this new Christian organization really want to reach nonwhites? It says yes, but its actions say no.

## HERE WE GO AGAIN

This organization is no different than many other white Christian organizations and some churches. It has a biblical, thus a worthy, objective all Christians can rally behind. Unfortunately, it also has the same old ineffective approach that has been and still is in practice today when soliciting minority participation. White Christians birth the project. Once it is up and running, minorities are only then asked to join, promote, and support this new work of God. Basically, minorities are an afterthought. No one wants to admit it, but it seems that the minorities who become involved are asked to participate specifically so they can promote this project to their own kind. Intentionally or unintentionally, minorities often feel used (see the discussion of "Plain Vanilla Christianity"[1] in chapter 1). They are wanted to help promote a program but not to help create it.

## THE IDEA STAGE

Christian minorities want to ask one question of their white Christian brothers and sisters (even though it seems some white males have more of a problem with equality than white women do), with whom they are going to spend eternity. This is it: "Why aren't minorities brought into the project during the idea, or birthing stage?" Before the idea goes anywhere, there should be prayer to determine if this idea is of God. It is here, especially, that minorities and women should be brought into the mix (actually *on board*). If this would take place, there would then be no embarrassment and no need for excuses to minorities for being an afterthought in regard to the project. This action would eliminate the need to worry about recruitment because everyone affected would have taken ownership. Recruitment would become a passion. The entire body of Christ could endorse this new project. This approach would also demonstrate to the rest of the body of Christ and the non-Christian world the unity Christ intended for His church from the very beginning.

One of my dear non-Christian friends—and tennis buddy— told me that when he was young, he used to go to church. He said that one Sunday some blacks wanted to worship at his church, but they were not allowed inside. Ever since that day, he has had no use for Christianity. He views Christianity as hypocritical. He does not understand prejudice. He is one of my best friends, and I want him to go to heaven with me. He puts up with me even though I am a Christian. Through the grace of God, I have been consistent with him.

## THE METHODOLOGY

The methodology of leaving minorities out of the planning stage seems to be condoned by many white evangelicals as normal and acceptable. Many white evangelicals are used to being, and expect to be, in charge. It is certainly all right with them if minorities want to participate in the projects they have initiated, but they don't think of minority participation at the beginning stages. Few white evangelicals (there is a small minority) actually know what is "happening" in Christian minority communities. It seems that only a few white evangelicals will join Christian minority-initiated efforts in kingdom building. It may not be intentional, but this action—or lack of it—is often translated as saying that minority projects are not important, thus not worthy of supporting.

## THE REASON FOR THE EXCUSE

The excuse for not including minorities from the beginning is usually fairly simple. A minority may hear, "We just did not think about it," or "We (white males) don't know any minorities," or "We heard he or she is 'liberal.'" (*Liberal* generally means that the minority does not belong to the right political party.) This response generally means that no minorities they know meet their standards. A minority never hears, "We prayed, and God told us not to include minorities."

## LOOKS CAN BE DECEIVING

On the surface, a naive individual may say that things are getting better. There *have* been improvements for minorities in evangelical circles. But a closer investigation reveals that the evangelical arena is still a good ol' boy system. Don't look at the boards of organizations. Boards only know what the organization wants them to know. No, look at the in-house, daily decision-making body of each organization. See if you can find any minority leadership in the upper echelons of management. Then see if there is any minority leadership over any areas other than minority-related ones. Count the number of minority presidents and vice presidents in the Christian organizations and look at their range of authority, budgets, and staff.

Check to see if these minorities are allowed to hire their own staff. Does the ministry promote its commitment to the minority publicly so that the organization cannot renege on its commitment?

All too often, minorities in Christian organizations are set up to fail from the beginning. They are almost always underbudgeted and understaffed. Their division or department is usually funded by soft money (grants or designated gifts). If the departmental budget is not a part of the regular organizational budget, then in all likelihood the minority is a two- to three-year experiment, which does not cost the organization one dime. As Dr. William Pannell, professor at Fuller Seminary (now retired), says, "The absence of minority presence in evangelical leadership questions the integrity of the Gospel proclaimed by these same evangelicals."[2]

The same is true of some large, predominantly white churches that are "integrated." It is uncommon to find in these churches a black staff person other than a black minister of music. This was true of two large churches here in Colorado Springs. One church finally hired a black staff person in a nonminority-related position. The other church told its black constituents that it was not going to put any blacks in positions of leadership because the church was afraid it would lose too many important white members.

People don't like to talk about it, but money, especially "old" money, can have a major influence in regard to integration. The influence of this money has, can, and will dictate to what degree a Christian organization, church, or school will be allowed to integrate.

When I was in seminary, the late Dr. T. B. Maston, who was white, mentored me. We walked around the seminary campus every other day until his health would not allow him to do so. He told me that when he was still teaching, the largest donor said that no blacks would live on campus as long as he (the donor) lived. Dr. Maston said none did until this donor died. Money talks! Dr. Maston also said there was an unofficial limit as to how many blacks could attend the school at one time. I kept track for the next five semesters. He was right. He said that if too many blacks came at one time, the "old" money would not come as often, nor would there be as much.

In the previous paragraph, I criticized Southwestern Seminary, of which I am an alumnus, for some situations that occurred during its past. I must just as passionately applaud Southwestern for having the courage, faith, and integrity to acknowledge some of its errors in regard to race relations and for its efforts to correct those errors. Southwestern president Dr. Ken Hemphill is to be commended for this. The seminary also dedicated almost an entire edition of the *Southwestern News* to Christian African Americans.[3] What an intentional step of faith! What a tremendous example to set for other institutions to follow.

The previous paragraphs may be difficult for some to accept, but we must attempt to understand the minority perspective on this issue if we are serious about improving race relations. It is hard for black Christians to comprehend how white evangelicals can have such a passion for strategic planning and five-year goals for their overall programs and yet lose this passion for planning when it comes to ministering to minorities and their communities. Therefore, when blacks hear of whites' desire to reach the inner city, for example, the effort they see expended does not appear to match the stated desire. This inconsistency, whether intentional or unintentional, gives minorities the impression of racism. This inconsistency may be expressed individually or institutionally or both.

## CAN I GET A WITNESS?

Recruiting black Christians with the idea of making them become just like white evangelicals is to miss the point of integration in the body of Christ. It seems that some whites tend to recruit with the idea of assimilation in the back of their minds, which means whites don't have to change, just the recruited blacks. This kind of thinking violates the biblical principle of diversity found in the study of spiritual gifts. In this study, it becomes clear that no one person has all the gifts. The divine purpose of this seems to be to develop interdependency among the congregation specifically, and the body of Christ in general. If a man and a woman have a good marriage, they know where one partner is strong and the other weak, and vice versa. They learn that instead of competing they must complement each other's strengths and gifts. This makes them stronger as they strive to become one. They know they are better together for God's glory than they are apart! This is what black and white Christians must learn.

It appears the biggest hurdle for many white evangelicals is understanding or even thinking about this principle. What many don't realize is that integration is an issue of faith. This is why the average tenure of a black in management in a white evangelical ministry is only about three to five years. Matthew 9:16–17 states:

No one sews a patch of unshrunk cloth on an old garment, for the patch will pull away from the garment, making the tear worse. Neither do men pour new wine into old wineskins. If they do, the skins will burst, the wine will run out and the wineskins will be ruined. No, they pour new wine into new wineskins, and both are preserved.

What some white evangelical ministries, churches, and individuals do not understand is that these verses are saying that you cannot do business as usual when another culture or race is to be included in ministry. The new patch (the minority) and the old garment (old traditions) will pull away from each other. Therefore, a climate for integration must be created that demands that some of the old traditions, which are not biblical, go before the minority even comes to work. This will require the evangelical mind-set to hire a minority consultant to assist the organization with this major transition.

Often these organizations, churches, and some individuals do not know what they are doing or what to do when they encounter someone who is different. Promise Keepers' tremendous influence has caused some ministries to integrate before they were ready and has caused others to integrate even though they didn't really want to but couldn't afford financially to be viewed as racists. These ministries quickly hire a black without knowing where they want to go, although they *do* know they don't want the black (who usually knows where to go and how to get there) to tell them what to do. These paternalistic efforts and lack of faith almost always guarantee that these kinds of actions will fail or end in frustration.

When white evangelical ministries and churches hire blacks to assist them in relating to minority communities, the unstated desire seems to be that the newly hired blacks will convince the minority communities to become white. Instead of understanding that it is the *white* ministry that must make the major adjustments and that the *black* who has been hired is the *expert,* they expect to make no changes themselves. What they should do is automatically propel the black Christian into the decision-making body because his or her very presence will influence the entire perspective of the particular ministry. But when the black Christian begins to share with the white ministry that what it thinks will be effective in the black community won't be—and may even be offensive—he or she is seen as a rebel attempting to turn the organization into a black one.

The white organization or church forgets that it asked the black to lead it in an area where it has never been effective with any measurable success. By asking for help, the organization implied that it has not been doing something right and thus needs to make some changes. The problem seems to be resistance to the needed changes.

For example, the organization will ask the black to evaluate its line of products, literature, and marketing. If the black is honest and says these products won't be effective in the black community, the organization will often be upset. Instead, it should ask, "What can we do to become more effective?" To become more effective will usually cost money, because changes have to be made. But instead of trusting God for the additional funding, too often no changes will be made because the black constituents aren't a sure market. There is no guarantee on the return of the investment. This leaves the black attempting to attract blacks to this organization with no products or literature to which blacks can relate. Then the organization gets upset with the black for not being as effective as it thought he or she should be.

Yet the black is only doing what he or she has been hired to do. In fact, this black is actually protecting the organization from needless mistakes that would result in criticism from the black community. Thus, in reality, the black Christian is the best friend the organization has in relating to the black community. Unfortunately, most times Christian organizations don't see it this way.

In fact, when this scenario occurs in an organization, it is not uncommon for the blacks who head these departments to all of a sudden have their authority reduced, or suddenly not be invited to meetings about their departments until major decisions are already made. They may even lose the right to hire their own staff so that the "right" kind of black can be put into the department. This sets in motion the old "divide and conquer" theory. It is usually the first step in replacing the black who is not working out with the "safe" black who is just glad to be there. The black who was originally hired to effect change now hears from his or her supervisor, "Why can't you be like so-and-so? He is black and he isn't complaining."

Of course, the new black usually can't see the big picture and often isn't looking long-term. Unfortunately, one of the traits of this new black is that he doesn't know the black community any more than the whites who hired him. This trait is what makes him so "safe" that he won't speak out against racism, because he doesn't understand the games being played at the corporate level. Without realizing it, the new black has been set up to fail, just like the original black was. The only difference is the original black will eventually be forced out of his ministry position, whereas the new black will simply be relocated somewhere else in the ministry, or someone else will be brought in to run the department. Then this parachurch ministry or church can tell the world it tried, but cross-cultural ministry was just something God hadn't called it to do.

This happens all too often. Numerous lawsuits have been settled out of court between black Christians and white Christian organizations because of this type of practice, which is by no means Christian. It is sad, but true.

The blacks to whom this is happening are questioning God as to why they had to have this experience. They are even questioning if they correctly heard God calling them to such institutions in the first place. The next step is to begin to question the salvation of some of the individuals in the white organization or church that has taken such actions in a business-as-usual fashion, with no remorse. It is all the black person can do to keep from going crazy.

Again, the problem is that the ministry is attempting to put new wine into old wineskins. The step of faith required demands that white Christians must trust God to work through black Christians. But many white Christians seem to struggle with the very idea of black Christian leadership, let alone thinking of actually experiencing it. This attitude by these white Christians is witnessed by many black Christians and builds the wall between the races higher instead of lowering it.

## DO YOU LOVE GOD LIKE YOU SAY YOU DO?

When people have a problem in the area of racism, it is because they have a problem with their relationship with God. It is a *sin* problem more than it is a *skin* problem. First John 4:20–21 says: "If anyone says, 'I love God,' yet hates his brother, he is a liar. For anyone who does not love his brother, whom he has seen, cannot love God, whom he has not seen. And he has given us [Christians] this command: Whoever loves God must also love his brother."

According to this standard, it appears from the actions of many white evangelical ministries that these people are sinning in the area of racism. Thus God is not pleased with them. This also means that God will bring judgment against these ministries in His time and in His way. Racism may also have incredible negative implications for revival happening in America! Think about it!

## THE FEAR OF BLACK MALES

White evangelicals also seem to have a problem relating to black Christian males. Evangelicals believe the media stereotypes that describe African Americans. There seems to be no difference in the way a black is treated, whether the black is a Christian or not. A portion of this problem seems to be motivated by fear. This appears to be very apparent if you examine the racial composition of these Christian organizations. The makeup of the decision-making bodies of these Christian organizations and churches is a clear indication of their practical theology versus their philosophical theology. What you will see is the practical application of the reality of what many evangelicals really believe.

This is very interesting, because even the "safe" black Christian males are very seldom on the decision-making bodies of these organizations. The odds are much better of finding one black *woman* on the board of the decision-making body. Yet women do not seem to receive equal treatment either. Therefore, having a woman in these positions is not a major statement unless there are enough women to impact voting decisions.

Recently, I ran into Dr. Cynthia James in the Denver airport. When she heard about the plans for this book, she told me that she was contacted by a white parachurch ministry in 1980 or 1981 that wanted to reach out to the black community. She and two black Christian males who also had Ph.D.'s were initially excited about the possibilities. Then she noticed the organization did not want to deal with the black males, even though she said they were more qualified than she for the position. The ministry hired her but not the more qualified black males.

We talked about the present-day evangelical community. As she walked away, she said nothing has changed. She told me many white ministries are not serious about serving the black community. The fear of black males is still there. When white ministries become serious, you will see black males in several, not just one, decision-making positions.

In an interview with Joyce Dinkins, who served as a Pan-African Christian Exchange Missionary, Dinkins responded to this question: "Is PACE open only to African Americans?" Joyce's response:

"No. PACE has sought to involve all people groups. For example, in October of 1994 a white male from Detroit joined the group to Kenya. He had special technical expertise to use at the well project. He went and served under Africans. This was done because PACE wanted to reverse the traditional model of black serving white. If real racial reconciliation is to be achieved, then the world needs to acknowledge Africans in the role of leadership."[4]

The result of all of this is that many blacks are leaving predominantly white organizations. Many all-black ministries are springing up as another result of the struggles blacks are having in white-dominated Christian organizations.

Again, the issue is one of faith.

### THE "SOUTHERN STRATEGY"

Many white evangelical Christians often look to conservative politicians to work to bring moral values and a Christian worldview to legislation before the Congress and to the political process in general. Yet the national party many of these evangelicals are likely to support, the Republicans, have made use of a political strategy—the so-called southern strategy—that is deeply offensive to African Americans and ultimately very divisive of unity between the races.

This strategy and its faults are discussed in an article "Rebels Yell," by Bob Jones IV, in the April 25, 1998, edition of *World* magazine. Jones frames his discussion by following the work of two Republicans, Rev. Earl Jackson, who is black and lives in the Boston area, and Mr. Bob Inglis, who is white and lives in South Carolina. Inglis, it says, "speaking at a historically black college in March 1997," argued that the southern "strategy was morally wrong and ought to be abandoned."[5] For this Inglis reaped the scorn of those who promoted the Confederate flag and was called disloyal to the conservative cause and even a liberal. Yet Inglis knows how the southern strategy affects black voters and further divides his party, which he wants to unify. Therefore, he is taking on an issue that may have been culturally and traditionally acceptable in the past but must be sacrificed today for the sake of unity.

At "party events and campaign fundraisers," party activists have told Inglis: "'Listen, you don't get it. You don't know how important race is to politics. You are leaving support aside. You are going to lose the devotion of many people.' Still, he professes not to be worried. The success of Promise Keepers, with its strong message of racial reconciliation, makes him think that at least the evangelical portion of his heavily religious district will respond to his emphasis."[6]

"But not all Republicans are eager to place racial reconciliation so high on the agenda," the article says.[7] Many minorities feel that though evangelicals have given the *message* of racial reconciliation a high priority on their agenda, the consequential *actions* of racial reconciliation are not high on the agenda.

> Mr. Inglis is careful to allow that many defenders of the southern strategy are not being *intentionally* divisive on issues of race, but he believes that their rationalizations miss the point: Whether or not the strategy is racist in its intent, it is undeniably racist in its impact. Black voters, he says, feel unwelcome in the Republican Party because of the way images and issues are manipulated to reinforce negative stereotypes. For instance, GOP campaign ads discussing Medicaid, welfare, and crime almost always feature black faces, reinforcing the impression that black people are the main perpetrators of violence or the biggest drain on the treasury.[8]

The evangelical community *must* come to understand this principle, of which it is also guilty.

> Ending affirmative action is another theme that plays especially well here, but Mr. Inglis has steadfastly resisted the suggestion that he make it a tenet of his campaign. Though he opposes affirmative action in principle and in his votes, he believes that leading with the issue would exploit voters' fears without making

*any positive contribution.* Instead, he seeks to be biblical in his approach: "I think it is true that affirmative action is an un-American concept. But speaking the truth in love means making sure to not use a backlash against black South Carolinians for my political benefit in seeking an answer to that question."[9]

Affirmative action may be an un-American concept, and so was slavery, but slavery was surely embraced in America, even taken to new heights. Someone must take responsibility for creating a "level playing field" that will right present mistreatment of blacks.

Inglis's approach is definitely biblical. He is not going to sacrifice his brother for personal gain. The evangelical community desperately needs to begin practicing this principle with minorities if we are to attain any kind of lasting unity.

For his part, Rev. Earl Jackson cites "a voter guide distributed in Austin, Texas, churches that used a black figure to represent the liberal position and a white figure to represent the conservative side. The message, he says, was clear: Black equals liberal equals bad; white equals conservative equals good."[10]

Evangelicals *do* tend to equate black with sin. Therefore, subconsciously, black is always bad. This typology has a tremendously negative effect on black youth. Some black youth don't want to be black or associate with other blacks because black is seen as bad by the government and American Christianity.

Jackson says that President Clinton's trip to Africa is another case in point.

> Mr. Jackson says Republicans just don't understand the PR value of the president's recent 11-day tour of Africa. "The first president goes to Africa and he's seen treating Africans as *equals.* It doesn't do anything substantively to change the life of a single black American," he acknowledges, but it works wonders in terms of lifting their spirits. "That is the sort of communication that Republicans are going to have to learn if they're ever going to

reach minorities in this country."[11]

The same is true for evangelicals.

Jackson is against affirmative action, "but he was dismayed by the plunge in minority enrollments following California's recent decision to ban racial quotas in its state universities. Blacks around the country concluded that 'the real agenda here is the re-segregation of America,'" Jackson says. "We know that's not true, but when you see dramatically declining enrollments, someone has got to step up and say: 'This is a concern for us all, and if affirmative action is not the answer, fine, but we've got to take this seriously and advance some positive agenda for dealing with the problem.'"[12]

Many blacks, Christian and non-Christian, tend to view white evangelicals who are against affirmative action as anti-black because when affirmative action in institutions in California was dismantled no positive alternative was put in its place. In the meantime, black youth suffer, and so do their futures. This is a typical example of actions being made without considering the consequences on minorities.

There *is* good news.

In 1996 state senator Stephen Newman, a white Republican who represents the district that includes Jerry Falwell's Liberty University, joined with his black Democratic colleague Louise Lucas to push a bill retiring the state song, which had lyrics many regarded as racist. Last year the two unlikely allies teamed up again, this time on an issue of more serious consequence: passing a ban on partial-birth abortions.[13]

Another political "odd-couple," a white Republican and a black Democrat, have teamed up "to introduce parental rights legislation that would guarantee the fundamental right of parents to 'autonomy in child-rearing.'"[14]

Mr. Michael Farris, president of the Home School Legal Defense

Association, says of the political situation in Virginia: "When we realize that many in the black community share our moral and social views, we come a lot closer to a working majority."[15] Author Jones says, "By coming together on social issues, both blacks and whites are able to flex their political muscle and show their independence from the party leadership."[16]

Evangelicals can learn a lot from some of these politicians. Just think what we could do together for the kingdom.

Remember: You can believe what you want to believe, but some things you may need to leave at home when trying to serve in a different culture.

## WHY RELATIONSHIPS AREN'T BUILT

Praise be to the Lord our God because there *are* people who are building friendships that cross cultural and racial boundaries. These friendships seem to be the exception and not the rule. For the majority of Christians, this does not appear to be the norm.

It is extremely difficult for black and white Christians to develop relationships in this context because there is little or no trust involved. If you remember the chapter that reviewed black history, Christian and non-Christian, there seemed to be little, if any, difference in the way most blacks were treated by most white Christians.

In conversations with whites who want to improve race relations, it has been amazing to hear how few have ever read any history about blacks written by blacks. This makes one question how serious they are about improving race relations—or is this just a fad, having a "brother of color."

## WHAT'S THE RUSH?

One of the major differences between whites and blacks is that whites appear to view programs as the solution to all problems. Blacks tend to be into relationships and generally follow people, not programs. Whites have a tendency to assess the black situation without ever going into the community or speaking with anyone from the community. Then they want to solve the problems with a program they have developed without any input from the black community. Yet, if they have not developed a relationship with the black community, the programs they create will have little chance of success. These programs will also be marked by an air of paternalism, even if not intended.

When whites *do* begin investing in the black community, they often want a quick return on their investment. Whites do not seem to understand that a relationship must be developed before any programs can or will be used. It takes time to build relationships. The issue of trust is critical for blacks, especially dealing with white Christians, who have not had a good track record in cross-cultural relationships.

A denomination wanted to have black representation so badly that it brought a black church into its fold. In no time flat, it had the church and pastor in its magazine, but now the denomination is asking questions about the church it should have asked before the church joined the denomination. Now the denomination is praying everything will work out. If it does not, it is the blacks who are likely to be blamed. That will make it more difficult for the next black church to join.

Often whites do not think any ministry is being done in the black community. Many times what is needed is not a new program, but financial support for what is already being done.

When whites decide to invest, they must give the best of their resources. You cannot play it safe and glorify God at the same time.

Ralph Ellison wrote the book *Invisible Man*. One of his points is that the concerns of people must be dealt with. Too often it seems evangelicals want to save souls without knowing about the concerns of the people they want to save. This is not the way Jesus did it. If the concerns of the people you are attempting to minister to aren't important to you, then, in reality, neither are the people.

## THE GREAT COMMISSION IS STILL RELEVANT

Another major hurdle for some white Christian ministries is

understanding the Great Commission in the context of America. As mentioned earlier, evangelicals do seem to understand how important it is to study the culture, learn the language, and acclimate themselves to weather and clothes when they are going overseas to minister. Unfortunately, whites do not apply this principle when they attempt to minister to blacks in America.

If many white evangelicals ever intend to minister effectively to blacks or any other minorities, they must go where the minorities live. This will allow these white evangelicals to learn things they cannot learn from a book or from the media.

Mark Brewer, a white pastor of Colorado Community Church of Denver, has developed a good relationship with some of the black pastors in Denver. The way he built these relationships was by going to the ministerial meetings, being quiet, listening, and learning. He did not go in and appoint someone as the black leader, as many white Christian leaders have done. Instead, he saw who the blacks themselves said was their leader.

Mark learned this principle from Jesus Christ. Christ was often criticized for associating with undesirables.

So many sincere, well-meaning white evangelicals have damaged the credibility of their efforts because they don't do this. They find a black who has gone to the "right" school, or select a black who is a friend of theirs, and set this person up as a "leader."

The first problem this creates is resentment from the black community for having the white evangelical community again being paternalistic. Thus, there is no equality or respect established by the white evangelicals in regard to the black Christian community. True equality means that white evangelicals will have to trust blacks to be experts on themselves.

A second problem is that this newly appointed leader by the white evangelicals is often not a leader in the black community. Therefore, he cannot effectively "deliver" the black community because the black community is not following him. In many cases, the black community doesn't even know who he is. But the evangelical community goes ahead anyway and makes him their spokesperson for all blacks. What is amazing is that even if the majority of black Christians do not agree with this new spokesman, the evangelicals will support him anyway. Then you hear these white evangelicals complaining in unbelief that the black community didn't show up. Some white evangelicals think there is only "one" voice who can speak for the black community. Unfortunately, some of these evangelicals come across as having all the answers to the black community's problems.

## WHITES MUST DO A BETTER JOB OF RESEARCHING BLACK FACTS

One of the most damaging problems I believe some white ministries have in their radio, TV, and communications areas is the tendency to do very poor research, or in some cases *no* research, when commenting on "facts" pertinent to blacks.

I am not going to name these individuals. There is documentation of the incidents, but these are godly men whom God has used and is using to touch lives for His sake. I know these men have certainly been used by God in my spiritual development. And I certainly will not in any way knowingly harm the Lord's anointed. Therefore, these men will remain nameless. Hopefully, they will read this book and make the proper adjustments.

My purpose is not to tarnish reputations, but to point out mistakes that need to be corrected for the sake of the body. The mistakes these men have made have been devastating to many of their black listeners and black financial supporters.

Let's consider the problem of poor research. One radio personality made the statement in one of his broadcasts that when President Lincoln signed the Emancipation Proclamation, "The slaves who were now free, simply stayed on the plantation." As you know from the history provided in this book and available in other history texts, this is not a true statement. Black and white historians alike have done tremendous research in this area. Yet, the research staff of this particular ministry did incomplete or no research. Then to make matters worse, the radio personality began to mimic how he thought a black slave would speak. (For some reason, there are radio personalities who take great joy in mimicking how they feel slaves would speak. It is always done with poor grammar and often accompanied by laughter. Several of these individuals have even spoken at events promoting racial reconciliation. These individuals need to make public apologies for their lack of concern for minorities. These apologies would open the door for some healing in the body of Christ.)

Have you heard the statement that there are more blacks in prison than in college? This may be true, but is it a fair statement? What would be a fair comparison would be to compare the number of college age (18–24) blacks in prison versus those of the same age group in college. You will find that there are three times as many black males in college than there are in prison, according to Farai Chideya's book *Don't Believe the Hype: Fighting Cultural Misinformation About African-Americans.*[17] According to the 1991 report of the 21st Century Commission on African-American Males, blacks receive longer sentences than whites who have committed the same crimes.

Kay Coles James, in her report as the Secretary of Health and Human Resources for the Commonwealth of Virginia to the Governor and the General Assembly of Virginia in 1995, "Study of the Status of Virginia's Families," pointed out that white women are having more babies out of wedlock than black teenagers.[18]

According to Harvard population researcher Nicolas Eberstadt,

[T]he out-of-wedlock lifestyle has gone "main-stream": Unmarried mothers are increasingly likely to be white, chronologically mature, and well-educated. The stereotype of the unwed mother as a black teenager is completely outdated. Less than one-eighth of the illegitimate babies of 1991 were born to African American teenagers— fewer in fact, than were born to white women in their 30s. So drastic was the change in norms over the past generation that illegitimacy ratios now appear to be higher for white women in their very early 20s than they had been for black teenagers in 1961.[19]

Doing a little extra research could go a long way in improving race relations among Christians. When poor research is done, it tears the body down, not builds it up. It also provides more ammunition for Minister Farrakhan and the Nation of Islam to criticize Christianity.

## THE EVANGELICAL COMMUNITY MUST ADMIT
## THAT RACISM IS ALIVE AND WELL WITHIN ITS RANKS

The secular world has had to admit that racism is alive and well within its ranks. It has had to come to grips with the fact that it is at war with racism.

For schools, coming to grips with subtle racism means coming to grips with its universality, Jack Dovidio advises. In the old view of racism, he says, the feeling was that "if you could fix the people who were prejudiced, everything would be fine. Modern racism, though, is rooted in subtle processes. Rather than [make assumptions about] who is racist and who isn't, we need to work on everybody. We all have the potential to be biased, and we have to get people to acknowledge that."[20]

And because of past abuses and discrimination, he says, "We have to understand the *importance of trust* in the whole process. We must understand we're starting from a position of distrust, and what we have to do is work toward trust."[21]

It is amazing that our secular society realizes it has a lot of learning to do. The evangelical community must also come to this realization and act on it!

## A CLIMATE FOR DIVERSITY MUST BE CREATED

Today more and more businesses are discovering they must embrace the concept of reaching different audiences and employing different people so that they can have the same types of people on their staffs internally as those they are attempting to reach as their client base. Christian ministries and churches could learn from secular businesses, which are years ahead of Christianity when it comes to integration. Diversity training from the top down for Christian organizations and churches should be mandatory if the goals of these organizations and churches include cross-cultural ministry.

Remember the Texaco scandal of a few years ago? A recent report in *USA Today* states that a court-created oversight panel concluded that Texaco has made "meaningful strides" in diversifying its work force in the past year.[22] The panel was created as part of Texaco's $175 million settlement of a bias suit brought by minority employees in 1996. The forty-five-page report said that 40 percent of some 8,900 new hires were from racial or ethnic minorities, and half were women. Of almost six hundred promotions, women received 44 percent and minorities 25 percent. The report also said that one of the oil company's top accomplishments was a 114 percent increase, to $298 million, in the amount of business it did with companies owned by women or minorities.

Texaco paid a high price for its racism, but it learned from the experience and turned it into a profit! The evangelical community could learn a lot from Texaco. Texaco learned to listen to the minorities it hired. In the process, Texaco achieved what it wanted all along: profit. The road to getting there was just a little different. The evangelical community must learn to listen to and trust the minorities it hires. Just like Texaco, the goals it wants to achieve will be achieved. It will just be by way of a different route.

It is amazing if you compare a two-year turnaround by a secular company and a Christian community that has not been able to make a similar turnaround in twenty years! Of course, Texaco had a court-created oversight panel—an accountability system. The evangelical community has no such accountability system—or does it? What is the Holy Spirit? Will there really be a Judgment Day, when our works will be judged?

Just think of the incredible things the Christian community could do for Christ if we were *one!* Think how we could impact our society if we were united in Christ! The Lord said in Genesis 11:6,

"If as one people speaking the same language they have begun to do this, then nothing they plan to do will be impossible for them." Think about evangelism, discipleship, marriage, and families. The world could be a different place!

Are you beginning to see how important ending this race problem among Christians is?

## LEAVE THE GUILT AT THE CROSS

As I compare experiences with blacks and other minorities who do cross-cultural consulting, one issue that always surfaces is the issue of whites feeling guilty and then becoming defensive. We, as blacks, would be hired to consult at the request of a white, usually Christian, organization or church—thus implying that the organization or church wanted to do something in the area of cross-cultural relationships.

In these meetings, when the cross-cultural consultants are asked to share the minority perspective of the majority race, the very people who hired us and asked the initial question begin to get defensive upon hearing the answers. It seems that becoming defensive is somehow related to feeling our "rights" have been violated. "Rights" tend to be related to selfishness.

The Bible has a lot to say about servanthood. As I understand it, a Christian who is a servant voluntarily sets aside his "rights" in order to serve. Jesus Christ has specific words to say about being a servant in Matthew 20:26–28:

Not so with you. Instead, whoever wants to become great among you must be your servant, and whoever wants to be first must be your slave—just as the Son of Man did not come to be served, but to serve, and to give his life as a ransom for many.

Maybe one of the problems with serving is that we do not see it modeled often enough. Servant leadership may be becoming a lost art, whereas non-Christian leadership styles and celebrity status seem to be the desired goals.

I think that we all as Christians need to focus more on serving. None of us needs to feel guilty if we have been to the Cross.

Remember, the purpose of this chapter is not to say that all whites are bad, just as not all blacks are bad, but to describe some practices that make it difficult for black Christians to trust white Christians. If you are white and are serious about improving race relations, you must understand what you may be doing wrong in order to make the corrections that are necessary if this goal is to be reached.

*Dear Lord,*

*Please forgive me if I have hurt any of my brothers or sisters in Christ who have read this chapter. I have so many in the body of Christ who are my family and are white, whom I in no way want to hurt. At the same time, Father, these are issues that must be dealt with if any long-lasting healing is to take place. I realize that most of the mistakes addressed in this chapter have not been made maliciously, but a few are.*

*Lord, help us realize that being a servant is not a weakness, but a strength.*

*Lord, help us realize that we can only serve people as we yield to the empowerment and guidance of the Holy Spirit.*

*Amen.*

## NOTES

1. Jo Kadlecek, "Plain Vanilla Christianity," *Ministries Today*, November/December 1996, 34–41.

2. William Pannell, *The Coming Race Wars? A Cry for Reconciliation* (Grand Rapids: Zondervan, 1993).

3. *Southwestern News* 56, no. 1 (October 1997): 16.

4. *Sunday Digest* 111, no. 2 (1996): 7.

5. Bob Jones IV, "Rebels Yell," *World*, 25 April 1998, 14. All quotes used by permission.

6. Ibid.

7. Ibid.

8. Ibid.

9. Ibid., italics added.

10. Ibid., 15.

11. Ibid., italics added.

12. Ibid.

13. Ibid.

14. Ibid.

15. Ibid.

16. Ibid.

17. Farai Chideya, *Don't Believe the Hype: Fighting Cultural Misinformation About African-Americans* (New York: Penguin, 1995).

18. Kay Coles James, "Study of the Status of Virginia's Families," Report to the Governor and the General Assembly, Commonwealth of Virginia, House Document No. 57 (1995).

19. Nicolas Eberstadt, "A Revolution in 'Family' That Is Eating Its Children," *The Washington Times,* 24 September 1993.

20. Jack Dovidio in Jo Anna Natale, "Education in Black and White," quoted in *The American School Board Journal* 185, no. 2 (February 1998): 21.

21. Ibid.

22. "Texaco Diversity," *USA Today,* 30 January 1998.

# 7

# The Responsibility of Black Christians in the Race Game

## We Can't Blame Whites for Everything

*[After becoming a Christian] I loved all mankind, slaveholders not excepted, though I abhorred slavery more than ever. I saw the world in a new light, and my great concern was to have everybody converted. My desire to learn increased, and especially did I want a thorough acquaintance with the contents of the Bible. I have gathered scattered pages of the Bible from filthy street gutters, and washed and dried them, that in moments of leisure I might get a word or two of wisdom from them.*

—Ex-slave Frederick Douglass

**A**ny remembrance of the racial situation between black and white Christians in America tends to make me sad, disappointed, angry, and tired of waiting to be treated with equality by those with whom I am going to spend eternity.

### HOW LONG SHOULD BLACK CHRISTIANS WAIT?

Many slaves never expected social changes here on earth, but they kept hoping society would be better for their children. Many slave songs spoke of receiving their due in heaven. During the civil rights struggle of the 1960s, Dr. Martin Luther King Jr. persuaded the masses of blacks to adopt the method of nonviolent protest. Many of the younger generation advocated violence because they were tired of waiting, but Dr. King was able to talk most of this generation into waiting.

More than thirty years later, black Christians are still waiting for equality and acceptance by the majority of their white Christian brothers and sisters. What should black Christians do? Should we back down in our fight for equality? No way! In fact, God's Word compels us to make those in the white evangelical community aware of the sins committed (and still being committed) against minorities. The biblical principle is found in Matthew 18:15: "If your brother sins against you, go and show him his fault, just between the two of you. If he listens to you, you have won your brother over."

Yet we must "speak the truth" with Christ's love (see Ephesians 4:15). As much as we may want to force many white Christians to change, we must understand that *this is God's job!* Only God can change people's hearts. When we attempt to do His job, we only frustrate ourselves. We must be careful not to allow this frustration to lead us to sinful action. We must also forgive, even though we are the ones who have been mistreated. Matthew 6:14–15 states: "If you forgive men when they sin against you, your heavenly Father will also forgive you. But if you do not forgive men their sins, your Father will not forgive your sins."

Thus, we must forgive and continue to wait for God to move. If we do not forgive, we will become just like the people who are persecuting us. More important, we will be sinning against our heavenly Father.

Our waiting is not one of inactivity. Psalm 46:10 says: "Be still, and know that I am God." Some Bible scholars say it means, "Relax, and know that I am God." The context here is that Israel was being tempted to ally itself with other nations for strength, as opposed to trusting God alone. He had not told Israel to form an alliance with other nations for military strength. The waiting spoken of in this passage would demonstrate a commitment to God and His sovereignty.

Therefore, for us this waiting includes a continued, consistent, patient, nonviolent protest against the racial inequality seemingly promoted by much of white evangelicalism as we pray for God to change hearts. We must also set an example of Christlikeness in the midst of injustice.

## WHAT TO DO WHILE WAITING

Now that we know as black Christians that we are to wait for God to touch the hearts of those who need to change, what do we do in the interim?

I realize some black Christians are saying, "I just can't wait any longer. I'm too tired." Some even say, "I just don't have that kind of personality." This is a subtle but bold statement. It means, I'm only going to take but so much off white Christians. The owners of such statements have a limited Lordship perspective. In Matthew 18:22, Jesus said, "I tell you, [forgive] not seven times, but seventy-seven times." The idea is to *keep* forgiving. This does not mean that we must continue to tolerate injustice. If you loan someone money and he never pays you back, you still are to remain friends and treat the person as though he does not owe you any money. Wisdom should tell you, though, not to continue to loan the person money! God has called all of us to be good stewards.

We continue to pray, preach, speak, and write against racial injustice among Christians, but we do so with a forgiving and loving spirit.

## "DON'T MISINTERPRET MY MEEKNESS AS WEAKNESS"

Rev. Vince Orange, former pastor of Freedom Baptist Church, oil executive, and former running back for Oklahoma State University, often makes the statement quoted above. Meekness is keeping under control the power God gave to be used at the appropriate time, but in *God's* time, not man's time. Man has a tendency to abuse power. God uses power for the good of man.

People who lived during Jesus' time on earth thought He was weak because He would not do *what* they wanted Him to do, *when* they wanted Him to do it.

It is only those who say, "God, even if You don't change the circumstances, I'm still going to follow You, Lord," who honor God.

Daniel 3:16–18 provides a biblical example of waiting on God:

> Shadrach, Meshach, and Abednego replied to the king, "O Nebuchadnezzar, we do not need to defend ourselves before you in this matter. If we are thrown into the blazing furnace, the God we serve is able to save us from it, and he will rescue us from your hand, O king. But even if he does not, we want you to know, O king, that we will not serve your gods or worship the image of gold you have set up."

Habakkuk 3:16–19 says:

> I heard and my heart pounded, my lips quivered at the sound; decay crept into my bones, and my legs trembled. Yet I will wait patiently for the day of calamity to come on the nation invading us. Though the fig tree does not bud and there are no grapes on the vines, though the olive crop fails and the fields produce no food, though there are no sheep in the pen and no cattle in the stalls, yet I will rejoice in the LORD, I will be joyful in God my Savior. The Sovereign LORD is my strength; he makes my feet like the feet of a deer, he enables me to go on the heights.

I realize that many of you who are black may feel this approach is a cop-out, but if God can't do what He says He can, then we are serving the wrong God!

## CHRIST AND CULTURE

Some black Christians actually put their culture before their relationship with Christ. If there is no strong black church in the area, they won't go to another kind of church, even if the Word of God is preached in such a way that they grow spiritually. Yes, some white evangelicals may have put their culture before Christ and continue to do so, but this is no excuse for black Christians to do this. Unfortunately, there are some cities where there are few good churches.

These black Christians need to ask God to reveal their hearts and show them whether they are racist or not. The Bible strongly indicates that knowledge is only knowledge when our actions match our talk (ouch!). The response needed is similar to the one Job made when he had lost everything and his wife told him to stop holding on to his integrity, curse God, and die. We black Christians must be careful to recognize the trick of Satan's using race as a way of tempting us to justify losing our integrity, cursing God, and dying.

Job answered his wife by saying, "'You are talking like a foolish woman. Shall we accept good from God, and not trouble?' In all this, Job did not sin in what he said" (Job 2:10).

If we lose our Christian integrity, we have nothing!

Please understand, I am in no way suggesting that we should not be proud of our culture and race. God made us and He doesn't make mistakes. There is nothing unbiblical in the title of the soul singer James Brown's song, "Say It Loud, I'm Black and Proud."

What I am saying is there are times when we may have to choose Christ *or* culture, or Christ *over* culture. What choice will you make? What choices have you been making?

## FIND REST AND REFRESHMENT IN THE LORD

For those who are tired but still want to wait on God to move, remember Isaiah 40:28–31, which says:

Do you not know? Have you not heard? The LORD is the everlasting God, the Creator of the ends of the earth. He will not grow tired or weary, and his understanding no one can fathom. He gives strength to the weary and increases the power of the weak. Even youths grow tired and weary, and young men stumble and fall; but those who hope in the LORD will renew their strength. They will soar on wings like eagles; they will run and not grow weary, they will walk and not be faint.

It is only through the supernatural power of the indwelling Holy Spirit that black Christians can and will be victorious over present and future injustices inflicted by our fellow Christians. Romans 12:12–21 gives God's instructions—actually God's *commands*—to Christians who face unjust treatment.

Be joyful in hope, patient in affliction, faithful in prayer. Share with God's people who are in need. Practice hospitality.

Bless those who persecute you; bless and do not curse. Rejoice with those who rejoice; mourn with those who mourn. Live in harmony with one another. Do not be proud, but be willing to associate with people of low position. Do not be conceited.

Do not repay anyone evil for evil. Be careful to do what is right in the eyes of everybody. If it is possible, as far as it depends on you, live at peace with everyone. Do not take revenge, my friends, but leave room for God's wrath, for it is written: "It is mine to avenge; I will repay," says the Lord. On the contrary: "If your enemy is hungry, feed him; if he is thirsty, give him something to drink. In doing this, you will heap burning coals on his head." Do not be overcome by evil, but overcome evil with good.

Many white Christians are in need of help from black Christians in the area of racial partnership. They are ignorant about racial relationships and sincerely want to know how they can deal righteously with persons of a different color or culture. Blacks can and should offer them instruction. It is also the responsibility of white Christians to attempt to understand the hurt of black Christians.

## WE MUST TELL OUR STORY TO OUR CHILDREN

We must continue to tell our children about their heritage as African Americans. We do this for a number of reasons. (1) Before you can progress, you must know your past. (2) It is critical for our children to know their identity as African Americans, for if their counterparts in white Christian evangelicalism continue to make distinctions in regard to equality, our children's self-image could be damaged. (3) There are white Christians who are genuinely sincere in their desire for racial equality but need education about our heritage so that they can effectively assist our cause. (4) The truth must be told whether it is popular or not. The Old Testament prophets were seldom popular, nor were their messages always obeyed, but because the message was proclaimed it eliminated the people's excuse of not having heard God's Word and thus not knowing the right thing to do.

## WE MUST TELL OUR CHILDREN "HIS" STORY

As Christians, we have a responsibility to tell our children the most important story of all, "His" Story! Our God's story—His sending Christ to earth to redeem man. We must instill in our children the biblical principles of victory over oppression. The understanding gained by a personal relationship with Jesus Christ will endow our children with a *freedom* no person or circumstance can take away! God's story must be told by us because He has commanded it. Christianity is always only a generation away from extinction. It must be passed on from one generation to the next.

## GETTING RID OF YOUR GOAT

Last winter, I was playing indoor tennis with a friend who does seminars for pastors and their spouses. On the next court, four men were playing doubles. One of the gentlemen has a reputation for being, well, not the nicest person (arrogant or a jerk). Their ball kept coming onto our court. Tennis etiquette demands retrieving their ball. Of course, this code of conduct also requires some expression of appreciation for the retrieval of the ball (remember, this is a gentleman's game). Unfortunately, their ball continued to come onto our court, particularly on my partner's side. He retrieved the ball twice without receiving any "thanks" for his efforts. The ungentlemanly gentleman was the one demanding the ball. The third time this happened, my partner got the ball but refused to return it until this particular individual said a begrudging "Thank you."

I thought everything was cool. I was winning the set (priorities), but I *did* notice the level of my partner's play decline. Could it have been my "wicked" forehand? I'm sure my forehand had something to do with it. But maybe more effective than my forehand was the fact that my partner's goat had been gotten! You see, my partner felt his "rights" had been violated. Thus, he demanded satisfaction, which he received (the guy did say "Thank you"), but it didn't satisfy.

The guy had got into my partner's head. My partner got so mad that he could no longer concentrate on tennis (we left-handers demand everyone's full attention on the court). My partner had voluntarily become the slave of the guy. After he lost the set, he could not play anymore, wasting the money he had paid for the court time. The ungentlemanly gentleman finished his match and left. He couldn't have cared less about how we felt about anything. Having run into this kind of individual in sports before, I knew the only way to gain his respect was by beating him on the court. My partner didn't seem to know this.

God has been stretching my partner in the area of cross-cultural relationships. God has opened a door for my friend to begin to serve the African-American community. His daughter's best friend since the second grade is African American. Thus, he has become extremely sensitive to any hint of injustice, which stimulated his anger against the ungentlemanly gentleman.

He said to me, "I don't know how you have dealt with all the racial injustice you and your people have had to face."

I responded by telling him of an experience I had with one of my former mentors, John Staggers, who is now with our Lord. I told him that I used to play tennis with a group of older gentlemen, of which John was one. John was trying to mentor me (I was a hard case). John and I usually did pretty well as a doubles team. During one particular match, however, an opponent kept saying certain things to me during the entire match. I got frustrated. My concentration was transferred from the tennis match to my increasing anger. The result was that we lost the match because I lost my temper.

After this match, as John and I walked back to the car, I tried to explain how I thought it was unfair for our opponent to talk to me like he did. John stopped in his tracks, looked me right in the eye, and said, "He got your goat tonight." Then John said something I've never forgotten. He said, "You shouldn't have a goat to be gotten!" John never changed the tone of his voice, but he might as well have shouted. He was right. He never said another word about that match. We went on to play many more matches. John's advice made me mentally tougher, which automatically made me a better tennis player.

More important than becoming a better tennis player (which was one result of heeding John's advice) was the spiritual application of the words God gave John Staggers that night in Landover, Maryland. I learned how to keep anyone from making me his slave mentally.

So almost twenty years later, God had me sharing this timeless principle with a friend who let someone get his goat. (Unfortunately, I haven't mastered it yet. Some days, I'm more yielded to God than others. I say this to my shame.)

As black Christians, it is critical that we learn this lesson. We must remember that God is sovereign and has planned for our best and not our worst (Jeremiah 29:11). We must remember not to worry about those who cannot destroy the soul. I am not suggesting some passive attitude. I am suggesting that we model the same attitude many slaves did against insurmountable odds.

Meekness isn't weakness!

## A STEP TOWARD FREEDOM

We must understand that, as Christians, all our causes against injustice belong to God. The results are His as well. Once we release ownership, we will find that less of our pride is involved, which makes it easier for us to let go of things. Letting go should not be interpreted as no longer caring. Letting go may reveal we care more. When we don't let go of things, they can become our "getable" goats. But if we turn these issues over to God, we can't be enslaved. Thus we can be free, no matter the situation. This perspective also lowers our stress. It allows us to think more clearly. If we are already free, we can be more objective in our thinking—and therefore more effective in our actions. We can hear God speak to us in difficult situations because this same freedom, whose source is God, allows us to keep our concentration on Him, "the author and perfecter of our faith" (Hebrews 12:2).

Oh, by the way, my tennis partner asked me if he needed to apologize. I told him he had to be led by the Holy Spirit. I *did* ask him how he thought the ungentlemanly gentleman would respond to his sharing Christ with him if he did not apologize. After hearing this, my friend went to find this man to apologize. He said he asked the man three times to forgive him. The man laughed at him, but finally accepted his apology.

## WE WILL NEVER GET AWAY FROM SERVANTHOOD (BUT THERE IS A DIFFERENCE)

As Christians, we are commanded to witness. We don't convert people to Jesus Christ. God does that through the Holy Spirit. But God *does* command us to witness.

As black Christians dealing with the issue of racism, we are God's witnesses to white Christians who struggle with prejudice.

One of the first things you learn in evangelism is that you should meet people where they are. Matthew 20:26–28 says: "Whoever wants to become great among you *must be your servant, and whoever wants to be first must be your slave—just as the Son of Man did not come to be served, but to serve, and to give his life as a ransom for many*" (italics added).

God has called Christians to be servants. Instead of being forced by a race to be slaves, as Christians we are to voluntarily become servants because we are motivated by our love for Jesus Christ. Our love for Christ must motivate us to make every attempt to serve white Christians by educating them in the area of institutional racism. As this is done, white Christians may become free, making racial partnership more of a practical reality than just a popular fad for our day. The integrity of our relationship with Christ will be called into question if we as black Christians will not serve with joy (this is a tough one, but God didn't say it would be easy, nor did He ask how we felt about this particular service to Him) by meeting white Christians "where they are" to assist them in overcoming their racism. This means continued patience with the white evangelical community on the part of black Christians. This patience doesn't preclude speaking out against institutional racism. There will be times when we may even have to boycott some white evangelical events to make our point. In order to do this, there must be solidarity among black Christians in these efforts.

## WE MUST BECOME PROACTIVE

We must continue to attempt to work with the white evangelical community, but more of us must begin to start our own ministries. Too much valuable time is being lost trying to measure up to white Christians' standards in order for us to be trusted. These ministries must provide employment opportunities for other blacks with expertise. There is no place or time for a "crab in the barrel" mentality. We must not try to pull each other down out of jealousy, but instead work to promote each other even if it requires some personal sacrifice.

We must develop support groups for blacks working in predominantly white churches and/or other Christian ministries in order to help them not just survive but have victory in those places.

We must think globally, and not just Africa, but the rest of the world. We must partner with other minorities.

## AN OLD-NEW ATTITUDE

One of my dear white friends who has been kind enough to share words of wisdom with me from time to time read a rough draft of this book. He said that one problem many white Christians have with blacks is the perception that most blacks have a victim mentality. He said this attitude is causing white philanthropists to stop giving money to blacks and begin investing in other minorities, because it is more profitable. He said that in the long run, if blacks don't change this attitude, other minorities will receive the benefits blacks would have normally received.

I didn't like hearing this, but I have to deal with it.

The comments of this Christian gentleman reminded me of my dad's comments to me when I was going to try out for a spot on the basketball team at the white school I was forced to go to because of integration. He said, "If you're not three times as good as the white players, don't expect to make the team." There was no speech about life's not being fair. He simply said, This is the way it is. My dad knew how to challenge me.

I also remember attending all-black schools all of my years except for the three just before I went to college. Our teachers worked us hard as they told us we had one strike against us because we were black. Therefore, discipline was critical. If we got spanked at school, we got spanked when we got home. The teachers were like our parents at school. There were also a lot of black male teachers in these all-black schools. The way integration was done in many places—demoting black high school coaches to junior coaches because most of the black high schools were changed to junior schools—ran most of the black male teachers into the business world. At the same time, positive role models and enforcers of discipline were removed from young black males.

Many of the discipline and drug problems today among black youth can be traced back to the way integration was instituted. No, I am not saying there would not be a discipline or drug problem among black youth if integration had been handled differently, but I am saying that the problems would not be nearly as bad.

We as blacks need to go back to the old attitude we used to have of knowing we had to be twice or sometimes three times as good as our white counterparts to succeed. This attitude didn't allow for excuses.

The music group the Temptations used to sing a song that said, "No matter how hard you try, you can't stop me now!" We need to instill this attitude in our youth. This is not to deny that we without a doubt have been victims, but we have got to move on because the consequences are too great if we pass this attitude on to our children.

## TIME FOR SOME HOUSECLEANING

In order for us as black Christians to have solidarity, some changes must be made in how we relate to each other. This may be difficult because some blacks have been blessed financially by the white evangelical community. Some of these individuals enjoy being the only black Christians "in the house." This allows them to be the center of attention and the "expert" on the black community. As the "experts," they are offered more speaking opportunities, which means "mo' money, mo' money, mo' money."

If you are white and reading this section, pardon my French, but brothers, we need to get these turkeys out of the "house." They need to be exposed for who and what they really are. This will be difficult, for those whites who are into "racial reconciliation" will protect these blacks out of ignorance and a sincere heart. Most will not know they have been taken advantage of. Some *will* know but will not want the world to know they have been tricked. Image generates money. Some white Christians seem to love having this black "expert" on board because he or she saves them from going into the black Christian community themselves to see who is actually impacting that community. There is a tendency on the part of the white evangelical community to seek to recruit black Christians who are just like them, which allows them to justify their incorrect views (mostly gleaned from the media and from the oral tradition of their families) and stay in their comfort zone.

These particular black Christians are then used by the white evangelical community to speak on behalf of the black community, even though many of these individuals have voluntarily or involuntarily cut off their ties with the black community. Thus, because the money is so good, they will say what the white evangelical community wants them to say. In the same way, some black Christians are using white Christians as an opportunity to make money through speaking engagements, consulting work, and seminar presentations. Obviously, these blacks have black skin, but that is about as far as it goes with regard to their commitment to the black community and honest efforts to improve race relations.

This kind of black Christian is dangerous, for when the white evangelical community isn't looking, he won't even speak with other blacks unless those blacks have some type of visible position. He will come into a predominantly white ministry or church and pass right by blacks who already work in the institution without speaking to them. This is sad but very true.

Let me suggest that ministries' or churches' budgets reflect ministries' or churches' priorities. Minorities should be a priority for Christian ministries that adhere to the Great Commission. Brenda and I do marriage seminars. We have learned that charging fees literally ensures the use of the marriage principles in the lives of the couples because it has cost them something. The same is true of evangelical ministries.

Perhaps most important, we as black Christians must be careful with the knowledge we have in the area of race. We know more about most whites than they do about us because they are the majority. Thus they have the majority culture that is imposed on us. We have no choice about this. In order to survive, we must master that culture, even though we still have our own. Whites made a critical mistake by making us sit in the back of the bus. By sitting in the back of the bus, we were able to study the white culture without being studied ourselves. Therefore, we often learned what they were going to do before they did it, learned their likes and dislikes, learned how to manipulate their system. By sitting in the front of the bus, whites forfeited the opportunity to keep an eye on us. This is why they fear us so much (fear of the unknown). This is why we blacks have made the progress we have, because we have learned the white value system.

The white culture seldom violates its value system because that provides its only source of security. Dr. Martin Luther King Jr. knew that by uniting blacks and whites in protest demonstrations he would slow down white attacks on the protesters. He knew that whites could not continue unleashing dogs on their own people or spraying them with fire hoses. Sooner or later, whites would have to stop attacking blacks. He knew the white value system. Whenever anyone in our society unites blacks and whites, he becomes dangerous to the traditional culture because that unity pecks away at the white power base. Usually such a method costs him his life. Of course, no matter how much truth we know, we must not allow ourselves to prejudge. Even Christians in the early church weren't immune from racism. Galatians 2:11–14 says:

> When Peter came to Antioch, I [Paul] opposed him to his face [Matthew 18:15], because he was clearly in the wrong. Before certain men came from James [Jews], he used to eat with the Gentiles. But when they arrived, he began to draw back and separate himself from the Gentiles because he was afraid of those who belonged to the circumcision group. The other Jews joined him in his hypocrisy, so that by their hypocrisy even Barnabas was led astray.
>
> When I saw that they were not acting in line with the truth of the gospel, I said to Peter in front of them all, "You are a Jew, yet you live like a Gentile and not like a Jew. How is it, then, that you force Gentiles to follow Jewish customs?"

Paul met this prejudice head-on. He had tremendous courage—but then he wasn't trying to impress men.

All Christians are required to build relationships. According to this passage in Galatians, we are not to go by first impressions or external appearances. In order to look at someone's heart, we need to take the time to get to know the person. If Christians followed this principle, racism among us could be eliminated because the fear of the unknown would be eliminated. Then we could concentrate on a unified effort in kingdom building!

Philippians 4:13 says: "I can do everything through him who gives me strength."

God is looking for Christians who can see the big picture no matter the personal cost—even if this means serving with joy those people who have mistreated us and continue to do so. This is where the supernatural power of Christ is seen in us!

I believe God is asking African-American Christians to develop the Habakkuk attitude found in Habakkuk 3:16–19. Even in certain doom, we are to trust in God. And not only trust, but *rejoice* and have joy in God our Savior.

God is looking for this kind of committed black Christian today, regardless of how the white evangelical community responds. In the Bible, neither Joseph nor Paul was treated fairly, but that didn't make them stop serving God, which sometimes meant serving their enemies with joy. We as black Christians can do no less! Will you join me in this effort? You can and will make a difference!

Read this true story of a Christian mother. It is an example for all Christians, regardless of their race, to imitate.

> Mamie Mobley's only child was brutally murdered in 1956. Her son, Emmett, was visiting relatives and friends in Mississippi. Outside a general store, with boys playing games on the front porch, the eleven-year-old decided to go into the store and buy some bubble gum and candy.
>
> As Emmett and some other boys came out of the store, someone asked Emmett, "How'd you like the lady in the store?" Young Emmett whistled his approval. Someone nearby heard his whistle and did not like an African American whistling at a Caucasian woman.

It was 2:30 A.M. the next Sunday when two men stormed into the house where Emmett was staying and took him at gunpoint. Three days later they discovered his badly beaten body. This was the hardest thing a mother or father is ever confronted with—the murder of their child. This tragic event would leave a mark on Mamie's life. And years after the tragedy she was asked, "Don't you harbor any bitterness toward the two men?" Mamie's reply reveals the depth of her faith: "From the very beginning that's the question that has always been raised. But what they had done was not for me to punish and it was not for me to go around hugging hate to myself, because hate would destroy me. It wouldn't hurt them. I did not wish them dead. I did not wish them jail. If I had to, I could take their four little children and I could raise those children as if they were my own and I could have loved them."

Mamie remembers her son when she sees children playing in the neighborhood and listens to friends talk about their grandchildren—something she realizes she will never experience.

When asked how she could say that, she said: "I was brought up in the Church of God in Christ. It preaches the Gospel of Jesus Christ with a different twist. I believe the Lord meant what He said, and [I] try to live according to the way I've been taught." Through this terrible ordeal she can honestly say, "I haven't spent one night hating those people."[1]

Allowing feelings of bitterness and hatred to fester in our lives will eventually destroy us. Jesus wants us to conquer not only the outer act, but the inner emotion as well.

*Dear Lord,*

*Give us eyes to see others as You see them; not by their external appearance, but by the sweetness of their hearts. In the Name of our Precious Lord and Savior Jesus Christ I pray.*

*Amen.*

# NOTE

1. Studs Terkel, *Race: How Blacks and Whites Think and Feel About the American Obsession* (New York: Free Press, 1992), 20–22.

# 8

# How to Relate to the Black Community

## Some Practical Steps for Fulfilling the Great Commission

*If you want to go somewhere you have never been before, you must be willing to do something you have never done before!*

—Alvin Simpkins, former National
Prayer Manager for Promise Keepers

*Not everything that counts, can be counted, not everything that can be counted, counts.*

—Albert Einstein

During the last eight years, I have been asked quite a few times to speak to various groups—churches, ministers, physicians, teachers—about the subject of race relations. These speaking engagements have introduced me to many sincere white Christians who passionately desire to be instruments used by God to improve race relations in some tangible way. My heart rejoices whenever I meet such individuals. It gives me hope, that maybe . . .

For those whites who are serious about improving race relations, this chapter is for you. I want to share a few simple suggestions you may want to consider. Please understand that no one person can speak for the entire black community because it is too diverse. But, hopefully, there are a few generalities that may prove helpful.

Before we get to the suggestions, there are a few non-negotiables we must consider. There are at least three issues that must be understood in order to be effective in the black community.

## DIGNITY, RESPECT, AND SELF-ESTEEM

Dignity, respect, and self-esteem must be taken into consideration, and in fact *encouraged*, when seeking to develop a relationship with a people who have been oppressed or feel they have been oppressed. Ephesians 4:29 says: "Do not let any unwholesome talk come out of your mouths, but only what is helpful for building others up according to their needs, that it may benefit those who listen."

Regardless of how you may feel about an issue, how do you express yourself in front of your spouse, children, and those of a different culture? Let's select the issues of affirmative action and welfare. Do you imply that those who are for these measures are the "enemy"? Or do you try to look at the issue from the perspective of those who may benefit from one or both of these programs? Is Christ glorified by your speech regardless of your position?

Suppose the people God is sending you to serve have different political views than you do—are you going to try to show "these" people the error of their ways? Or can you simply meet them "where they are" by letting them see a loving reflection of Christ in you?

If you are serious about serving the black community, or really *any* community, then political issues must become secondary and people and their needs must come first. Hebrews 10:24 says: "And let us consider how we may spur one another on toward love and good deeds."

## WHO IS IN CHARGE?

The question of authority must be understood in order to be effective in the black community. The African-American Christian community will no longer give credibility or support to anything in which the community has not already been involved during the decision-making process.

A few years ago, I was visiting a city in the South. I was doing some cross-cultural consulting. A white Christian gentleman expressed his frustration with the black Christian community. He told how he and some of his Christian business friends planned an event *for* the black community. They rented an auditorium on an all-black university campus. They contracted a famous black person to come and speak to the black community. They advertised it. They sent letters to the black pastors. The white community was extremely excited about this event!

The day for the event came and *very few* blacks attended. This white Christian gentleman told me he was extremely upset and wondered what could he do about it. I asked him one question: "When you got this idea and began to share it with your friends, how many of those friends were black?" He said none. I asked a second question: "Did you ask blacks to evaluate the black speaker you selected?" He said no. Next, I asked him: "Do you realize that this particular black speaker does not relate to the black community even though whites love him? Do you have a relationship with and do you pray with any of the Christian leaders in the black community?" Again, his answer was no. Finally, I asked him: "Suppose someone from another neighborhood left you out of the decision-making process and told you to come to some event in your own neighborhood—would you attend it?" All of a sudden, a light went on! He realized what he had done. This was good, because some people never wake up.

## WHO HAS AUTHORITY OVER THE FINANCES?

In order to be effective in the black community, the relationship of money and power (or authority) in the project must be worked through. The two go together. The question most blacks are concerned with is not *how much* money, but *who* is going to make the final decision as to how it will be used. Often, well-meaning wealthy whites will want to give money to blacks for their community but don't allow the blacks they want to serve to have any input as to how the money will be used. Blacks really don't want paternalistic assistance.

These three issues must be answered in your mind before you try to serve the black community.

Now, if you are still interested in how to relate to and serve the black community, here are some practical suggestions.

## KNOW GOD HAS CALLED YOU TO SERVE IN THE BLACK COMMUNITY

If you were to ask me, "How can I relate to the black community?" I would ask you, "Why do you want to relate?" It is imperative that you ask God to examine your heart and motives. Psalm 139:23–24 says: "Search me, O God, and know my heart; test me and know my anxious thoughts. See if there is any offensive way in me, and lead me in the way everlasting."

You need to have pure motives if there is to be any eternal fruit that will honor God. Having a black friend is the popular and even the spiritual thing to do right now in our Christian society. Fads come and go, which is OK for *things,* but can be devastating for *people.* We can't just put people on the shelf when they bore us or make us uncomfortable. Therefore, ask God to search your heart.

If your motivation for ministering in the black community is to save a soul and get people to heaven but not to deal with the issues they face here on earth, check your motives.

If your motivation for sharing Christ is simply to keep blacks from joining Farrakhan's Nation of Islam, check your motives. It may be that you are desiring to control society and not serve people.

If your reason for sharing Christ in the black community is to show blacks the way politically, then you need to reexamine your motives.

If your motives are anything less than serving the whole person and understanding the issues of the black community, then there is an excellent chance that your ministry will neither be accepted nor effective.

A condescending attitude of superiority will be spotted immediately and will be met with resistance. Few of us warm up to people who think they are doing us a favor by helping us, even if that help is needed. People have to be treated with respect. There is no place for an attitude of superiority or inferiority in ministry. Make sure God has called you to serve this community. If God has called you to do so, then do it and don't quit.

## BE YOURSELF: YOUR GREATEST GIFT

God may have called you to serve the black community, but you may feel inadequate (you are, but we *all* are apart from God) because you may have never had a black friend. Don't tell anyone, but God is more concerned with the condition of your heart than the color of your skin! Therefore, you don't need to try to be black or speak slang or know the handshake. The answer to the question "Can I trust you with my life?" is infinitely more important than skin color! Remember Mr. Erickson and his work in the inner city of Chicago with the Scripture Kids? It's too bad that so many evangelicals have bought into Satan's lie that we must be of the same race in order to minister effectively. This is not true in the black community. In Washington, D.C., a white family, Bob and Sharon Mathieu and their children, have lived in one of the tougher neighborhoods in that city for approximately thirty years.

If God has called you to serve the black community, remember to *be yourself!* The greatest gift you can give to anyone is to be who you are in Christ! You can't be anyone else anyway. Many times when nonblacks attempt to act black, it turns blacks off. Forget the racial jokes. They may be a sign of a more serious problem. Your calling may not eliminate your nervousness or even the fear of the unknown. Most preachers and speakers I know are a little nervous before they speak. They say that is usually a good sign because they know they will have to depend on God and not themselves. Remember, it is not the initial response but the end result that counts with God (Abraham and Sarah, Moses, Peter). Let things happen naturally. You don't need to be afraid of silence if people aren't speaking to you all the time. Relax and be yourself and serve.

## STUDY BLACK HISTORY

Serving another culture requires a *willingness to learn*. Your ability to do this will probably be the key to your success or failure in this area of ministry. A teachable spirit will take you where you want to go in establishing long-term relationships. You will probably receive much more than you give. Effective missionaries learn about the people they are attempting to serve from someone of that particular culture. If you desire to serve the black community, it is crucial that you learn about the black culture from a black perspective, i.e., read books by Christian and non-Christian black authors concerning history, religion, and culture. Here are some books you can use as a starting point:

Aptheker, Herbert, ed. *A Documentary History of the Negro People in the United States.* Vols. 1–4. Secaucus, N.J.: Citadel Press, Carol Publishing (an imprint of Stuart, Lyle), 1989.

Beals, Ivan A. *Our Racist Legacy: Will the Church Resolve the Conflict?* Notre Dame, Ind.: Cross Cultural, 1997.

Cameron, Robert J. *The Last Pew on the Left: America's Lost Potential.* Lafayette, La.: Prescott, 1995.

Ellis, Carl F. *Free At Last: The Gospel in the African-American Experience.* Downers Grove, Ill.: InterVarsity, 1996.

Emerson, William O., and Christian Smith. *Divided By Faith: Evangelical Religion and the Problem of Race in America.* New York: Oxford Univ. Press, 2000.

Gates, Henry Louis Jr., and Nellie Y. McKay, eds. *The Norton Anthology: African American Literature.* New York: W. W. Norton, 1997.

January, Jerald. *A Second Time.* Franklin, Tenn.: Cool Springs, 1996.

McCray, Rev. Walter Arthur. *The Black Presence in the Bible and the Table of Nations Genesis 10:1-32, with Emphasis on the Hamitic Genealogical Line from a Black Perspective.* Chicago: Black Light Fellowship, 1990.

McKissic, William Dwight. *Beyond Roots: In Search of Blacks in the Bible.* Wenonah, N.J.: Renaissance Products, Inc., 1990.

Terkel, Studs. *Race: How Blacks and Whites Think and Feel About the American Obsession.* New York: Free Press, 1992.

Usry, Glenn, and Craig S. Keener. *Black Man's Religion: Can Christianity Be Afrocentric?* Downers Grove, Ill.: InterVarsity, 1996.

Weary, Dolphus. *I Ain't Coming Back.* Wheaton, Ill.: Tyndale, 1995.

An important step to take before you begin to serve in the black community is to go and observe. See who the leaders are. Attempt to identify three or four Christian African-American individuals who have ministries in the community. This will keep you from possibly duplicating a ministry that is already up and running. It will also keep you from being viewed as competition. Instead, you can be seen as a friend if you come and work beside those who are already ministering. Seek to develop relationships with several different pastors of different denominations in the community. These pastors can help you with your orientation and protection as well. Developing relationships with several pastors will keep you from being accused of having a "favorite" pastor friend.

## INVEST IN IMPROVING RACE RELATIONS

Commitment must be demonstrated. More and more, black leaders are beginning to say publicly that certain white Christian churches and parachurch ministries have racist agendas. Naturally, the churches or ministries that are named become hurt, angry, and defensive. Even though their agendas may not be intentionally racist, they never, or at least very seldom, seem to be inclusive in their actions relating to minorities. For example, when some predominantly white Christian organizations plan a marketing campaign or prepare promotional material, it is not uncommon for all of the pictures to be of whites, with maybe one minority picture. This church or organization may believe it is doing a superb job, but minorities feel slighted (again).

What these churches and organizations fail to understand is that inclusion means serving everyone in such a way that the people they are attempting to serve feel ministered to. In order for this to be accomplished, a minority perspective must be developed. This minority perspective will not become a reality if it is not actively *supported from the top by the executive leadership!* Minorities need to be hired in nonracial positions. If the church or ministry is serious, these minority individuals should be empowered to do what they have been hired to do. They must have the opportunity to fail in order to have the opportunity to succeed. Let these individuals lead your church or organization in their areas of expertise, unless you just hired them for image maintenance.

## DEVELOP A PARTNERSHIP MENTALITY

The understanding of differences is crucial to the success of this partnership. Most people can and will observe differences, but few appear to respond positively to those differences. Apply Proverbs 3:5–6 when you get nervous or tense: "Trust in the LORD with all your heart and lean not on your own understanding; in all your ways acknowledge him, and he will make your paths straight." Most minorities are more relationship oriented than program oriented. If there is no relationship, there is usually no understanding.

Proverbs 4:7 says, "Wisdom is supreme; therefore get wisdom. Though it cost all you have, get understanding."

Don't allow yourself to be intimidated. Remember, you are in Christ and you must find your confidence in Him!

## STUDY SOME OF THE CULTURAL DIFFERENCES

Cultural differences do not indicate superiority or inferiority, just a difference. You already know to study history. Be sensitive. Racial jokes are rarely a positive sign of being sensitive. They are not always, but may sometimes be, a sign that there is a problem. Be willing to work through some of the differences. This process will develop bonds of trust. This trust in turn will lay the foundation for a close friendship. Take time to step back and appreciate the differences God made. Learn to thank God for those differences.

## PRAY, PRAY, AND PRAY SOME MORE

Your prayer life is the most important aspect in ministering. Therefore, prayer should not be the last thing, but the *first* action you take in preparation for ministry. Prayer will guide you in determining if God is leading you into cross-cultural ministry. Build a prayer support group consisting of persons from different cultures, if possible, and ask them to pray for you and the people you are serving. The combined wisdom of the different cultures and time in prayer will open your spiritual eyes to see God in different dimensions.

This group can also serve as a support group and provide wise counsel. Take time to study the history of black/white relationships in the state, city, town, and community in which you are trying to serve. You will need to pray against the strongholds of racial prejudice in the community where you are serving. Often, the lack of visible results can be traced to the lack of *specific praying* against these strongholds. A stronghold is a place where Satan has a strong foundation that will not easily be destroyed. These strongholds are usually developed over a long period of time. Thus, it takes time to pray them down. Ephesians 6:11–12 states:

> Put on the full armor of God so that you can take your stand against the devil's schemes. For our struggle is not against flesh and blood, but against the rulers, against the authorities, against the powers of this dark world and against the spiritual forces of evil in the heavenly realms.

Pray for yourself and your family, because you and they will most likely be attacked by Satan. The purpose of this attack is to tempt you to back off on certain issues or commitments you have made with blacks. When whites back off of commitments made with blacks, the damage is worse than if the commitments had never been made! The Bible mentions in many places that it is better not to vow than to make a vow and not keep it. Another purpose in Satan's attack is to get you to quit altogether. Keeping your word reveals your character and your trustworthiness. Therefore, *follow through on your commitments!* You don't have to be perfect, but be consistent and be sincere.

## QUESTIONS BLACKS ARE THINKING BUT MAY NEVER ASK YOU

Why are you here in my neighborhood? Why now? Why are blacks so popular with white Christians now? What is in it for you? How long will you be here before you stop coming just like the others did? Why should I trust you? When you go to the black neighborhood, the black community may well see you as coming and offering them your suburban Jesus. When you tell individuals in the black community that you love them, they may wonder: If you *really* loved us, why did you move away from us to the suburbs? Why did you want to live away from blacks? Now you are coming to give them Jesus, and they are not sure that they want "your" Jesus. If you really love blacks, they may ask, why are you raising your kids away from black kids?

These are questions you will have to answer, one way or another. You may say that these questions aren't important in regard to salvation, but they *are* because they are on the minds of African Americans. You must meet people "where they are." Jesus did so with the woman at the well. Paul did so with the Greeks who worshiped the "unknown" God. Peter did the same with the Jews at Pentecost. Some of these questions are the ones the late Tom Skinner shared with Campus Crusade for Christ at one of their staff training sessions in 1971. It is amazing that nothing significant has happened in the area of Christian race relations in the more than thirty years since he spoke.

## DON'T LOOK FOR QUICK RESULTS

Sometimes it may be years before you can measure any tangible results for your efforts. Our society has developed a microwave mentality. Unfortunately, this mentality can exist in Christian churches and organizations where the "bottom line" is often money and numbers. Too often salvation or encouraging souls is not the deciding factor in ministry decisions. This mentality will be devastating if it is carried into attempts to develop cross-cultural relationships. You can't undo in a year or two what it took hundreds of years to develop. The situation is similar to couples with marital problems, who often want a marriage counselor to solve in one session the problems they have allowed to accumulate over years.

We need to look at developing cross-cultural relationships with spiritual eyes and not worldly eyes. Second Corinthians 4:18 says: "We fix our eyes not on what is seen, but on what is unseen. For what is seen is temporary, but what is unseen is eternal."

We have no idea how God is using us to impact people. Sometimes the thing we do that we think is unimportant may be what touches a heart. Let's practice obedience and let the results rest with God.

## AN AMERICANIZED JESUS MAY NOT WORK IN THE INNER CITY

If you bring an Americanized white Jesus into the black community it may hinder your ministry. As we have discussed earlier, many white conservative evangelicals have embraced the Founding Fathers, yet many blacks feel very negatively toward the Founding Fathers. Many blacks see the Founding Fathers as non-Christians or as hypocritical Christians at best. These same blacks will see you as a hypocrite if you are idolizing these men. You can believe what you want to about the Founding Fathers, but if you are going to minister in the inner city, be careful how you express that belief, if you express it at all.

Be careful of your attitude. You may say, "Why can't these blacks get over this?" The problem is that the black community still sees the white community as perpetuating a system that oppresses them. Therefore, the connection to slavery is still very real and painful.

Remember, you can believe want you want to believe, but you may have to leave some things at home if you are planning on serving in the black culture.

## EXPECT INITIAL REJECTION

Don't be surprised if you are rejected initially. This is a test given to all "outsiders," even other blacks who are not from the community. This test is to determine your "toughness." The ability to survive is a key element in the black community. It is also a type of rite of passage, or initiation to the community. You need to understand that many well-meaning—and some not-so-well-meaning—whites have come to the black community before, saying the same things you will be saying. Few have kept their promises, which is why God may be calling you to serve this community. So you must understand that you will have to earn the trust of those you desire to serve. Expect to be moved out of your comfort zone!

Suffering will be a part of moving you out of your comfort zone. God will stretch you more than you ever anticipated. There will be times when you will want to quit. When this happens, you are just about ready to become useful to God. Some of the suffering will be humiliating. Obedience to the call and to the Word of God, regardless of the circumstances, must be your foundation. Answering the questions mentioned earlier, earning trust, and experiencing an initial rejection are almost certainly, but not always, guaranteed.

Therefore, don't run home and quit after your initial rejection, if you are rejected. Instead, try to find out *specifically* why you were rejected and learn from it. This knowledge will assist you in ministering more effectively in the black community. And that is your goal, isn't it?

## COUNT THE COST

God is a God of change in regard to His ministry. This is so even though He is always the same in essence and character, as Hebrews

13:8 says: "Jesus Christ is the same yesterday and today, and forever" (NASB). Jesus Christ was in spirit form in the Old Testament, incarnate in the Gospels, and is now in His glorified form. He works on earth in many differing ways.

Jesus Christ sacrificed His life for us. I strongly believe we must be willing to change our own learned behavior as Peter did when God told him to go to Cornelius. We must be willing to change our own thinking patterns because our thoughts often lead us to action. Therefore, we must be *flexible*. Some are not willing to change because change requires faith, as described in Hebrews 11:6: "And without faith it is impossible to please God, because anyone who comes to him must believe that he exists and that he rewards those who earnestly seek him."

We must also be willing to let God out of *our box!* Theologically, God is bigger than we think! Culturally, different may just be *different,* not better or worse, nor good or bad.

## A STEP IN THE RIGHT DIRECTION

I believe Focus on the Family is beginning to make some steps in the right direction in relating to the black community. In January 1998, Dr. Dobson interviewed Dr. John Perkins and the late Spencer Perkins about civil rights on Dr. Martin Luther King Jr.'s holiday. The idea for the show came out of a conversation Dr. Dobson and I had almost a year earlier. Recently, Dr. Dobson interviewed three young African Americans, Rev. Linda Woodall, Dr. Harold Davis, and Mychal Wynn, who are involved in mentoring African-American youth, males in particular. What is important about this particular broadcast is that Focus addressed an African-American issue. These three African Americans were not the most well-known blacks, but they were and still are on the cutting edge in regard to doing ministry in the black community.

These are good *first* steps, but neither can Focus nor any other parachurch group or church that has begun cross-cultural ministry afford to back up. In fact, most if not all must seek to include all people of color in *every aspect* of each particular ministry. This is what most people of color really desire.

Again, these are good first steps, but we have to do more than talk in order to establish long-lasting relationships. The commitment to partner with the African-American community must be seen in everything the evangelical community does from now on. This will be true of any ministry planning to have a long-term relationship with any minority group, whatever that ministry's strength is, be it mass communications, literature, videos (these should feature more than one person of color, and sometimes the person of color needs to be the star), or resources. In the May 4, 1998, edition of *U.S. News and World Report,* Dr. Dobson warned the Republican party to make good on its political promises. He says, "We've got to see the proof." In the same way people of color have to see "the proof" from the evangelical community.

It took all of my three years at Focus to get to this point, and it has a long way to go, but I think Focus is beginning to get an idea of what the vision for doing *effective ministry* with the black community requires. Perseverance by minorities and whites will be critical in this effort. Focus began celebrating Black History Month in 1998 and in 2002 hired an African-American consultant to assist them in their cross-cultural efforts. For some organizations, it is easier to listen to a person of color who is outside of the organization than to listen to a person of color who works within the organization.

Once again, evangelicals must understand that they are viewed as intelligent by the African-American community because evangelicals have so many resources. Therefore, it is difficult for people of color to view exclusion as anything but intentional, even though the exclusion may actually have been unintentional. Whether exclusion is intentional or unintentional, people of color are waiting for the thinking patterns of the evangelical community to change. These actions are often interpreted as not caring.

## ETERNAL SPIRITUAL BENEFITS

You must realize that what you do will have *eternal* consequences. Know God is shaping you more into *His image* as you serve Him by serving others. Don't worry about being "perfect," but do be sincere and consistent.

As you go, make the idea of partnership the foundation of your service. The idea is to work together with all peoples.

Now, am I going to see you in the black community?

*Dear Lord,*

*Help those of us who desire to serve others cross-culturally to allow Your Holy Spirit to examine our hearts and our motives. Please give us the wisdom and courage for our actions to be consistent with our words. There is no way for us to count the extent of the cost because You always stretch us further than we ever anticipate, but please let our faith in You be all the motivation we need to be obedient to You. May we not attempt to share in Your glory, which some people may try to shower upon us as You bless the cross-cultural actions we do that others may refuse to do. All that is good comes from You.*

*Amen.*

# 9

# Winning
# the Race
# to Unity

## The Rewards of
## Racial Unity

*Behold, how good and how pleasant it is for brothers to dwell together
in unity! It is like the precious oil upon the head, coming down upon
the beard, even Aaron's beard, coming down upon the edge of his
robes. It is like the dew of Hermon coming down upon the mountains
of Zion; for there the Lord commanded the blessing—life forever.*

—Psalm 133:1–3 NASB

Having talked about race quite extensively, suppose we do all
that has been suggested? What will be the payoff? Will all the
hard work be worth the effort? What will we do if we do not see the
expected results we had hoped for anytime soon?

Psalm 133:1–3 seems to emphasize a bond because of race but
also, more importantly, a bond because of a covenant relationship
with God. Unity here is for one purpose: worship of the Lord. In
worship, the emphasis is on giving, not receiving. The nature of worship is that as you give, you will receive. You can't be in God's presence and not be blessed. The oil is the fragrant anointing oil that
was the divine commissioning of the priest. The dew is the divine
refreshment that is the result of the experience of this spiritual unity
or partnership. Thus, the fellowship of God's people is refreshing.
Zion is the place of Yahweh's appointment and blessing. Whenever

God's people are living together in unity, God sends His blessings.

So it seems that unity among Christian brothers and sisters will result in spiritual benefits from God. We know that God is glorified by our unity because this unity reflects obedience to Him. Our unity reflects the integrity and legitimacy of our worship.

## REWARDS REQUIRE INVESTMENTS: NO CROSS, NO CROWN

The Bible says that in order to make friends, one must himself be friendly (Proverbs 18:24 KJV). Thus, the Bible seems to imply that if we want to make a friend, we must demonstrate friendliness. This principle requires us to initiate efforts to make friends, which means we do not wait for people to come to us. Notice that the Bible doesn't refer to the color of the skin of those people to whom we are to show ourselves friendly.

The first obstacle to fulfilling this principle is that it requires us to make the first move. The problem with this is that almost none of us will do it. The reason is that most Christians have bought into the American mind-set of being comfortable. Trying to make friends with people will definitely move us out of our "comfort zones."

The second obstacle to taking the first step in making friends is that it requires faith. If we are honest with ourselves, many of us, even though we are Christians, do not like living by faith. We struggle with living by faith because living by faith means we are not in control, and we are not sure exactly what God may ask us to do. But we *do* know that whatever God asks us to do won't be easy!

The third problem we have with showing ourselves friendly is that we fear people will reject us. People may think we are strange or even call us names. An attempt at initiating relationships with people may even affect our reputation in the business world, at church, or in the evangelical community within which we work, which could negatively affect our earning potential.

I wish I could assure everyone who attempts to improve race relations that nothing bad will happen to them, but I can't.

## OBEDIENCE IS BETTER THAN SACRIFICE

One of the benefits of attempting to improve race relations is that God commands it. How? Everyone is our neighbor (see the story of the Good Samaritan in Luke 10:25–37). Therefore, every Christian is commanded to treat everyone in a way that glorifies God.

We must never confuse the issue of *results* with the issue of *obedience*. Some Christians of all races have the mind-set of "I will do this as long as I get the results I want. If I don't get the desired results, forget it! I'm not going to do it." This attitude and subsequent actions are just the opposite of obedience to God.

Obedience is what God has commanded of every believer. Obedience is simply doing what God has commanded us to do—period! The results belong to God. That is His work, which He does through the indwelling Holy Spirit. If we get caught up with results, we will have a tendency not to demonstrate the grace God has given us.

## CROSS-CULTURAL BLESSINGS

One of the most important benefits for me in my cross-cultural experiences is that God continues to use these situations as test grounds for my faith to grow. Every time I think I have a handle on race, God gently reveals to me that I have a ways to go. Maybe you can relate?

A few years ago, one of my ministry trips took me to my hometown, Winston-Salem, North Carolina. Originally, I was scheduled to preach at a black church. To make a long story short, I ended up preaching at a white church. I'm cool with that most times. But here the pastor told me that no black had ever preached in his church before. This church was founded in the 1700s! That was the last thing I wanted to hear. I was forty-four. I don't need to be, and shouldn't be, the first black anything, anymore, especially in the Christian community! I am usually leery of white pastors who want to get a black person to come and preach to their congregations about race, especially when I am the first one.

I was dreading going to this church, and my traveling partner,

Phil Williams, said I had a funny look on my face. I wasn't even sure what I should preach. I decided not to preach on race. As we walked in, people were staring. They didn't seem to be glad that I was there. This was all the encouragement I needed. Now I *really* didn't want to be there.

All too soon, it was time for me to preach. I preached about marriage. The folk began to laugh at my jokes. Therefore, they could not be all that bad!

After the service, the people were warm and genuine. I had to stop and thank God for His guidance and anointing for the sermon, which seemed to scratch where this church was itching. The ladies began to hug me. Perhaps two of the most important confirmations of the impact of the sermon had to do with a young boy who said the sermon kept him from going to sleep. Later this boy was eating some Cheerios and shared them with me. It reminded me of an experience told by a member of the 10th Cavalry. He said that he knew he was accepted when a white soldier let him drink out of the same canteen.[1]

All of this made me ashamed and embarrassed at myself and my own prejudging. I wouldn't have believed that these folk would be so accepting of me (sad, but I'm just being honest). I'm glad I have a God who loves me enough to continue to put me in situations like this so that I might grow spiritually. I wonder if any of you have had experiences like this—or did you bail out before you had a chance to see the people's heart (1 Samuel 16:7)?

The most memorable of my cross-cultural blessings I experienced when I was playing basketball in West Africa for Sports Ambassadors during the summer of 1974. We seemed to average no more than four to six hours of sleep each night. The team was either playing a game every day and/or conducting a basketball clinic. In St. Louis (pronounced *san louie*), Senegal, our game for that evening was canceled. Being the spiritually mature giant that I am, I went straight to bed. Elridge and Ken, my roommates, went out on the streets to witness. One of them, I can't remember which, got on some kind of platform and started preaching. Someone from the crowd began to interpret because this was a French-speaking community.

Late that same evening, Elridge and Ken returned with two teenage boys (aged about sixteen or seventeen) who were Muslims. As Elridge continued to witness, one of the boys asked why Ken, who was white (he still is, and I don't hold it against him), was in the room. Elridge told them Ken was our roommate. These boys could not believe it. Then Elridge really "blew them away" by telling them that Ken was our brother because of Jesus Christ! This they could not accept. They stayed and asked questions about Jesus until three o'clock in the morning. The love of Christ that can overcome racism and the peace that Christ provides was shaking the foundations of their faith in their religion.

The next morning, *early* the next morning—they woke us up—they said they wanted to ask Jesus Christ to forgive them for their sins and to come into their lives as their Lord. We prayed with them. Afterward, we were all bouncing off the walls with the joy of the Lord!

Then Elridge, Ken, and I were all challenged because the boys had to leave home forever, as their parents attempted to kill them because of their new faith. The rejection of Islam is a social rejection as well. Christians in America may talk about choosing Christ over culture, but these boys accepted Christ as their Lord and Savior knowing the consequences.

As we parted ways, the boys asked us to pray that God would provide an opportunity for them to share Christ with their parents. The boys went to live with the missionaries in the city.

## THERE IS ONE WHO STICKS CLOSER THAN A BROTHER (PROVERBS 18:24)

One of my best friends is Gary Jennings, a white guy from Texas. We worked for the same Christian organization for one year. When God made it clear that it was time for me to move on, one of the hardest things was leaving Gary and his family. Our families had become family.

Just when I thought I knew Gary pretty well, he threw me a curve. Bo, his oldest son, had just won the boys' state eighth-grade basketball championship. Gary asked me if Bo could stay with me for two weeks so I could prepare him for high school basketball. I was deeply touched that he trusted me with his son.

Brenda readily agreed that Bo should come. During Bo's first week with us, I was teaching evangelism at a Southern Baptist conference called Black Church Week '97. There were a few whites there, quite naturally, but the majority of people were black. Just imagine, this black family going all over the conference grounds with this six-foot, one-inch, 200-pound young white man. He was part of our family. My girls consider him their big brother.

One of my new best friends, Gerrit, an Afrikaner from South Africa, and his family came over for dinner during Bo's stay. Gerrit later told me that it surprised him to see Bo there, but he was glad to see him. Gerrit also said that Bo appeared to feel right at home.

God has also given me several Hispanic friends. Pastors Ron Griego and Mike Mestas were used by God to help me make an important decision concerning the ministry last year.

The second most difficult time of my life revolved around the death of my mom and being called by God to leave the pastorate in order to serve Him in a different capacity. We had not yet sold our house, but I had to report to work. Earlier in the year, I had spoken at a revival at Southwestern State University in Oklahoma. When the Baptist student director there heard that I was moving to Springfield, Illinois, he told his brother, Dwight Morrison, a Springfield resident. Dwight called me and offered me his son's room because he (Evan) was moving out. I still don't know why I accepted, but I did. I guess I felt if someone was kind enough to invite me to stay in his home, I should accept, unless I had a good reason not to (my mom's influence). I could also sense Dwight's humble and sweet spirit.

When it came time to go to Springfield, I was late starting out because I didn't want to leave home. This was the first time I would be leaving my family for an indefinite period of time. It was an eight-hour drive to Springfield from Tulsa, Oklahoma. When I got there, it was dark and late. I could hear two large dogs barking. As I was unloading my car, Barbara, Dwight's wife, came right over and gave me this big hug! You would have thought we were family! We were—I just didn't know it! Barbara has enough love for ten children! She had three and made me feel like the fourth. The hug she gave me was like the Lord's saying "It's going to be fine." Barbara's love helped me work through my mother's death. Here God was using this white woman and her family to love me.

It was funny to hear and see the reactions of some of the people where I worked when they heard where I was living. One comment was priceless: "They're white, aren't they?" My response: "They were the last time I looked."

Then there is Bob Cook, who initially touched my life through the life of his son, Robin. Robin and I met during the summer of 1975. We were in training camp preparing to go overseas to share the Gospel of Jesus Christ through the medium of basketball with Sports Ambassadors (formerly Venture for Victory), playing national and Olympic teams. Robin's humor and his walk with God caught my attention, and I never forgot him. Robin is now the director of Sports Ambassadors in Colorado Springs.

The move to Springfield brought me into contact with Bob. After knowing Bob for some six months, I asked him to mentor me. He told me, "All that I have is yours." I knew he meant it. I found out later that Bob financially helped to put a black man through law school. This black man later became a successful attorney and a political figure in the state of Illinois.

Bob has been mentoring me for the last three years. We spend time in the Word together when I am in town. God has used Bob to peel away some painful layers of sin in my life. Bob has introduced me to many friends of his, such as Mike Singletary, the former Chicago

Bear and Hall of Famer; Chuck Colson; Walt Henrichsen; Gordon Loux; Bob Foster; Winston Parker; Fred Smith; and other godly men who have touched my life in one way or another.

Naturally, there are many black brothers and sisters all over the country to whom I am indebted. They provide words of spiritual wisdom and prayer support from having gone through the circumstances which I am presently experiencing. I could not survive without them! But because I am emphasizing cross-cultural relationships, I will not expound on these relationships.

*Dear Lord,*

*It has been a long journey with some mountains we have all had to climb. Thank You for the mountains because they have enabled us who have climbed to the top to see things more from Your perspective, things we otherwise would never have seen. Father, help us to share what we have seen of You with others whom You will bring across our path. Lord, help us to share Your perspective in the power of the Holy Spirit, with Your love. Help us to also leave the results of our sharing with You, since it is Your job to change hearts, not ours.*

*Father, may all people see in us a "loving reflection of You."*

*Amen.*

## NOTE

1. Jeffery C. Stewart, *1001 Things Everyone Should Know About African American History* (New York: Doubleday, 1996), 206.

# 10

# Look Who's Talking

## Cross-Cultural Is More Than Black and White

*"I have other sheep that are not of this sheep pen. I must bring them also."*

—John 10:16

As America *browns*, it is critical for us to understand that cultural/racial issues extend beyond just blacks and whites; we must begin to think inclusively. With this in mind, I've asked some friends of mine from different cultures/races—some are Christians and some are not—to write about their best and worst cross-cultural experiences. I have also asked them to comment on what role they see the media playing in race relations. In the following pages are perspectives from those who were able to respond to my questions: an Afrikaner, an Asian American, a Caucasian, a Hispanic (Latino), a Jew, and a person of mixed racial heritage. I also asked a Native American (First Nations), and an Iranian, but they were unable to respond.

# WINNING THE RACE TO UNITY

## GERRIT WOLFAARDT, AFRIKANER

*Best Cross-Cultural Experience*

My (indeed, our entire family's) best cross-cultural experience was, undoubtedly, in Richmond, Virginia, where we resided in an African-American neighborhood from 1993–97.

We were welcomed with a warmth that we have not felt elsewhere in the U.S.A. Neighbors came to introduce themselves and offer help if we needed it. We had this big old apple tree in our yard, and when the apples ripened, an elderly lady came by and said that she had picked the apples for many years and would we mind if she continued the "tradition"? Of course we said it was OK. And a few days later, she brought us the most delicious apple pie we had ever eaten!

The family whose home was opposite ours had yearly "blockbuster" parties with massive loudspeakers and good soul music. They always invited us (the only "whities"). We had the privilege of mingling with this family and their friends, everyone making us feel right at home. Our introduction to real "soul food" also came during these times, and we just loved the experience. That same neighbor, Ira, would sometimes come home with a paper bag full of spiced crabs and bring it over so that he and I could sit under the apple tree and talk *man's talk!* He shared his innermost feelings about the race issue in America, his disappointments, and especially being on the wrong end of discrimination on the basis of his skin color.

What blessed me about these *heart talks* was the fact that our neighbors treated us like one of their own and did not see our family as different from themselves.

My son, Thabo, started a lawn-mowing business in the area and was signed up by a number of our neighbors. One elderly gentleman said to him, "Now I never thought I'd see the day when a *white* boy came to mow my yard!" and promptly gave him more than he had asked for, just because he had the guts to ask for jobs in the "hood." We miss our friends and will always cherish our time among them.

*Worst Cross-Cultural Experience*

My (our) worst experience was when Chris Hani, leader of the Communist Party in South Africa, was assassinated in 1993. Blacks regarded him as a great leader, even if they did not all vote in the elections for the party he ran under, the African National Congress (ANC). More than 90 percent of the population voted for the ANC, the ruling party in South Africa. The ANC came to power in the first democratic elections held in South Africa in 1994, resulting in Nelson Mandela being the first democratically elected president of the country. They received more than 60 percent of the total vote. The other parties, the National, Democratic Alliance, Inkatha, Communist, etc., split the balance. (The ANC also won the next election when Nelson Mandela stepped down and Thabo Mbeki was nominated as president to replace him.) Chris Hani was a hero to millions of blacks who admired him as a person of great courage who had laid his life on the line to fight apartheid and to gain their freedom.

On the day he was assassinated (by a white right-wing extremist), we arrived in the area where I was to teach on reconciliation at a mission organization. My wife, Celeste, and I were in shock. I phoned his widow, Mrs. Hani, to apologize and ask her forgiveness. However, it was impossible to get her at the time.

As we arrived at the mission, several young black missionary trainees welcomed us (they had experienced my ministry of reconciliation in the black townships). They were all obviously very distraught. We discovered that some of the white missionaries had applauded the assassination, because Hani was a "communist" and it was "good riddance." Instead of placing themselves in the shoes of their black colleagues and consoling them, they were shocked that "Christians" would mourn for such a communist villain (in their eyes). Some of the black young people were crying and extremely angry. We had a huge challenge on our hands!

Fortunately, over the next two days, I was allowed to teach. Biblical truths were able to bring resolution and some reconciliation to the situation. In one case a "right wing" Afrikaner broke down and asked forgiveness, which led to a time of deep healing. However, and sadly so, some of the whites never understood the hurt and pain their black friends had undergone during that time, and I am afraid some scars will remain.

## The Media's Influence

I have thought about the media issue, but I cannot come up with a definitive take on the media and their influence on race relations.

It is very obvious to anyone who watches the news channels in the U.S.A. that there is a conspicuous scarcity of black news-readers and anchors. So we are mainly fed the white viewpoint, be it conservative or liberal. Some folk mean well, but it is obvious that they have no experience of what black folk in this country really have to put up with. They have no experience of what it is like to live on the "other side of the tracks" as we were privileged to experience during our stay in Richmond, Virginia. So my main take on this is that TV, radio, newspapers, and magazines are really trying to interpret the news happening in the black community from a white perspective.

A recent event showed a young man of color in California being savagely beaten by a policeman, including getting his head slammed on the trunk of the car. I found it hard to even watch the clip being played over and over. But what shocked me even more was that some radio and TV stations had talk shows running the next few days somehow trying to justify why the white policeman may have had the right to act that way! Well, that just fuels the fire as listeners/viewers subconsciously start placing the blame on the victim (black) and exonerating the perpetrator (white). The outrage dies down, and silently people start believing the young black man got what he deserved. Here is the result: Blacks are outraged, and whites cannot see their point. Outcome: People drift even further apart. Trust cannot be built in such an environment. Is the media to blame? Yes, I would say so, but it is hard to prove. It is more underneath the covers than out in the open. It is just my sensitivity to racism that makes me see these things through a different grid. Because I am white (only in skin, brother), white folk talk freely around me, so I know that what I am saying is true, but not easily provable.

***About Gerrit:*** Gerrit Wolfaardt was a litigation attorney and partner in a South Africa law firm for a number of years. After becoming a Christian, he joined Youth With A Mission. He later was ordained as a minister in the Church of England. He became a missionary and Bible teacher. Presently, he is the National Director for Veritas College in the U.S.A. He continues to teach racial reconciliation here and in Africa. A movie of his life—his persecution of blacks in South Africa, his conversion to Christianity, and his new lifelong passion for racial equality—has recently been released; it is called The Final Solution. One of the sponsors for this movie is former NBA player A. C. Green.

## CHRIS P. RICE, CAUCASIAN

*Best Cross-Cultural Experience*

My greatest cross-cultural experience was, for over seventeen years, participating in the life of an interracial congregation in the so-called racial "eye of the storm" in Jackson, Mississippi. There, on a terrain the size of a zip code, I joined several hundred African Americans, whites, and others who shared rare intimacy. We had a daily life of living on the same streets, worshiping together, raising our children together, and working side by side to love our neighbors and confront the powers of brokenness and hopelessness in a marginalized and forgotten urban community.

During these years, a group of about twenty whites and blacks from our congregation began meeting every week, studying the Sermon on the Mount and telling our life stories. We weren't interested in simply "talking noise," in nodding our heads at one more nice biblical truth, and continuing life as usual. We wanted to live out what Jesus taught. Step-by-step, we wove our lives together in practical ways in a small common fund, doing work projects. Our eventual journey toward sharing houses, incomes, and daily life was organic; it seemed like the next logical and scary step in becoming a more faithful community of friends. Eventually eleven of us bought a six-acre property with a hundred-year-old farmhouse on it, and we moved in together to form an intentional Christian community called "Antioch."

The Antioch Community was a motley crew; our members included a computer programmer, a social worker, a single mother, and a secretary. One member grew up on Southern California beaches and in suburbs and won straight A's, another was a farm girl who won a milking contest, another grew up a foster kid who was once driven to the desperate point of searching for food in garbage cans. For twelve years whites and blacks shared kitchens, incomes, meals, and outreach to neighbors. Dozens of people lived with us over the years, from eager-beaver volunteers to men just out of prison. We shared a kind of "kitchen spirituality"; common meals and hospitality were central to how we cared for each other and our neighbors. Dinnertime was an informal education in race, and many people were shaped by those conversations. Someone described Antioch's mission this way: "Caring for each other, forgiving each other, and washing the dishes." When you do those simple things across racial lines, it's a very powerful experience and witness.

What Voice of Calvary and Antioch taught me is that most of us don't know what we're capable of because we don't allow our lives to become interrupted by the possibility of becoming a new people. Central to the story of Voice of Calvary church and the Antioch community is that we were hardly perfect saints; we were broken, flawed people full of weakness. But we did not accept "the way things are" as the way things must be. We dared to imagine a different world, to give ourselves to it through fidelity in sickness and health, and to seek God's help. Only by plunging in over our heads did we become capable of discovering the power of God to carry us places that only the Spirit could take us, of developing the distinctive

Christian skills which made a new life possible over the long haul, and of finding the joy of seeing God give gifts to sustain us when it seemed we could go no further in our own strength.

Voice of Calvary and Antioch gave me a new racial story to live by, one that resists the story that is automatically handed down to us within this society with the insidiousness of an invisible, unconscious legacy. Mississippi showed me the possibility of different "races" disciplining our bodies into a common space of fidelity and forgiveness, as a new life together became visible in our midst.

But oddly enough, Antioch's existence would have been impossible without what was, without doubt, *my worst cross-cultural experience.*

### Worst Cross-Cultural Experience

In 1983, two years after I moved to Jackson and Voice of Calvary, a group of African-American church members began to confront us white members about race problems within our own congregation. Until then, I thought I was living in a paradise of racial harmony. I was flabbergasted, confused, and angered by their charges of our racial privilege. America's racial fault line, I discovered, ran right through the heart of Voice of Calvary. Until then, I thought I was part of the solution, not the problem. But the reconciliation meetings proved the distrust was personal and that black folk didn't trust me; now I didn't trust them either. It turned out that whites and blacks had very different understandings of race. White folk saw the race problem as being people who wore hoods and used the n-word. But black folk saw the race problem manifested in more subtle ways, like how mostly white people were running our different ministry programs. They were very blunt and emotional about what they saw, and it was difficult dealing with their anger and their charges of racism. I remember walking from one meeting alone down the street, full of confusion. *Why do black folk have to talk about "black" and "white" so much? Don't they know I'm here to help?* Mentally I began packing my bags. I didn't need angry black folk telling me what was wrong with me.

Over the year, after those reconciliation meetings, with the help of the new friendships with African Americans that developed within the Bible study that eventually became Antioch, I underwent a painful transformation, a kind of "second conversion." I finally came to see that being white gave me certain privileges. For example, for me dealing with race was *optional*. I could take it or leave it. I could move across town, move into an all-white world, join an all-white church, and not be bothered by race again, unless I chose to be. But I saw that black people had to deal with race whether they wanted to or not.

I also saw that I carried a great deal of anger toward the black people who ran the reconciliation meetings. I saw I had to forgive them, to release myself from their anger so I could be free to see their truth. And the truth was, I realized that I had struck a deal: I would do justice for all, as long as I could look in the mirror and see the squeaky-clean face of goodness and innocence, and as long as I could stay in control. Hey, I was a big fan of justice for all, as long as it didn't limit justice for me. After learning about the bitter racial experiences of new black friends in the Bible study, I finally understood what a high price black folk at Voice of Calvary had paid all these years, and how deeply they had forgiven by choosing to stay in the same church with us. All these years black folk had been hanging on to white folk "in spite of," and here I had been tempted to leave at the first sign of conflict. All of this was a transformation that to me felt like a difficult, painful conversion. But in the end, it released a great new joy in my life, as trust and friendship and common mission deepened across divided lines.

## The Media's Influence

I do not claim to know how to dissect all the ways that the media view race relations between whites and African Americans. But what I do know is that what underlies much of the media's coverage of race, indeed, their obsession with it, is the assumption that the most we can hope for is tolerance. But this must be rejected on theological grounds. For the witness of Scripture is that what the Cross and Resurrection has brought is "one new humanity." What I see in the history of African-American people and in their life as a church, and in the history of Voice of Calvary in particular, is something that is not to be merely received with tolerance, but that has the possibility of transforming me, of re-creating my existence as a white man, and forming me into a different kind of person and a more faithful disciple.

The historical trajectory, which Christians must resist, is one that has disciplined our racialized bodies for separation, inscribing separation and exclusion into our very choices about marriage, whom we worship with and study the Bible with, and where we live. In the end, the division of white and black lives into separate spaces has become normal to us, and quite comfortable actually. "Black." "White." "Black churches." "White churches." How readily those categories and descriptions are accepted in the media and in our culture! They have become fixed, permanent categories and the only way we can imagine our existence.

In the face of this, some want to say that being Christian means transcending race. And if that is not true, if our Christianity and the grace of God cannot ultimately triumph over the power of race, then we are indeed people without hope. Others see the Christian task as racial realism: The past and continuing history of terror, inequality, and difference is real. African Americans still have to work twice as hard to get half as far, and we ignore this history at our peril. After all, if African Americans do not keep the truth of the past alive, the memory of evil, resistance to it, and knowledge of how the past continues to form us, who will? And if we deny that race continues to haunt the national landscape and our daily lives, then we are playing tiddlywinks.

Against complacency, we must engage history by the agonized truth of the Cross and enter the messiness of engaging our racial history and how it has deformed us. Against despair, we must proclaim the hope of resurrection and God's fullness and the possibility of newness breaking into our life as the church. As we give over our spirits, our minds, and our very bodies to the Spirit who is the Giver of Life, the promise of God is that "one new humanity" becomes material reality, a people within this world whose existence challenges history, a people who imagine a different world and a world shaped by the Cross, the Resurrection, and the power of Pentecost.

*About Chris:* Chris P. Rice is the author of the memoir *Grace Matters: A True Story of Race, Friendship, and Faith in the Heart of the South* (Jossey-Bass, 2002), which tells the story of his years in Mississippi. His book *More Than Equals* was coauthored with the late Spencer Perkins. Chris has been a research associate for the Boston University Institute on Race and Social Division, a columnist for *Sojourners* magazine, and he has spoken and taught extensively on racial reconciliation. He is currently pursuing studies at the Divinity School at Duke University.

## DAVE TAENZER, JEWISH

Jews are a tiny minority in the United States. We are just over 1 percent of the population. I am reminded of this fact every year on the Jewish High Holy Days of Rosh Hashanah and Yom Kippur. These are the two most important days of the year for a Jew. Jews who rarely go to our weekly Sabbath services come to the synagogue for these holidays. Coming to the synagogue on these days is almost like a minimum requirement for considering yourself a Jew.

Most people in the United States do not understand the importance of these days to Jews and sometimes schedule important events on these days. Rosh Hashanah is the Jewish New Year celebration. No one in the United States would schedule an important business meeting or an important test in school on January 1, but they think nothing of doing this on Rosh Hashanah.

Yom Kippur is the holiest day of the Jewish year. It is called the Day of Atonement. Jews worship together at their synagogues, spending the day thinking about what they have done in the past year and how to do better in the coming year. We forgive people who have wronged us, even if they have not apologized for their actions.

It is a very solemn day that really has no equivalent in the Christian calendar. The closest thing to scheduling an important event on Yom Kippur would be scheduling that event on Easter Sunday. Since our population is over three-quarters Christian, no one would think of scheduling important events on New Year's Day or Easter.

Unfortunately, this happens every year for most Jews. Schools are normally in session, and, often, important tests are given on Rosh Hashanah or Yom Kippur. This happened to my son last year at his high school. When he came back to class, the teacher was reviewing the test and told my son he had to leave the class since he hadn't taken the test yet. His teacher is a nice man and certainly not anti-Semitic. He just didn't understand the importance of Yom Kippur to a Jew and how insulting his actions were to us. His actions were based on ignorance, not hatred.

Rosh Hashanah and Yom Kippur are normally displayed on almost all calendars, but people do not understand their significance. I used to work for a large corporation. As a manager, I was invited every year to the yearly manager's conference. This was a critical event where important topics were discussed and planning was done for the corporation.

The first year I worked at this company, I discovered that they had scheduled this conference on Yom Kippur. I explained that I would not be able to attend because of this conflict and asked them not to schedule it on Rosh Hashanah or Yom Kippur the next year. They apologized to me and said that they would be careful the next year to avoid scheduling the event on the Jewish holidays.

The next year, it happened again. I got a letter from the president of the company apologizing, but it happened again the following year. It was a large corporation that said that it took diversity very seriously. All employees had to take special diversity classes. There were more than a hundred managers attending this conference, but almost all were white Protestant men.

It was hard for me to take their corporate diversity policies very seriously. In fact, one year they scheduled a corporate-wide diversity conference on Yom Kippur. When I called the person running the conference, he said that he did not schedule the event and it wasn't his fault. They, of course, did not change the schedule. It was like something I would expect to see in a Dilbert comic strip.

This kind of problem happens every year to someone in my family. It is a reminder of what a tiny minority we are. When someone schedules an important event on Rosh Hashanah or Yom Kippur we are excluded from participating. It makes us feel like second-class citizens in our Christian country.

I am a leader in the Boy Scouts. This year, my district scheduled an important adult training class on Yom Kippur. When I talked with the person running the class, he told me that he did not schedule the class and perhaps I could take it next year. The Boy Scouts organization encourages its members to actively participate in the religion of their choice. It says it encourages all religions, but often I participate in events where a prayer is used that refers to Jesus as our Lord or Savior. This is obviously awkward for Jews or any other non-Christian members.

The anti-Semitism that was common in this country fifty years ago has been replaced by ignorance and indifference. I hope that we can all learn more about people who are not like us. We have people of many races, cultures, and religions in our country. I think we will all be much better off if we make a real effort to understand each other and treat each other with respect.

*About Dave:* Dave Taenzer is a software consultant. He and his wife, Lynn, and their three sons live in Aurora, Colorado.

## WENDY CHISHOLM, AFRICAN-AMERICAN AND JEWISH

I have a hard time categorizing experiences into "best" and "worst," because even though I have had some painful racial encounters I have seen how the Lord has used them to either make me more sensitive to racial concerns and justice issues or as a teaching opportunity for my own personal benefit or for the benefit of others.

I am in a cross-cultural situation in almost every arena of life. There are very few groups that I have been a part of that identify with the various biracial concerns that are unique to the African-American and Jewish cultures simultaneously. I have grown to see that the Lord has graciously given me this cultural heritage to color the way I perceive life issues. I look at my heritage as a gift, and I try to use this unique racial perspective as a tool to teach sensitivity for racial concerns in ministry situations. My biracial heritage has afforded me unique inroads into both cultures: African American and Caucasian Jewish, which give me invaluable learning opportunities. I have endured many painful racial experiences over the years, but I have really seen how the Lord has transformed this pain into the message of my call. Ministry opportunities have revolved around a strong concern for multicultural ministry and a deep concern for racial justice.

## Best Cross-Cultural Experience

One of the best cultural experiences for me was living in the Austin community on the West Side of Chicago, a community whose residents are predominantly African American. (While I consider myself African American if I classify my race, I found that the Midwest culture and the economic and social issues varied from the way I was raised.) The community was extremely tense with many of the prevalent issues that go along with gang and drug activity, but I found that that experience challenged me to address some pervasive prejudices that I had been taught by the media.

For instance, I realized that I had fear of my neighborhood that was not founded on my experience, but on how the media had portrayed tense neighborhoods and the people who become involved in illicit activities. I had learned to fear; however, as I became more comfortable in the neighborhood and began to own the issues that

myself this new perspective until I was able to adopt it and override the media perceptions that were etched in my mind from an early age.

I came away with the life lesson that presence is everything. What I mean by that is I could see the good and the bad because I was in close proximity to the issues that would have never touched me had I lived in another area. My life would not have been so full of the rich blessings that I received from the community had I allowed the fear to abort our decision to move where all our friends told us was not a wise place to move to. I also realized that I could not allow the fear that I learned to keep me from the ministry that God had called me to. It became quite evident that the stereotypical problems and joys of families that are promoted in the media are shallow and not representative of the entire culture. Good cross-cultural experiences expose us to the heart of people making us able to see a fuller picture of life.

In evaluation, I have also come to see the strengths of mono-cultural situations. To this point I had always championed the cause of multicultural situations, and I still believe in the necessity of developing this type of environment for all so that true maturity can happen as people of different races explore difference and diverse cultural strengths together. I have come to believe, however, that there are true strengths for having monocultural situations if those situations will benefit the strength of the respective communities' voice in the multicultural setting. The Austin community was a place where African Americans could have voice, which was stripped of them in the broader society. This community boasted of many heroes molded into gracious caregivers who didn't allow the broader society's prejudice to influence their drive for success. Many of the community residents could be models for the church to teach grace, perseverance, and longsuffering. These voices are squelched or invisible to the media. The voice of evil, which is such a minor voice, is louder than the voice of grace.

Other beneficial cross-cultural situations for me have been

relationships I have developed with people from different countries. I am privileged to learn about the respective cultures through these friendships, but more importantly my view of God has broadened. I have seen God through the eyes of persecuted saints and saints of humble means, each with their unique view of God. The faith of these believers is astounding. Many of them have left everything to serve God, and their appreciation for everything has challenged my apathy. My faith is challenged as I pray with these believers for the minutest details of need. Their faith is contagious, and they regularly experience faith that moves mountains. My hope in God has increased, and I feel so privileged to see God through different lenses.

My mother positioned us to be accepting of any culture, which I am sure stemmed from the prejudice she faced as a young woman and her interpretation of Jewish culture, which she credits with a strong sense of justice for all people. She lived in a predominantly black community with my father, and she witnessed the victimization of a people and became sensitive to the social concerns unique to that community. She always positioned our family to have this same concern for people. I adopted many of my views for cross-cultural ministry from her model. We entertained people of various cultures in our home and were accepting of people from all walks of life. Because of this I find that I operate with ease in most cultures and position myself to explore unique settings that place me near people who are different from me. They only serve to enrich me as a person, and I am deeply grateful for the way I was raised.

## Worst Cross-Cultural Experience

School was a very troubling world for me, because it was there that I faced a lot of prejudice that the broader society was dealing with. I sensed great acceptance and love in the neighborhood I was raised in. However, when I entered school I realized that there were children who held different views about race than I was taught and that some of them had ill-founded hatred for children who were mixed. I specifically remember another young boy who got beaten up because he was mixed like I was, but he wore a Jewish Star of David. The African-American children threatened to beat him up, and I became quite frightened for him and myself.

I was raised in an era just after the civil rights movement when the world was deciding what integration should look like. Busing was a huge concern for many of the neighborhood schools, and there was volatility in these forced mixtures of people. Busing was popularized to achieve this integration. Kids were bused from all over the city to my junior high, and the races rarely mixed during the social hours like lunch and breaks. I found it hard to make friends because I didn't fit in any of the groups. I was too black for the white students and too white for the black students. I became a loner.

One day I asked for a Jewish holiday pass so I could be excused from school to attend holiday services at temple. The teacher denied me that pass and told me in front of the whole class that I wasn't black, that I didn't think like a black person, and that he wouldn't give me the pass. I thought I would die right then and there. Through that experience I began to learn that prejudice is a problem that is in the heart of the one who voices the prejudice and has nothing to do with the one that the stereotype is directed at. Because of that experience and others, I hated to be biracial. I wanted to be all African American and nothing else. In retrospect the pain of the prejudice drove me to deny who I was, and so I would classify these experiences as negative.

I struggled while at Moody Bible Institute because I found that many of the students had had limited cross-cultural experiences. I had one young man take me to lunch and confess that he had a sin problem. I was shocked at first, but I agreed to hear him out. He told me that he had never met a black person before and that now that he met me he realized that the way he was taught to hate black people was wrong. I was surprised at his honesty, but in my genuineness I remarked, "I had read about people like you in books, but I didn't really believe you existed." I had not realized that there was a whole sector of society that never had to see someone of a different race. I had always been raised in the city, and my mother went to great lengths to get us into schools that were multicultural. I wrestled with this experience for a long time. It was the first time I realized with great clarity that prejudice is taught; it also taught me that God's heart is to uproot these negative views.

## The Media's Influence

Media tends to color the way we perceive cultures based on prejudicial macro-cultural trends. It is a constant struggle as a Christian to counteract these biases by intentionally developing cross-cultural relationships that challenge these prejudices. The media takes the problems and the joys of lives and gives the viewer a shallow perception of the captured experiences. Life is fuller than what can be captured by the glimpse of life the media can portray.

*About Wendy:* Wendy Chisholm is pursuing studies at Fuller Theological Seminary and has a Master's degree from NIU in Adult Education. She has been a teacher and adviser, GED coordinator/instructor, and women's basketball coach. Wendy has been married for fifteen years to Greg Chisholm, pastor of Chinese Faith Church, and they have a daughter, Zhita-Lynne, who is three years old. Wendy is a stay-at-home mom and heavily involved in the ministry with her husband as a Bible teacher, nursery coordinator, and play-group leader.

## JONATHAN LEW, ASIAN AMERICAN

As an Asian American, I often feel "neither here nor there" when it comes to my place in this society. The title of a video I saw many years ago summarizes my experience well: *"Between Two Worlds."* I feel "between" in many ways. I am third-generation Chinese American, which in a nutshell means that culturally I'm not fully Chinese nor fully American, but some combination of the two.

I am also "between" in the sense that racially I am neither white nor black—the major paradigm under which race relations have been viewed in the U.S. At times, individuals from both of those groups have been unsure how to categorize people like me. In a crowd of white faces, my black hair and tan complexion stand out, leading some to include me in the category of "minorities" or "people of color." Others, however, noting the way I speak, the clothes I wear, or the music I listen to, have concluded that—except for my last name or the color of my skin—I might as well be "white."

I have struggled with my ethnic identity in the midst of these different perceptions of who I am and where I fit, and I have basically come to the conclusion that I am a unique individual with a mixture of cultural influences and choices. Where I used to see my being "between" as a liability, I now see it more and more as a blessing. It gives me the freedom to move among different groups, forming friendships with people of diverse backgrounds, and looking at the world through others' eyes.

## Best Cross-Cultural Experience

My best cross-cultural experience was not one in which I crossed cultures, but one in which someone else crossed cultures in order to understand me. When I was in college, a group of Asian-American students sponsored a demonstration and teach-in to protest stereotypical, patronizing portrayals of Asians in a musical that was being performed on campus. I had mixed feelings about demonstrating, but decided to go and support my friends. When I got there, I was surprised to see a few white students I knew from the InterVarsity Christian Fellowship group who were there to learn more about the reasons for the demonstration. What impressed me was that they were not there to criticize or argue with us, but to ask questions and learn. I will never forget one white student in particular who took the time to sit down with me at the teach-in and listen to speaker after speaker, some of whom in their anger and emotion were lashing out at whites! Yet my white friend did not get angry or defensive in return—or if he did, he didn't show it—but instead I could tell that he was really trying to understand why people were upset, to step out of his own skin and into others' shoes. His was a simple but powerful expression of love and humility to me. It continues to give me hope for race relations to this day.

## Worst Cross-Cultural Experience

My worst cross-cultural experience, which also happened during college, was the only time that I can honestly say I was the target of blatant, hostile racism. It happened as I was driving my car with a Jewish friend of mine in the passenger seat. We were stopped at an intersection when two white men in another car yelled out some ethnic slurs directed at me. My friend could not take it and yelled something back in my defense. Provoked, the two men proceeded to chase us in their car through the streets surrounding the college. At one point, they succeeded in getting in front of our car and blocked the road, forcing us to stop. One of the men got out of the car and walked toward us. He made some comments to me to the effect that "your people" should "stop buying up all the good property in this country" and "go back where you came from." Then, having had his say, he turned around and left. The whole incident reminded me that no matter how American I might think I am, there will always be people who will consider me a "foreigner" and judge me by their stereotypes.

## The Media's Influence

My opinion is that the impact of media on race relations is very mixed. On the one hand, the media have helped to expose the problems of racism and injustice to a wide audience. It is difficult to watch TV footage from the Civil Rights Movement of the 1950s and '60s, for instance, and not wince at the sight of policemen with clubs, dogs, and fire hoses attacking peaceful demonstrators.

On the other hand, I also believe that the media often overdramatizes, oversimplifies, and even omits important information when it comes to the complex issues surrounding race and culture. During the riots in Los Angeles in 1992, much of the news coverage seemed to portray the looting and violence that occurred as an African-American-versus-Korean-American situation. Yet, as more information came to light, it appeared that the situation was much more multi-dimensional, with large numbers of Latinos also in the picture as both perpetrators and victims of crimes.

One thing about the media that is frustrating for me as an Asian American is how much we tend to be overlooked or ignored in the media. The movie "The Joy Luck Club" was groundbreaking because it was a mainstream, box-office hit featuring a majority Asian-American cast, but there have been very few films that have Asian Americans in starring roles (and even fewer TV shows!). Many of the movies or TV shows that historically have portrayed Asians have limited them to stereotypical roles: for the men, either house servant, martial arts expert, nerd, or enemy soldier, and for the women, the exotic "geisha girl" or submissive "picture bride." Even in the news media, Asian Americans are often left out when it comes to surveys or polls.

## The Relationship Between Asian Americans and African Americans

It is difficult to make generalizations about the relationship between Asian Americans and African Americans, because it can be as different in any two locales as it can be between any two individuals. The two groups have different histories (and within each group, there are different histories among the subgroups), and yet there are more similarities than the average person would expect. The legacy of slavery is obviously something that sets African Americans apart from any other group; yet Asian Americans have faced their share of prejudice, segregation, racism, and hardship as well. There are many well-documented examples of both *legally enforced* and illegal acts of discrimination against Asian Americans. Two prominent examples are the forced relocation and internment of Japanese Americans during World War II and the Chinese Exclusion Act, which brought Chinese men as cheap labor into the U.S. but virtually forbade their wives and other Chinese women from immigrating!

As in any relationship, there are ways that the two sides can respect or disrespect each other. There can be a general lack of knowledge on both sides about each other's history, which leads to a lack of appreciation and understanding for the other's current situation. Some Asian Americans have a genuine admiration for African Americans for paving the way for other minority groups in securing civil rights and a more just society. Other Asian Americans may carry the stereotype that African Americans don't work hard enough or have the same value for education held by Asian Americans. On the other side, some African Americans admire the apparent success of Asian Americans academically, professionally, and economically, while other African Americans lack respect for Asian Americans because they perceive Asian Americans as being weak in physical, social, or verbal skills.

Overall, my personal relationships with African Americans have been positive and mutually enriching. I have come to appreciate and admire what I perceive to be cultural strengths among many African Americans, including a greater freedom to express their thoughts and emotions (in speech and in worship), as well as a rich legacy of music, art, and sport within African-American communities that has greatly influenced the broader society. I have also been blessed to know African Americans who have taken a deep interest in the cultures and histories of Asian Americans and other groups, and who have sought to learn from us as well. While I am aware of real differences and tensions that continue to exist between groups like African Americans and Asian Americans, I am hopeful that there can be strong bonds of mutual trust, affection, and partnership—especially within the body of Christ, where we are called to "act justly and to love mercy and to walk humbly with [our] God" (Micah 6:8).

*About Jonathan:* A graduate of Claremont McKenna College, Jonathan

Lew also has an M.A. in Intercultural Studies from Biola University and is pursuing a Ph.D. in Higher Education at Claremont Graduate University. He has experience in both campus ministry and higher education administration, having worked at the University of California at Irvine, Azusa Pacific University, and the Claremont Colleges.

## ALBERTO RODRIGUEZ, HISPANIC

Not a homogeneous group, Hispanics defy customary classifications. For example, the Census Bureau, recognizing the differences between all the Hispanic origin subgroups, does not use Hispanic/Latino as a race. Hispanics come in many different colors and shades. Their heritage comes from Natives: direct descendants of the ancient civilizations like the Aztecs in central Mexico, the Mayas in Guatemala and El Salvador, the Incas in the Andes of Peru, and many other indigenous groups; from Europeans; from Africans brought to America and the Caribbean as slaves; and from Spaniards.

Growing up in Puerto Rico, I was unaware of racism as I'm aware of it today. My ancestors came from the Canary Islands in Spain and from Cuba. Having fair skin color and coming from a hardworking, middle-class family with a strong Christian faith, and living and relating mostly to the same social strata, kept me insulated from being the object of direct discrimination. My parents were not very mobile and kept the relationships within their immediate family, the church, and work circles. At the age of ten, I was given the opportunity to play basketball for the YMCA in tournaments in the U.S. We visited Indiana, Illinois, and New York City and played against clubs and in areas that were very segregated. It was an eye-opening experience, even when most of the families involved opened their homes to us wholeheartedly.

Later in life, as I graduated from medical school, I moved to Philadelphia to complete my postgraduate training. Again the segregation in the community, the churches, and even the hospital were as shocking as my sudden immersion in a totally different culture. In the "City of Brotherly Love," skin color became an issue as I walked the streets of the "war zones"—the frontier between the Hispanic *barrio* and Afro-American "hood." My wife Debbie, who is also very fair skinned, was denied jobs and given low-paying assignments (stuffing envelopes in a factory), even when she had a college degree in business. She saw an interviewer write in her employment application "the Puerto Rican girl," after asking where she got her accent. She never received a call from that agency again. Several times, despite our education, we were treated as if we were not able to understand or were unable to accomplish the tasks at hand.

We moved to North Carolina for me to pursue additional medical training. While there, Debbie was denied service at a local grocery store because she was an "alien." We experienced and also witnessed more overt racism in the South than in any other area we have ever lived before. We have been involved in many churches from different denominations and traditions and with several ministries in our journey. We can honestly say that those have been "the best of times and the worse of times." Some Christians have been like the family we left back in Puerto Rico: supportive, inclusive, real friends, and partners for life. Some of these people did not start out being our friends, but they made an effort to walk out of their comfort zone, so did we, and it culminated in great friendships. But in some other instances there has been sharp segregation and discrimination, poor communication, suspicion, isolation, lack of support, and what I call a "pharisaic attitude"—the crossing to the other side of the road in order to avoid finding a person in need whom they really don't want to serve or who will be an inconvenience. It may require time, involvement; it may be too risky and out of our comfort zone to help, become involved, or even shake a hand.

The Anglo church in general has been very willing to help Hispanics, and especially the poorest of them, by providing social services, monetary help, educational assistance, etc. This is good and necessary, but what I have observed is that building close relationships and working together, sharing responsibilities and authority, and trusting each other is usually "too close for comfort." "I have no idea how to minister to *your* people"; "It will be much better for you to build a separate organization, department, ministry so Hispanics can have total control of their own organization"; "Hispanics are not in the '10/40 window'"—these are typical comments that I have heard from Christians, churches, and Christian organizations as they excuse themselves from relating to Hispanics individually and in ministry. The greatest need of the Hispanics in ministry is to be part of it—to belong, to be included, and to be in partnership with others (Anglos, Afro Americans, other Hispanics or Asians). The great majority of the problems that arise for most Hispanic churches and individuals, including pastors and leaders, can be traced directly to being isolated.

Token positions for Hispanics in Christian organizations and churches do not meet the needs of the individuals involved, and they will never meet the needs of the organization. The organization/church needs the input and help of the ethnic group as much as the ethnic group needs the organization. We really need each other, close and personal. At a minimum, having diversity in the organization will cause internal adjustments and changes, which in turn will cause growth. Isn't that what Christ is after in our lives?

If we are not relevant and do not really love our neighbors, those neighbors that we can see, how can we expect to reach those who are far away? Of course we can reach them, you may say; but can you really reach them with your heart? Churches and Christian organizations need to be aware of the changes in their communities so they are able to present a relevant message to their world. Sometimes they are blind and deaf to the needs of ethnic groups just across the street or across the pews. In being unaware and insensitive to their needs, they are also missing out on the skills, resources, and contributions that these ethnic groups can provide to individuals and to the community of faith. It seems that it is preferable to many to be a missionary in an exotic place far away than to get to know the neighbor for whom Christ also died and who in His sovereignty was placed right next to you, in your community.

The Hispanics in the United States present a challenge and an opportunity for Christians, the church, and Christian organizations. What will be our response?

As our Afro-American brothers have said, we are not seeking reconciliation, but a relationship: a partnership, inclusion, and assistance as well as receptivity to the gifts and resources that God can give you through us. I pray that besides supplying for the physical and financial needs of those who are poor, all of us may become visible parts of the body of Christ, needing each other and supplying the needs of each other as we build lasting relationships full of God's grace.

*About Alberto:* Alberto J. Rodríguez has been a family physician with private practice in Hartford, Connecticut, for the past sixteen years. He is a graduate of the University of Puerto Rico. He obtained his postgraduate training at Hahnemann University Hospital and Medical Center in Philadelphia and a Teaching Fellowship at Duke University in North Carolina. He is an Associate Professor for the University of Connecticut Medical School and in the teaching faculty of Yale University Medical School. He is serving as President of the Connecticut Academy of Family Physicians. He and his wife, Debbie, give leadership to the marriage small groups in their local church. Presently, he and Debbie serve as the Directors of FamilyLife's U.S. Hispanic Ministry. The Rodriguezes have been married for twenty-four years and have four children.

> *Dear Lord,*
>
> *I pray that as we read this chapter, it will help us to develop a greater appreciation of those You have made who are different from us. May our sensitivity and grace toward others increase. May we live out Revelation 7:9 before we get to heaven.*
>
> *Amen.*

## THOUGHT QUESTIONS FOR THIS CHAPTER

1. How do you feel about what you just read?

2. Could you relate to some of the shared experiences? Can you talk to a friend or class about it?

3. Did you learn anything new as a result of reading this chapter? What was it? How do you feel about this new information you now possess?

4. Will you look at other people differently since reading this chapter?

5. Do you think that you will be more patient with people who are different than you?

6. Are you surprised to read about how another culture views your culture?

7. What do you honestly think about other cultures/races and why?

8. What are some practical things you can do as a result of reading this chapter? Individually? In your church? In your school? In your Christian ministry/organization?

## FURTHER RESOURCES:

Center for immigration studies—http://www.cis.org.

Fong, Ken. *Pursuing the Pearl: A Comprehensive Resource for Multi-Asian Ministry.* Valley Forge, Pa.: Judson Press, 1999.

Katz, William Loren. *Black Indians: A Hidden Heritage.* New York: Atheneum, 1986.

Lin, Tom. *Losing Face & Finding Grace: 12 Bible Studies for Asian-Americans.* Downers Grove, Ill.: InterVarsity, 1997.

Ortiz, Manuel. *The Hispanic Challenge: Opportunities Confronting the Church.* Downers Grove, Ill.: InterVarsity, 1993. (Statistics and Ideas).

Rice, Chris. *Grace Matters: A True Story of Race, Friendship, and Faith in the Heart of the South.* San Francisco: Jossey-Bass, 2002.

Suro, Roberto. *Strangers Among Us: How Latino Immigration is Transforming America.* New York: Knopf, 1998.

Twiss, Richard. *One Church Many Tribes: Following Jesus the Way God Made You,* www.wiconi.com.

U.S. Census Bureau, Minority Populations in the U.S. from the Census Bureau. (Statistics – Most Statistics from 1990 and 2000 Census).

Yep, Jeanette Peter Cha, et al. *Following Jesus Without Dishonoring Your Parents.* Downers Grove, Ill.: InterVarsity, 1998. Written by a team of Asian-American Christians.

# 11

# We Don't Know What We're Missing

## Biblical Diversity in Everyday Life

*". . . and a little child will lead them."*

—Isaiah 11:6

When my twin daughters, Christina and Michelle, were eleven years old, and Andrea was nine years old, they would often play with our then next-door neighbor, eight-year-old Amy (who has since moved away).

It was not uncommon for Amy—who happens to be white—to ask to sleep over at our house. She had no problem being the "person of least color" in our house, nor was she ashamed to be seen with my girls in public. Amy just liked hanging out with my girls, and they liked being with her. That's what friends do.

Though they didn't really know it, these four girls were practicing biblical diversity, and they were doing it for one simple reason: They had (and still have) a relationship. They didn't go to events where they listened to a speaker and were suddenly convicted of their racism, cry, make a public declaration, and then go back to life as usual. They simply loved (and still love) each other and enjoyed (and continue to enjoy) being together. Like all children, they had their problems, but unlike adults, they didn't seem to have the difficulty of forgiving each other, even if some of their more difficult problems meant bringing their parents into the picture. They moved on to what was most important to them—being *genuine* friends. They had come to realize what they would be missing if they stopped playing with each other.

We could learn a lot from these girls.

In fact, I believe we can draw a parallel in the body of Christ in regards to culture and race relations. Christians often don't know what we are missing cross-culturally because it seems we seldom allow ourselves to be in situations where we can learn and benefit from our racial and ethnic differences for the glory of God. And because we usually don't miss what we've never known, we have African-American urban churches, Caucasian suburban churches, Korean, Latino, First Nations (Native American), Chinese-American churches, you name it. Rare are the congregations across our increasingly diverse nation that not only integrate such cultures but actually celebrate them for Christ's sake. Though for the past forty years many secular colleges, corporations, and city councils have taken critical steps to represent this land of nations (often amidst growing hostility), the church sadly has taken little initiative to do the same. And I believe we are missing out not only on the blessings of relationships—like the ones my girls know and experience—but on an opportunity to reflect God's kingdom to a world desperately in need of a love that transcends cultural boundaries.

The Bible teaches us that all Christians from all tribes and nations will spend eternity together. Yet it seems that here on earth, we struggle even to get to know each other, let alone develop mutually beneficial, lasting relationships with each other, especially if we are from different cultures and ethnic backgrounds.

Why is this? How can we be a family as is clearly said in the Bible, yet fail to interact with one another—in all our differences and similarities—in a way that honors our heavenly Father?

Which brings me back to my original point: For a variety of reasons, the body of Christ, which is one in a theological sense, does not know what it is missing collectively and individually. Perhaps the first reason is that it is human nature for us to gravitate toward people we perceive are like us, rather than live in harmony with individuals whose skin color and culture varies from our own. For example, one of my white friends asked me, "Am I prejudiced because if I see an all-black team playing a white team, I pull for the white team?" I told him, "I don't know, but I tend to do the same thing, unless that all-black team is playing against my favorite school team." We both probably need some help, but both of us are simply human. In other words, it's easier to choose the path of least resistance than the higher calling of diversity.

A second reason could be because the church in the United States has done so little to acknowledge, let alone improve on, our country's tragic history of segregation and racial injustices. And, finally, I believe we lack an authentic vision for what the body of Christ is and what it should look like.

Granted, all of us who are striving to improve race relations among Christians are indebted to groups such as Promise Keepers, Mission Mississippi, etc.—whose greatest contribution may have been to acknowledge the race issue at all, and then to view it as an integral one for unifying the church. And in what was perhaps the first time for evangelicals in America, Promise Keepers created a climate of openness in which Christians of varying backgrounds could begin to discuss cultural and racial issues with intentionality and purpose.

## CREATIVE UNITY

I'm thankful that Promise Keepers and such groups at least got people thinking and talking about the issue. But the blessing of biblical diversity is much more than a cause on an agenda. It is as natural a part of the Christian lifestyle as prayer, worship, Bible study, and seeking God's desire (Revelation 7:9). Why? Because as my girls are teaching me and others who observe them, it is simply about building daily friendships—at any cost. That is part of the very purpose of Christian discipleship, isn't it?

Before that can happen, though, I believe God must first give us a new vision for the church. That takes us to Scripture. The church at Corinth seemed to have a similar problem to that of modern day evangelicals. The apostle Paul offered a few godly words: "The body is a unit [unity], though it is made up of many parts [diversity]; and though all its parts are many [diversity], they form one body [unity]. So it is with Christ. For we were all baptized by one Spirit into one body—whether Jews or Greeks, slave or free—and we were all given the one Spirit to drink" (1 Corinthians 12:12–13).

This passage seems to indicate that diversity and unity not only can coexist, but are prerequisites for the church to experience and reflect the best of God's rich blessings. Neither does union require everyone to be exactly alike. Unity allows for diversity and creativity, even though we are all on the same team. Unity allows for getting to the same place at different times and not having the exact same route, even though going the same general direction. If we aren't careful, our attempts to find unanimity can be the enemy of unity. This is an intriguing concept I am learning from Walt Henrichsen, author and former Navigator staff member. Therefore, our *God-given* differences—something we tend to forget—are an asset for Christ's body, not a detriment. Unfortunately, the sinful aspects of the dynamics of a majority/minority system created at the founding of our country have had, and seem to continue to have, a greater influence in the body of Christ than we dare to admit.

Paul goes on to share more of God's design and wisdom regarding diversity and unity in the body of Christ: "Now the body [unity] is not made up of one part but of many [diversity]. If the foot should say, 'Because I am not a hand, I do not belong to the body,' it would not for that reason cease to be part of the body" (1 Corinthians 12:14–15). Obviously, a human body functions as one body when all its different parts are working together. That's a medical fact as well as a reality we all experience each morning we wake up. If I play enough tennis, eat enough greens, and sleep enough hours, I know that my legs and stomach—very different parts—are going to cooperate with my head and my heart—equally different parts. You get the idea.

Likewise, the diversity and unity found in the body of Christ are based on fact and not on feelings. Our mutual salvation is based on the perfect work of our Lord and Savior Jesus Christ and not the feelings we might (or might not) express in response to it. They co-exist for the mutual benefit of each other. In other words, every congregation is comprised of different folk (some more different than others), and we all know that a congregation will be at its best when each of those folk is working together for the good of the congregation. Unity brings together people who are different. And the whole purpose of diversity is unity; otherwise, you have chaos and disorder.

Last summer, our family had the opportunity to have a vacation on the East Coast. We also were provided with some extra work to help pay for our vacation. One of these work opportunities was conducting a marriage seminar for Salem Baptist Church of Atlanta, pastored by the legendary preacher Rev. Jasper Williams, along with one of his sons, Rev. Jasper Williams III.

Our girls' godparents, Jim and Kim, live in the surrounding area, so we left the girls with them and their children so we could facilitate the marriage retreat.

While we were at the retreat, Kim took the girls swimming. At the pool, one of her neighbors, an African-American woman, saw Kim with these three black girls. Kim and Jim had previously had her and her husband join them at Kim's parent's house for a swimming party, so she and Kim were friends. In the process of natural conversation, Jim and Kim's relationship to these three black girls was revealed.

Did I forget to mention that Jim and Kim are white?

As Kim explained to her neighbor that she is the girls' god-mother, something immediately changed in their relationship. It deepened. Kim told me the African-American woman seemed to become much more comfortable around her. She now began to call Kim "girl" (as in "girlfriend").

When people see us in action, it can change their impression of us. Jim and Kim's actions matched their talk. Life is funny, isn't it?

So the *fact* of the church is that diversity and unity are at the heart of both its mission and its nature. All Christians belong to the body of Christ, even if some members treat others as if they don't, and even if some only identify with those like themselves. God will deal with these individuals in His own time and His own way; in the meantime, these folk are missing out! And *these* folk impact us as well with their disobedience.

## DIFFERENT PARTS

Taking it a step further, we see that verses 18 and 19 of 1 Corinthians 12 provide deeper spiritual understanding of God's design for diversity and unity: "But in fact God has arranged the parts in the body, every one of them, just as he wanted them to be. If they were all *one part,* where would the *body* be?" (italics added). These verses reflect God's sovereignty and His love for diversity and unity. But they also boldly suggest that cultural identity must not be denied nor assimilated into a majority culture. If anything, a celebration of the unique cultures (body parts) for the sake of the One whole body is the only thing that seems to fit His agenda.

Verses 21 through 26 may be where people of faith err the most, because it seems that we do so little together. There is a tendency to think of ourselves as superior and of others as inferior to us, to be divisive by majoring on the minors (like differences) rather than on the major beliefs we share. We don't seem to realize that when one part of the body hurts we all hurt. Do you remember the girls? If Michelle was sick and in bed, Amy wasn't the only one who was sad her friend could not play with her. The other girls were also sad, because when one hurts, they all hurt. It's just not the same.

Likewise, when one of the girls did well in school, they all got excited for her. This is something evangelicals haven't been very good at either. A Christian executive once rejoiced in my presence when he heard that another Christian organization was having financial difficulty. His organization was older, and he was embarrassed when the younger ministry's annual budget had become larger than that of his organization. It is sad but true that we rarely rejoice in the Lord when one part of the body is honored. Yet if we are not honored specifically, we are honored in general because we are all part of the same body. This requires learning how to serve each other by honoring those from another culture, not offending them. Our ability to do or not do this reflects the level of maturity of our relationship with Christ. And maybe this is the critical key. It is our personal relationship with Jesus Christ that empowers us to act like Christ with all people.

Bill, one of my disciples (sort of) and a donor of our nonprofit ministry, calls me periodically to check up on me. Bill and his family recently moved from Houston to a suburb of Minneapolis. A consultant on Bill's job is an African American and a Christian. He lives in Atlanta, but his job frequently has him traveling to Bill's company. Bill invited his friend to his small group from his church. Bill called me concerned that only two of the seven guys in his small group took the time and initiative to greet his African-American friend. He said that the women were much friendlier.

As we talked, I tried to share with Bill the possible perspective of some of the white guys in his small group. Regardless of our skin color, we need to meet people where they are in their understanding of cultural/racial differences. Our ability to meet people where they are, like Jesus did, parallels our spiritual maturity. It is so easy to want people to be just like us; then we don't have to live by faith.

I told Bill that in his part of the country, there are very few people of color with whom whites can interact. I also told him that the only place these guys may see people of color, particularly African

Americans, is on television, on the front page in trouble with the law, or on the sports page (unfortunately, they can now also be in trouble with the law there too). Additionally, there is the fear of the unknown. We tend to run from or kill what we fear.

## LEADING THE WAY

In order to learn how to honor other cultures/races, then it is mandatory that we learn about other peoples' histories from their perspectives. Christians—and the organizations and the schools of which they are a part—should lead the way in learning about other peoples' histories and cultures, if for nothing else because of the church's commitment to home and foreign missions. Christian educators must begin to realize that their students will be global adults in a world where 70 percent of people are non-white.[1] Yes, it is more work for Christian school administrators and teachers, but the rewards of a greater sense of oneness in the body, more opportunities for evangelism, and more examples of God being glorified are worth the extra efforts.

Of course, Paul's description of Christ's body makes it obvious that we have a lot of work to do if we are to reflect a vision of heaven on earth. Dag Hammarskjold said that he learned a radical lesson from the Gospels: "All men are equals as God's children and should be met and treated by us as [by] our master." Theologically, few Christians will disagree with this statement; but our actions in the evangelical community clearly demonstrate we don't believe it. Why do I think so? As we look at many denominational organizations and parachurch ministries, we find few people of color in decision-making positions. We find even fewer Christian resources than in corporate America that are inclusive in their marketing approach and appeal to nonwhites.

So if the body of Christ is serious in practicing the parallel applications of truth in 1 Corinthians 12, our vision must be focused on our unity now so that we will be ready to share our heavenly home together. We must see anew with the eyes of our hearts how Christ's body is to function in the here and now as we prepare for eternity together. *We need each other.* And so we must allow our differences to unite us.

What else can we do? We must realize that we wrestle every day with the dynamics of a majority/minority system that is rooted deep in the history of our country as well as in the sinful hearts of men through the ages. Often those who comprise the majority will say from their "king of the hill" position: "Those people of color are oversensitive. Things are much better today for them than they were in my parents' day. Why don't they just get over it?" The one who asks such a question is not ready for anything more than a superficial cross-cultural relationship at best.

People of color may agree that some things are better for them than in their parents' day, yet they continue to struggle in an unrelenting quest for equality. People of color tire of being told they are equal in the body of Christ and simultaneously hearing, "It just takes time to make those *kind* of changes," or "That's just the way the system is, and I didn't create it. It's not my fault." Few in the majority culture seem to be trying to correct the problem.

An equally critical issue is the sharing of leadership, which translates into the sharing of power. If we are honest with each other, we'll admit that few people—regardless of culture or skin-color—naturally want to share the power they hold. We want it for ourselves.

The corporate world exists by claiming and holding onto power, yet this seems counter to the Gospel of the kingdom that defines greatness by the relinquishing of power and serving others, especially those in the household of God (Galatians 6:9–10, italics added —"Let us not become weary in doing good, for at the proper time we will reap a harvest if we do not give up. Therefore, as we have opportunity, let us do good to *all* people, especially those who belong to the *family* of believers.") It seems that for most whites, the issue is often one of faith, control, and/or trust. The questions many whites may be asking—though no one may ask aloud when nonwhites are present—are: "What will the leadership by people of color look like? What will it do? What will be my role? Will I be mistreated because they have been mistreated or they perceive they have been mistreated?"

For many people of color, the issue is often one of vulnerability *again*. I say "again" because people of color often feel they are at the mercy of a system in which they have little or no influence regardless of whether the system is Christian or non-Christian. It is basically a system designed without people of color in mind; so their questions are: "Can I really *trust* these people? Will my own people understand what I'm trying to accomplish by being the first person of color working in an organization that doesn't have a good track record with people of color, that I'm not an 'Uncle Tom'?"

Hard questions like these must be asked and answered if lasting and productive change is to occur. And a vision of eternity must guide us as we build relationships with each other on earth, knowing that when we do, everyone benefits. And when we don't, well, everyone misses out.

Just ask my girls and their friend Amy.

## WILL WE EVER GET IT TOGETHER?

Not long ago, I received a call from a prestigious Christian school in California, requesting my help because the school was experiencing some racial problems in teacher/student/parent relationships. White teachers were calling African-American students "cute little monkeys," which the teachers saw as an affectionate term, and one they'd also use for white children, but which is considered derogatory by African Americans because of subhuman connotations. I worked for a white Christian organization in the 1990s that had never heard of Farrakhan until the Million Man March. But then I think, *Why should white Christians who live in the suburbs, who have little or no contact with African Americans, know anything about African-American issues if they are not affected by them?*

The school's executive director sincerely communicated his

commitment for racial unity. Money wasn't an issue. He even asked his pastor to have me preach at both services specifically as to how to improve race relations, as well as to meet with a group of local pastors, representing several cultures and/or races. I was received well. While I was selling and signing my books in the foyer of the church, an older white gentleman in his seventies or eighties came behind and said the sermon helped him to realize his prejudice. With tears in his eyes he said, "I'm going to do better." I asked him if I could hug him. He said yes, and we hugged.

The next day, I spoke to faculty and administrators, leading them into a question-and-answer session, which resulted in more awareness. I also suggested some easy, doable, measurable first steps for faculty and administrators to prayerfully consider. They were an example of good Christians who theologically have no problems with biblical diversity but do have problems living out the practical consequences of cross-cultural relationships that go beyond the surface.

As mentioned earlier in the book, race relations can be improved upon. My life is so much richer because of all the men and women of many different backgrounds who have invested and continue to invest not only in my life, but the life of my family as well. They are African (including Afrikaners), Asian, Caucasian, Native American, and Hispanic. I am anxious to have more people who are different from me in my life and in the life of my family.

I am constantly trying to align myself with people regardless of their culture/race who want to go beyond window dressing to build win/win, lasting, cross-cultural relationships in the body of Christ. And I'm also building relationships with people outside of the body of Christ.

For example, the last week of August, on my return flight from speaking to the Christian school in California, I was upgraded to first class (suffering for Jesus) and happened to be seated by John Kobara, an Asian American who is the senior vice president for Sylvan Learning Systems's online higher education program. John is just as passionate for cultural/racial diversity as I am. He sounded much like me as he told me stories about informing his daughters about diversity. His wife's responses to his passion for diversity reminds me of Brenda's concern for me going overboard in teaching our girls. John and I are simply trying to protect our children from pain as well as attempting to teach them how to be proactive cross-culturally.

John is also well connected and often speaks on diversity to Fortune 500 companies. John immediately began to recommend books, such as *The Shape of the River* (Harvard research on affirmative action beneficiaries—twenty years later), as well as people he knows that he feels I should meet. I don't know if John is a Christian or not. I do know that our connecting was a divine appointment, not just for me to share Christ with John if he doesn't know Christ, but also for me to be taught by John about his beliefs and Asian history, successes, and struggles in America. This new relationship, this knowledge, and my recent trip to Singapore and the Philippines make me more sensitive toward Asian Americans. Shouldn't we as Christians be sensitive regardless? Yes, but the reality is that little happens outside of relationships.

It is exciting watching God move in this area! I know my meeting John is a God thing. It is comforting to know that I don't have to try to force cross-cultural relationships because God orchestrates them.

It isn't easy, but it is *possible*. The key is a faith that moves us beyond rhetoric to biblical action. This action, our obedience, glorifies God, who then because of His grace and mercy blesses us, always resulting in a heavenly win/win situation and sometimes one on earth as well.

## REFLECTIONS

As I reflect upon these cross-cultural relationships, the first thing that comes to mind is that God crossed all of our paths. There was usually no intentional going out of the way to develop a cross-cultural relationship. I realize that most of the motives are pure in these efforts, but many times the emphasis on making a friend of a different culture comes across as what I call "spiritual affirmative action." What is interesting is that many who support this *spiritual* affirmative action movement oppose the secular affirmative action that will touch lives holistically.

Another benefit of cross-cultural relationships is that they are a tremendous witness to the world. During the days of Roman persecution in the early life of the church, it was not unusual for a Christian to sacrifice his life for another Christian. In fact, the quote we have from the Romans watching this was "Oh, how they love each other!" John 13:34–35 says, "A new command I give you: Love one another. As I have loved you, so you must love one another. By this *all men* will know that you are my disciples, if you love one another" (italics added).

The world is still waiting to see Christians love each other in a practical way. Don't get me wrong. I was at the Stand in the Gap Assembly and was proud to be there as a Christian. Obviously, the world took notice. In fact, I believe it scared the world just a little bit. The key question is how the commitments made there in regard to race will take shape in everyday life. Will Christian institutions that have been listening to blacks for years now have the faith to put into practice what they have heard? Will they put up the money to match what they have been professing? When this begins to happen, and minorities (not just blacks) can become excited about partnering with Christian organizations and churches, then the world will take notice as Christians take their rightful place as leaders in improving race relations.

Presently, the world is doing a much better job than Christians, and the world knows it. One of the strikes against Christianity is that the world can sit back and show many examples of racism among Christians. This has got to change! Our integrity as Christians is at stake if we continue with business as usual.

As we are obedient to Christ, we will experience peace, a fruit of the Spirit. This peace will usher us into a closer walk with our Lord and Savior. This intimacy will be reflected in our servant attitude and actions in our dealings with our spouses, children, extended family, church, and ministry to people we know and people we don't.

This kind of spiritual environment will set the stage for us to become encouragers. This ministry of encouragement will lead us to a better understanding of who God is. If people are made in His image, then the better we understand His image, the better we will understand Him and ourselves. Learning about other cultures will seem natural because God intended for us to be one. It will require a humble, teachable spirit for this kind of learning to take place. Learning about different cultures and developing cross-cultural relationships will provide special experiences that will sometimes be difficult to express in words.

When this kind of closeness is developed, a foundation for spiritual maturity has been built. A foundation of spiritual maturity allows people in these relationships to ask questions about each other's differences. This acceptance of the differences is to be without condemning the differences. It is not so much *earning* the right to ask personal questions as it is *being given permission* to ask those questions that lead to spiritual oneness!

This spiritual oneness will lay the foundation for working together that is motivated by the love of Christ. And this takes us back to John 13:34–35. This is the kind of love our Bibles tell us the world will see!

Alvin Simpkins, who helped me write part of chapter 8, is a tremendous prayer warrior. He has gotten men of many cultures and races around the country to get up and pray on Wednesday mornings from 4:00 A.M. to 7:00 A.M. Alvin shared Revelation 7:9–10 with me. It says:

> After this I looked and there before me was a great multitude that no one could count, from every nation, tribe, people and language, standing before the throne and in front of the Lamb.

They were wearing white robes and were holding palm branches in their hands. And they cried out in a loud voice: "Salvation belongs to our God, who sits on the throne, and to the Lamb."

The message of the Gospel is all-inclusive. It always has been. Now we must live it in our everyday lives, not just with words, but with our actions. It seems many are praying and fasting for revival. Our failure to heed this inclusive Gospel may be one reason we are not experiencing revival.

Remember, "Without faith it is impossible to please God" (Hebrews 11:6). Living by faith always stretches us because it means God is in charge and not us. Are you living by faith in the area of race relations?

Ferrell Foster, former editor of the *Illinois Baptist*, a state denominational paper, is one of my dear friends and someone I consider a brother. He wrote an article seven years ago regarding the issue of race. His words are good ones to consider.

There's a day in my past that embarrasses me. The year: 1968. The occasion: a violent death. I didn't do the killing. It's my reaction to the homicide that still troubles me. News accounts said Martin Luther King, Jr. had been slain. A 12-year-old boy in Texas felt no sadness. Instead, he thought maybe all the racial turmoil would finally cease. The kid with no black friends or acquaintances had come to see King as the cause of so much discontent and strife. The boy was me.

[King's] dream, however, is still only a dream 30 years later. One could even say the situation is worse. It seems impossible to approach any social issue or relationship without reference to race.

Chicago pastor Don Sharp, an African American, took me to lunch on the south side of Chicago. I was the only white guy around, but I did not feel uncomfortable in the least because I was with a friend. Don seemed surprised when I confessed to past racial prejudices. "What changed you?" he asked. "The Holy Spirit, I guess. That's the only way I can explain it," I responded. It wasn't like I set out to change. I just changed.

The truth is, I've found race doesn't matter much when it comes to liking people and enjoying their company. I have more in common with some black people than some whites. I respect some black people more than some whites. And the opposite can be said. But saying that, a truth still remains—I'm white, not black. I bring some cultural baggage to cross-racial friendships, just like blacks do. I like being white, not because it is nonblack, but because it is who I am. I expect black friends to like who they are.

In the body of Christ, there should be a coming together of believers into a oneness that transcends culture without denying it. African Americans have been coming into Anglo settings for some time now. Whites have a chance now to go into black settings.

We need to be open and honest with one another, hearing different perspectives on what it means to serve Christ. To be open and honest, we're going to have to also be sensitive to one another—the needs, the hurts, the fears. And all of us are going to have to make some changes.

Those changes will be difficult if we lean upon our own understanding. They will be made easier if we lean upon Christ.

Martin Luther King, Jr. spoke of children in his 1963 message. His words took new meaning for me one evening a couple of years ago as my young son played with three African American children in his room at home. They were living King's dream. They did not judge each other by the "color of their skin, but by the content of their character."

But those children were able to do that because two sets of adult parents had chosen to reach across racial barriers and embrace something new in their lives—a relationship where race did not matter. We can allow God to make something new so our children will reap the rewards.[2]

The three African-American children mentioned in this article were Christina, Michelle, and Andrea—my little girls. God bonded my heart with Ferrell when I worked for the Illinois Baptist State Association (I was the first black to serve on this state convention staff). Our families became *family*. What an incredible experience God provided for us.

Cross-cultural relationships give you the best of two worlds or more, depending on how many cultures or races with which you choose to interact. Race should not be an attraction—but neither should it be a deterrent.

I pray you won't settle for less than God's best for yourself and for the body of Christ!

*Dear Lord,*

*May our hearts be like those of the four girls in this chapter. It seems children are accepting, teachable, and usually willing to work through difficulties, which leads to intimacy. May our hearts be the same as You may desire to teach new things through new people, and may our lives and the lives of those around us be richer for it.*

*Amen.*

## THOUGHT QUESTIONS FOR THIS CHAPTER

1. Why is it easier for children to accept others who are different from them racially than for adults?

2. What can we learn from children regarding race and difference?

3. How can we practically celebrate God-given diversity? In our church? In our Christian school or organization? How can we practice celebrating diversity in our family, by celebrating our differences (different ages, different genders, different interests and skills)?

4. How can we practically celebrate unity?

5. What would biblical diversity and unity look like in your church, Christian school, or Christian organization?

6. What would be some practical, measurable, obtainable first steps for your church, Christian school, etc.? What would be your very first step? Why?

7. Why do you think Christians struggle so much with biblical diversity and unity?

8. Why do you think Kim's African-American neighbor seemed to become more relaxed when she learned that Kim is the god-mother for three African-American girls?

9. Why do you think the women who attend Bill's small group were friendlier to the visiting Christian African American than most of the white males in the group? Have you ever been in Bill's situation? How did you respond? Why? What were the results?

10. How do you think students, new employees, or people who are different from you would be received in your classroom, church, or Christian organization? Would you do anything if they were being treated badly? What would you do if they were being mistreated? Why?

11. What would be necessary in order to achieve cross-cultural unity in your local Christian community?

12. Have you ever been under leadership of a person of color? If yes, what was your experience? What do you think contributed to your cross-cultural experience being what it was?

13. Why do we fear difference and change?

## NOTES

1. According to the Freeman Institute (Freemaninstitute.com).

2. Ferrell Foster, *Illinois Baptist,* 20 November 1996.

# 12

# Transforming Our Theology into Reality

---

## Making the Workplace a Safe Place for Women and People of Color

*"God created all people and any inequalities among us was due to unequal opportunities."*

—Hattie Anne Virginia Fisher, born a slave 1855[1]

**W**hat's the deal with the gender issue? In reality, if the workplace is not safe for women, it is probably not going to be safe for people of color. And it is often women, officially or unofficially, who help to make cross-cultural transitions successful.

In the last few years, racial discrimination lawsuits have been filed against major corporations (for example, Denny's Restaurants, Texaco, and the Coca Cola Company).[2] These cases demonstrate that even with all of the technological advancements our country has enjoyed in the past century, cultural and/or racial problems have yet to be solved. Recently on a flight, I spoke with a woman executive who had more than twenty years with her secular organization. She told me about her frustrations, especially how difficult it was to get into the "boys' club." Given how many businesses are struggling with ethical situations these days, I wasn't surprised to hear her story. What is more disappointing to me, though, is that the Christian community seems to be light years behind the world in practicing gender and racial equality in the Christian workplace.

Time and time again I have seen examples of this. For instance, after completing a biblical diversity session with a well-known Christian organization, the CEO invited his senior executives to lunch to secure feedback from them. His team consisted of all white males and one white woman. During this lunch, the woman, who had demonstrated her brilliance throughout the session, never said a word. As we were walking out of the restaurant, I asked her why she didn't say anything. She looked at me and quietly responded, "It's not a *safe place.*"

I was blown away. Here was a Christian white woman with twenty-plus years with this organization and yet she didn't feel she could express herself in a Christian white male arena, with brothers with whom she will spend eternity!

That conversation and many, many others with women mentors as well as the men in my life got me thinking. I began to dream about how we could, in fact, make the Christian workplace an authentically safe place for women and people of color. I found myself asking questions like: What attitudes need challenging? What issues need to be addressed? What Scriptures speak to the importance of creating a safe workplace? It even motivated me to create a new consulting seminar on the topic and to further explore this crucial subject as we decided to update this book. And as I've conducted some of these seminars with a variety of Christian organizations, I've found them to be extremely eye-opening—particularly for white males as they are often hearing and beginning to *understand* women's issues and the pain they experience *for the first time!*

### WHAT'S NOT SAFE?

Typically, a Christian organization is not a safe place for women and/or people of color to work. Why? First of all, women and people of color are seldom viewed or treated as equals. For instance, women at many Christian companies rarely receive the same salary and opportunities for advancement as their male counterparts doing the same jobs. And one need only glance at the board of directors of some of these same Christian agencies to see how few people of color or women sit on them.

Part of the reason for this "unsafe" corporate structure lies in the thinking that has set it up. A theology that has promoted white males as dominant leaders in this country has been partly to blame. And a lack of biblical understanding has also been part of the problem. I'm not talking about theological disagreements on the role of women, say whether or not women can be pastors. In the corporate Christian world, the issue is whether they can "be in the room" as members of management or the board. And if they're allowed to be in the boardroom, the issue becomes equal treatment.

But instead of pointing fingers, let's focus on how to move from this unsafe environment to one that is safe and freeing for everyone. That leads us to re-examine Scripture. For instance, Galatians 3:28 says, "There is neither Jew nor Greek, slave nor free, male nor female, for you are all one in Christ Jesus." We are all equal before God.

Our present situation must be transformed from what is really a lose/lose situation into a win/win for all. We need Christian white male leaders who are willing to implement biblical diversity in the workplace, creating a safe and beneficial place for all (not perfect because none of us are). We need them to stop simply talking about it or playing the "window dressing game," but to act accordingly.

What is the *window dressing* game? The window dressing game is hiring a person of color or a woman who doesn't necessarily relate to his or her own culture or gender; in fact, in numerous cases, this person disdains his/her race or gender. She is easily hired by white Christian organizations because she fits in comfortably; she is perceived to be just like the people who hired her, and is therefore not a threat to disrupting the status quo.

Of course, this arrangement is doomed from the beginning to be unproductive (and is anything but safe for everyone). It is like having a battery with two positive or two negative charges. A battery must have a positive and negative charge in order to work. In other words, "sameness" does not produce good and lasting fruit for God's kingdom.

Therefore, organizations hiring these people will not meet the goal they say they have of influencing masses of people of color or women. In order to glorify God the most and to be the most productive, Christian organizations must implement biblical diversity, that type of diversity seen in 1 Corinthians 12, which we talked about in the previous chapter.

Another insidious aspect of the "window dressing game" is that many of these same organizations know that foundations give tremendous sums of money to urban projects. So they think that having an African American or any person of color in their department, or having such an urban emphasis, uniquely "qualifies" them to apply for this money. One organization I know secured $300,000 to start a ministry for people of color. This organization actually gave the new department $100,000, deducted the director's and his assistant's salaries from this amount, leaving the department approximately $30,000 to start up and effectively run a ministry to people of color. The remaining $200,000 went to the Republican party because a Christian organization can donate up to 2 percent of its budget to a political party without losing its non-profit status.

Oh, the games people play in the name of Jesus.

Such organizations usually hire people of color who aren't necessarily visionaries or leaders. They are foot soldiers who must be told what to do. They are passive and will never create a challenge or cause a problem or an embarrassment to the organization. They are good "boys or girls" who know their place. In fact, they are just glad to be there. They won't inform the white Christian organization when it is about to make a cross-cultural mistake, often because they themselves don't know or they are too afraid they'll lose their job. They simply provide Christian organizations with the excuse of saying they tried to make a change, but it failed. This excuse allows the organization to shut down the department, or else let it continue to exist so it can continue receiving money from well-intentioned foundations and misappropriate those funds.

## THE *MISEDUCATION* OF EVANGELICAL LEADERSHIP

One way to move past these unsafe working environments is through the process of education. Unfortunately, though, educating traditional evangelical leadership has been a problem. Why? First of all, many leaders seem to believe that racism in Christianity isn't a problem, or at least it's not *their* problem. Their silence condones the present state of affairs.

Second, leaders from these same organizations, now having a person in management who is a person of color that they perceive to be just like them, can now say with authority that people of color should be just like the one they hired. They can now imply through subtle communication that people of color who aren't like the person they hired are intellectually and/or morally inferior and defiled.

An example of such thinking is a statement made by the super-intendent of one of the Christian schools in Colorado Springs. He said that African Americans don't care about education. He obviously had not studied the history of African Americans: that countless African Americans taught themselves to read and write during periods in our country's history when it was actually illegal (and punishable by jail or death) for a black person to learn to read. Or he didn't know that African Americans have become one of the strongest markets for book publishing companies in recent years. Thousands of other examples confirm that the vast majority of people of color *do* care about education.

When leaders like this Colorado Springs Christian educator make such misinformed statements, it's bound to affect both his professional actions and those of his subordinates—administration and faculty—subconsciously and/or consciously, in their attitudes and consequential actions. This is critical to understanding how the continued *inaccurate* information about race is so often perpetuated within the white Christian community. It is both amazing to me and sad that an educator wouldn't do his homework concerning the facts on a particular issue before making such a statement. But if you believe people of color aren't really important and you live in a city with a small percentage of people of color, what difference does it make? The local Christian community certainly did not say anything in response, since many of their children attend this school.

Nor did anyone seem to notice when a local church held its vacation Bible school for children and used an evangelistic tool that uses colors to teach the Gospel: Black represents sin, red is the color of Christ's blood, white equals purity, and green represents growth. Where in the Bible is sin called or described as black? (Answer: nowhere.) Imagine being the parent of a black child and having that child being told her color represents sin. You have got to immediately correct this error while explaining how the white people were sincere, but were just ignorant. Then you have to deal with the question of why these "good Christian people" were so insensitive, which is usually not the first—or last—time such an incident will have occurred. One of the African-American members warned the vacation Bible school leaders not to do it, but they did anyway. African-American parents were offended. And then the white leadership of the church wonders why attendance from blacks spirals downward rapidly!

## GETTING IT RIGHT AT WORK

Obviously, these same uneducated attitudes find their way into the Christian workplace. If it isn't a safe place for women and people of color, what does this reveal about most Christian organizations? It reveals an imbalance, resulting possibly from the deeper issue of the sin of prejudice and racism.

That's why those in leadership must begin to recognize that hiring qualified women and people of color for decision-making positions is not so much affirmative action as it is creating a biblical balance. This would provide opportunities that were previously withheld because of bias, resulting in a more effective and God-glorifying Christian organization.

If we can learn and apply the biblical principles from 1 Corinthians 12 on spiritual gifts, we will understand that *all* members of Christ's body are necessary. Revelation 7:9 says, "After this I looked and there before me was a great multitude that no one could count, from every nation, tribe, people and language, standing before the throne and in front of the Lamb. They were wearing white robes and were holding palm branches in their hands." This verse reflects the whole body of Christ. We also learn from it that in order to produce God's *best*, diversity and unity must simultaneously coexist.

The goal of every board member, trustee, and CEO or president should be for the organization that he is serving as God's steward to bring the most glory possible to God as the organization attempts to reflect God's splendor. A practical strategy for attaining this is discerning individuals' abilities and mentoring them into positions of leadership. Equally important is for the organization to make Christian ethics such as integrity, respect, humility, compassion, servant leadership, etc., the priorities that drive the company. Too often, Christian organizations operate like secular ones, and human nature takes over.

So if the workplace is not a safe place for women and people of color, where (and how) should Christians begin rectifying this non-Christian situation?

The American workplace, Christian or secular, generally functions from the top down. Therefore, the first place to begin in changing this unbiblical situation is with senior executives. It would be advantageous for the president/CEO to have one-on-one talks about the biblical mandate for biblical diversity with executive staff, upper management, the human resources department, and, not to be forgotten, the women and people of color of his/her organization. An assessment of the *strengths, weaknesses, opportunities,* and *threats* of the organization—as they relate to the issues of race and gender relations—should be taken. Next, management at all levels should consider the value and diverse contributions of female and ethnic leadership (historically and recent).

Education usually alleviates fear of the unknown. A study of secular organizations' practices on diversity may be needed since Christian organizations are so weak in this area. Teaching males, especially white males, how to hear women and how men and women and people of color differ in communicating is a great starting point. These differences don't mean inferiority, and acknowledging the reality that there are different perspectives on how to handle conflict can be a helpful approach.

## PRACTICAL STEPS (MAKING IT REAL)

An organization could take a variety of practical steps to make its environment a safer place. (Many of these suggestions have come from seminars and interviews with women.) First, CEOs/presidents should have their vice presidents plan strategies to create a "safe" place for women and people of color. It is critical that women and people of color are included in these strategy sessions. The question they must then ask is, "How can the organization create a plan for someone or a group of people without *everyone's* insight?" If this step is not taken, it would be like a group of men planning to market a product for women without having any women involved in the planning sessions.

Next, executives should secure a review of last year's promotions from the human resources department. Somehow, prayerfully attempt to create an HR system allowing anyone to anonymously file a grievance so that the individual would not feel threatened by stepping forward. I realize that this could be difficult, if not impossible to do, but you get the idea.

Some companies might hire a diversity consultant to assess attitudes, perspectives, and opportunities in the organization regarding women and people of color, beginning at the top. Your organization may need to apply categorical resolutions to problems of gender and race. For instance, in corporate Christian and non-Christian America, the African-American male has the most difficult challenge of all minorities of advancing in a predominantly white-male-oriented organization. Next are females, especially African-American females, in advancing in white-male-dominated organizations. (Because of their hard work and qualifications and because African-American women cover two issues, people of color and gender, some organizations looking to fill quotas promote them faster than they promote African-American men).

An assessment then needs to examine the underlying issues that might prevent women and people of color from advancing up the organizational ladder. If the executive leadership can't make this transition, their usefulness in following Christ's desire for their particular organization may cease to exist, and this needs to be communicated. Finally, the board should not be forgotten in this appraisal. The objective is to create a *climate* for biblical diversity among the top two or three layers of management with a three- to four-month timetable and an evaluation process built-in. This question must be answered, "What needs to be done to integrate a harmony of talent/skill/contribution within our organization? What obstacles are keeping us from accomplishing our goals?"

## OBSTACLES WOMEN AND PEOPLE OF COLOR FACE

Numerous women and people of color currently working in Christian organizations graciously granted me interviews to help me better understand how to create a safer workplace. They expressed their concerns as follows:

1. Women feel they are seldom heard by men; people of color feel they are seldom heard by whites.

2. Men often tend to brag and are used to hearing other men brag. If a woman doesn't brag, men think she doesn't know much.

3. Women also say that unless they yell, scream, and keep interrupting, they will not be heard by men. The difference seems to be that women often say things in an *indirect* manner, but men usually communicate in a more aggressive way. The "bulldozer"

approach is viewed as a sign of strong conviction and a quality of a good leader, but women's suggestions are often ignored because women don't appear to show the same conviction as men.

4. Women and people of color face subtle prejudices, discrimination.

5. Women encounter subtle or open sexual harassment.

6. Sometimes men have perceptions of women's commitment and motivation being limited ("playing work"), especially if they are mothers.

7. People of color and women often fail to receive equal pay for equal work.

8. All people *need* to be understood, treated as a person first, not as a member of a group, and people don't want to be tolerated or seen as window dressing.

9. Too many promotions are still based on the "good ol' boys' club," versus merit, and surmised ability to work late on future projects if required. Nor are women believed to be able to handle intense pressure (contrary to evidence).

10. Managers often have the idea that women won't work as hard as male peers and people of color won't work as hard as white peers.

11. In interviews and performance reviews, managers show intrusiveness into women's and people of color's personal life by asking incredibly personal questions that males or white males wouldn't be asked. (For example, it is illegal to ask whether a prospective employee has children, but many women reported being asked how many children they have and their ages, as though the employer were figuring out how much time off will be involved. Others have been asked about their marital status and their husbands' jobs. One woman told me she'd been asked, "Are you still with the baby's daddy?")

12. Many of the people interviewed expressed the problem of not *empowering* women and people of color to adequately perform given tasks or giving women and people of color supervisory positions with no one to supervise. Recent studies reveal that white women and women of color make up only 5 percent of top level senior management.

13. People of color and women can be subject to stereotyping, the glass ceiling, and denial of credential-building experiences. When employers hire unqualified women and people of color, they then can use their experience to "prove" the stereotype was legitimate: "See, I told you she/the person of color could not do this work."

14. Women and people of color who are assertive are deemed a "threat" to men/whites.

Though these concerns are real and need to be addressed, I believe there are also certain responsibilities that women and people of color have as well. If all males and whites were removed from the workplace, would the workplace be perfect? No. The nature of human nature and sin is not limited by color or gender, nor is any of us perfect.

Although there are well-documented inequalities in the workplace, women and people of color should feel called to the Christian organizations for which they work, trying to see the big picture as to why God has called them to be where He has planted them. Women and people of color also must develop thicker skin, but not a blind eye. I am not suggesting we justify inequalities, but rather ask God to give us staying power. Also, when there are differences with people in the corporate structure, it may help not to assume malice but consider that the problem may be the other person's ignorance.

For those women and people of color who are the first ones in the organization or in a decision-making position, we must make things better for those who will follow us and for the sincere white males who also believe in and take personal risks promoting biblical diversity. Additionally, women and people of color need to be sensitive as to how we treat each other. Why should we demand that people of different cultures or races treat us with respect and equality if we are not treating people within our own race appropriately? Some people may look at the way we treat each other and think, *If they don't treat themselves with respect and equality, why should they expect me to do so?* Sometimes we are our own worst enemies in Christian organizations, so we must examine our own hearts in the process of creating safer places.

Even with the lawsuits against major corporations, the vast majority of women and people of color who have worked in both Christian and secular organizations say that secular organizations are much better places to work, citing better treatment and better pay and benefits. In order to make Christian organizations safe for women/people of color, abusive power must cease. Such power only perpetuates the gender and race war. Power rooted in mutual respect can become beneficial to relationships by sharing power with all, rather than rationing it among a few. This will revolutionize Christian organizations and challenge the fact that some of the problem has been that some Christian leaders built kingdoms to themselves. Leaders must learn to see women/people of color as peers and partners rather than inferior. There are scores of examples of how God uses women and people of color that should inspire us to keep going. We need to seek to battle our common enemy and not each other. If someone gets hurts, then no one truly wins.

CEOs can demonstrate this same commitment by creating task forces for diversity that can enact policies that promote it. They should then hold their executive staff, directors, managers, etc., accountable for progress by including diversity in all strategic business plans. Performance appraisals, compensation incentives, and other evaluation measures must reflect this priority. In the process, organizations would do well to prepare women and people of color for senior positions by establishing mentoring programs. As leaders understand the benefits that diverse thinking brings to problem-solving for their organization as well as a larger share of the market, they will see their productivity increasing.

## CROSS-CULTURAL CONFLICT ON THE JOB: WHAT YOU NEED TO KNOW

In a marriage relationship, there will be conflict because not only are there two different people, but there are also two different genders. Marriages that become stronger and in which intimacy is developed are not those without conflict. The absence of conflict is not reality; relationships that are honest will experience conflict. Intimate marriages are those in which both partners work through the conflict to understanding. This understanding includes realizing that each partner may respond to conflict differently. Most marriage counselors agree that in most instances, during conflict, it is the man who wants to walk away and the woman who wants to talk it out. Couples that do talk it out develop intimacy.

Dr. Martin Davidson, an associate professor of business administration for the Darden Graduate School of Business Administration of the University of Virginia, believes this is true cross-culturally as well, specifically for whites and blacks. In a recent research project, Davidson interviewed sixty whites and sixty African Americans attending an MBA program and asked them to respond to a scenario of a cross-cultural team of two working on a project for months. When the presentation is made, one person does the entire presentation, thus getting all the credit. Naturally, there were varied responses due to individual personality. But Davidson concluded that there were certain consistencies that could be based on race.

There are tremendous generalities, but his observation of 120 students can't be disregarded. The following are certain consistencies that surfaced:

- In heated conflicts, whites are more comfortable backing off and giving distance (to get under control and be rational before discussing the issue).

- African Americans, in general, look to engage and have discussion (which is considered an issue of courtesy/respect—lack of respect is to walk away).

- Not only are the behaviors themselves significant (patterns of withdrawal and engagement in heated conflicts), but how each participant interprets the behavior affects the relationship.

- Conflict plus subordination complicates the issue if a white must report to a black or vice versa.

Subordinate relationships between blacks and whites usually are damaged when:

- An African American subordinate has a conflict with someone he/she believes is racist, reports this to his/her white supervisor and the white supervisor argues whether or not the action was racist. A better approach would be devising some way to test actions in order to evaluate if action was primarily racist or not.

- A white subordinate whose black supervisor has reported a problem with his/her work goes to several whites in the office who think he/she is fine and shares that with the black supervisor, thus indirectly discounting what the black supervisor has told the white subordinate. This basically says the problem is the black supervisor.

- When there is conflict, and the white subordinate goes to the boss's managers and peers, but doesn't inform the boss (the white subordinate usually has this choice since the organization is probably primarily white—a black subordinate seldom has this option). This may be unconscious, but the action demeans a boss if the boss is a person of color.

If stress between the parties is handled well, there is no behavioral difference between the races after the conflict has been resolved. If stress is handled poorly, especially if the perception is that the situation is race-based, the African American tends to concentrate on the technical aspects of the job and isolate himself/herself socially. The lack of support and/or minority colleagues is the reason. It's difficult to correct a situation with this response.[3]

Successful African Americans in the white corporate world must have mentors, including white supporters, according to David A. Thomas, a Harvard University professor. Thomas is a widely recognized expert on this area of organizational behavior and has explored conflicts in the context of career development.[4]

Conflict on the job, whether it is with parties from the same culture or cross-cultural, isn't bad, but in fact normal. Whites should not lose hope if something doesn't go according to plans the first time; nor should blacks quit, become defensive, or assume the worst when things don't go their way initially.

Cross-cultural conflict, like in marriage, can be a tool to produce intimacy between races if those of difference cultures/races are spiritually mature enough to work through the problem, realizing that they are on the same team and that the problem, not the other person, is the enemy. They must also understand that the relationship is worth having because with work, it can be mutually beneficial.

## LOWERING THE FEAR OF CHANGE

One practical way of at least lowering the fear of the unknown is to place magazines written by people of color for people of color in break and lunch rooms, as well as libraries of companies and schools. Betsy Holden, CEO of Kraft Foods, Inc., has councils representing the different cultures/races and women in her company. She says it has been successful because it creates awareness and acceptance.[5]

In Christian schools, especially kindergarten through twelfth grade, it would be wonderful if stories of Christian heroes from many cultures and races were taught as well as having their pictures placed in classrooms and libraries. Christian schools could have Christian speakers of various backgrounds come to speak, not just on race, but in all fields. These schools could also celebrate special days of other cultures if they don't oppose biblical principles. Such an education would be distinctively Christian, encouraging missions and unity, and lowering prejudging among a significant group of Christians.

As it is today, Christian schools have a terrible reputation when it comes to racism. A Christian college president told me that he wanted more African Americans to attend his institution because it would provide a more rounded education for the white students, and I agreed. But I asked him how would attending his school benefit people of color? I asked, "Shouldn't this school be a win/win for all who attend?" This president was unable to give me an answer. Such institutions will not be safe places for people of color.

## IS IT REALLY TAKING A CHANCE OR LIVING OUT OUR FAITH?

Finally, it is extremely common to hear leaders of Christian organizations say that they desperately want to hire *qualified* employees, not just minorities. This is another easy way out since today there are more qualified women and people of color than ever in the history of the United States. The real issue is that the white Christian community is unfamiliar with the culture and community of women and people of color. I occasionally headhunt or help companies find people of color for Christian organizations who desire to diversify their workplaces, and I have always found this to be the case.

Three or four years ago, I was asked by two Christian organizations to headhunt for them. They specifically wanted African Americans or other people of color. I knew the presidents of both companies. One said that he was impressed with the candidate that I brought to him, but that he didn't know anything about fund-raising, which would be 25 percent of the job. Because we were good enough friends, I could speak directly with him. I said, "The issue is whether or not he is smart enough to pick it up."

A few days later the candidate, who was and is also a friend, called to tell me he had been offered the job. I immediately called the president and asked him why he changed his mind. He said that he asked himself, "Where would the candidate go to learn how to fundraise?" He said, "I realized that fund-raising is a 'good ol' boy' network. I know that he is smart enough to pick it up." So that president hired an African American to be his vice president. The African American is now the president of this predominantly white Christian organization. The former president moved on to a larger Christian ministry. He later told me that one of the most difficult things in accepting the position was leaving his vice president, whom he had grown to love like a brother.

When I was asked to do this particular headhunting assignment, I knew the two of them would work well together because of their relationships with Christ. I actually served with the former president as fellow elders in a local church. The candidate, unfortunately, had been forced out of his position at a Christian organization, even though he was bringing money to this for-profit organization and had received the highest bonus in the history of the organization. I also knew that this organization would be a "safe" place for the candidate. The question I had before the candidate's call was would this Christian African American go to work for another predominantly white Christian organization after being burned? It was a faith issue for both. God was glorified by their union and is still being glorified by their relationship. It can be done.

The second headhunting assignment was for an executive assistant for a strategic Christian organization, which influences numerous other Christian organizations, especially in the area of missions. The president's statement to me regarding the candidate I presented was, "She doesn't know anything about missions, and I don't have time to teach her." I asked him, "Why should any African American know anything about traditional American evangelical missions?" I didn't need to elaborate because he knew what I meant. He knew how mission organizations had mistreated Africans and African Americans who wanted to be missionaries (which is why, even today, many African Americans go to the mission field on their own, instead of through one of these organizations). Then I threw out my famous question, "Is she smart enough to do the job?"

A few weeks later, she was hired. The president trusted her with running the entire office and often asked her opinion on major issues. Not only does the president love her work, but he loves her family as well. It turned out to be a win/win for all concerned. It can be done, but it requires godly people who are willing to live by faith.

Both presidents wanted to implement biblical diversity and needed to fill positions with talented people, but they initially felt that my friends were not qualified by criteria to which the African American had no exposure. Thankfully, these leaders were Christian men of faith and prayer and so decided the best thing for everyone was to hire the right people for the jobs. Their decisions affected the white and African-American communities more than either of these presidents realize. These hirings say to the African-American community, "Some white men can be trusted and are fair. So I can't lump all whites together." To the white community, at the very least it says, "There some African Americans who are certainly qualified and some of my white Christian brothers are actually hiring people of color in decision-making positions."

## WILL WE CHANGE?

Companies like Texaco and Coca Cola are trying to learn from their expensive mistakes, and, as a result, are almost becoming model companies in relating to women and people of color. In fact, Coca Cola is spending $500 million with minority suppliers in launching a formal mentoring program and creating a series of celebration days modeled on its "We'd like to teach the world to sing" advertisement. That a company can bounce back from a troubled history is evident from our No. 1 company (best companies for minorities to work for), Advantica. The owner of Denny's Restaurants was hit with a series of legal claims in the early 1990's but responded with aggressive minority hiring and a supplier-diversity effort. It has led our ranking for two years in a row.

"Yes, lawsuits are a powerful motivator," says Virginia Clarke, the co-head of the diversity practice at executive search firm Spencer Stuart. More important, however, is the growing realization that there's a correlation between financial performance and a multicultural work force. Clarke is fielding more and more calls from companies looking for minority leaders for top-level posts—even in a slowing economy. "There is a strong business case [for diversity] now," she says. If you have any doubts about it, just look at the 2000 census figures. A third of all Americans belong to a minority group. Peak or trough, a diverse workplace isn't a luxury—it's a necessity.[6]

Well, since lawsuits are a powerful and effective motivator for the secular world, what will motivate Christian organizations to change? Is our love for God enough, or is our consistent struggle an evaluation of our love for God (1 John 4:20–21)? For corporate America, diversity isn't an option if a company wants to compete globally, and any Fortune 500 magazine article will tell you the motivation is money. In fact, in many companies in corporate America, your salary increases, bonuses, and even promotion can be impacted if you are not diversifying your area of responsibility. Can you imagine being penalized for not diversifying! What if there were similar forms of accountability in Christian organizations as well? It is sad to even think about, but it appears that the world's love for money is greater than our love for Christ and our brother (if actions are evaluated).

Only time will tell if present Christian senior leaders have the faith and courage to lead their organizations in representing all of God's people in their workforces. Without the perspectives and partnerships of women and people of color, the Christian community will be incredibly limited in its ministry efforts to reach America and the world. The body of Christ certainly can't and won't produce God's best without manifesting biblical diversity. God-given differences produce God-blessed resources, and amazingly safe working environments for each member of the body!

*Dear Lord,*

*Thank You for inspiring me to write this chapter. Thank you for the women who provided so much insight. I pray for all the women who have been intentionally or unintentionally wounded by me and/or other men. May we men use this chapter to educate ourselves and then do whatever is necessary to make the workplace a safe and more productive place for our sisters in Christ to work for Your Glory.*

*Lord, I also want to pray for men, especially white males who are in positions of leadership, who have courageously read this chapter and for those who were unable to finish. My prayer is that those who finished this chapter will see it as a way they can make a difference as opposed to feeling guilty for being a white male. As an African American who has been discriminated against, I still don't know how it feels to be a woman who has been discriminated against. I may never know, but I can develop my sensitivities and actions to lower discrimination.*

*Because of Your Amazing Grace,*
*Clarence*

## THOUGHT QUESTIONS

1. Is your church, Christian school, or Christian organization a safe place for women and people of color? If you are in management or have decision-making authority, look for some way to allow women employees and employees of color to honestly tell you their perception of the workplace (perhaps an anonymous survey or small-group interviews conducted by someone the groups in question consider to be an advocate).

2. What makes your institution safe or unsafe? How do you evaluate and correct if necessary?

3. Is your organization becoming more diverse numerically? What do you attribute to your organization's growth, lack of growth, or decline in diversity?

4. If your organization is not a safe place for women and/or people of color, what is the first necessary step toward safety?

5. Do you have women or people of color in decision-making positions? Why or why not? Do you think this is a reasonable possibility for your organization? Why or why not?

6. Does your organization have a glass ceiling?

7. How diverse is the daily decision-making body of your organization?

8. How diverse is your organization's board of directors?

9. How do you think women and people of color regard your organization? Is your organization one that they willingly promote by word of mouth, or are they just surviving until they can find another job?

10. How and where do you recruit for women and people of color, or do you recruit for your organization, school, etc.? If not, why not?

## NOTES

1. From *The Substance of Things Hoped For: A Memoir of African American Faith,* written and read by Samuel DeWitt, Proctor Simon & Schuster Audio.

2. Jeremy Kahn, "Diversity Trumps the Downturn," *Fortune,* 144, no. 1 (9 July 2001): 122. Coca Cola had to pay more than $192 million to more than two thousand African-American employees and set up diversity programs in November of 2000, $36 million in diversity reform programs according to *USA Today* and *Fortune.*

3. Davidson's research appeared in the September 1, 2001, issue of the academic journal *Sex Roles: A Journal of Research* under the title "Know Thine Adversary: The Impact of Race on Styles of Dealing with Conflict." 45(5-6): 259–76. It is also analyzed in Jordan T. Pine, "On-the-Job Conflicts: How Blacks and Whites React Differently," DiversityInc.com, December 14, 2001 (http://www.diversityinc.com/public/1958.cfm).

4. Pine, "On-the-Job Conflicts."

5. Annie Finnigan, "Different Strokes," *Working Woman,* 26, no. 4 (April 2001): 42.

6. Kahn, "Diversity Trumps the Downturn."

# 13

# Where Do We Go from Here?

## Will You Be Part of the Problem or Part of the Solution?

*"Like anybody, I would like to live a long life. Longevity has its place. But I'm not concerned about that now. I just want to do God's will. And He's allowed me to go up to the mountain. And I've looked over, and I've seen the Promised Land. I may not get there with you, but I want you to know tonight that we as a people will get to the Promised Land."*

—Martin Luther King Jr., address in Memphis, Tennessee, April 3, 1968, the night before his assassination

A few months before I sent the final manuscript of this book off to my publisher, I asked a friend to read a rough draft. Fred Smith, a successful businessman in Dallas, has been used by God to touch many lives. So I value his input. When he finished reading, he looked straight at me and asked, "Well, Clarence, what are your solutions to the race problem among Christians?" I laughed nervously. Then I stalled. But finally, I told him that if I had the solution, I would have straightened people out a long time ago!

Of course, it's much easier to discuss the problem of race relations in our country than it is to recognize—let alone put into practice—the solutions. Yet I strongly believe this book is a step toward the solution. Why? Because if this book is about anything, I hope it is that building effective, lasting cross-cultural relationships is a process, one that spills over from our lives with Christ. It is a journey that takes a long time—as Dr. King's statement and life shows us—and one that requires an intentional commitment to improving race relations. I also believe that if anyone can show this country how to do that, it is those people who love Jesus Christ, who know they are God's people—the church.

And yet the evangelical community has much to learn in this area and must be held accountable for its role in making racial relations better for everyone. Churches that say they want to minister cross-culturally (both in world missions and in their communities) must have their actions closely examined to see if they are consistent with what they profess. The same is true of parachurch ministries.

Wouldn't it be great if the leaders of the evangelical community came together to find solutions to problems of race and to examine their particular church's or parachurch's measurable commitment to improving race relations within their own institutions? Wouldn't it be exciting if in addition to holding Bible studies and prayer services, Christian leaders organized creative ways to build lasting and mutually beneficial cross-cultural friendships? And what if they began to ask each other questions—like, "Where do we go from here?" Sometimes we spend time arguing over how bad the problems are, instead of agreeing to work together to get beyond the superficial and aim for honest, deep relations now and in the future.

The questions are important as we continue learning how to practically and daily live out biblical diversity. Our credibility as a church is at risk. Many in the Christian community outside of the United States, for instance, see our hypocrisy and wonder why it continues. I discovered to my surprise on my recent trip from the Philippines that the Christian Filipinos I met said that they view the United States as racist because of how African Americans have been treated in America. Why did that surprise me? Because American media had given me the idea that African Americans will be treated with suspicion and hostility anywhere in the world that we might travel. Even some white South Africans complain about the racism they see within the evangelical community in America. They know that not only have we been ineffective in combating our country's history of racial tensions, but we have made little progress in coming together as a unified body. Our divisions and prejudices affect many people on many levels throughout the world. It is amazing when you think that South Africa had apartheid, no Civil Rights movement, yet it has had a person of color as president.

Unfortunately, though, those who are not as seriously committed to improving race relations probably didn't read this far. Since *you have,* my hope is that some of your thinking has been challenged and your vision renewed so that your life will reflect God's desire for unity. In other words, since we usually think before we act, then if our thinking is changing, right actions may soon follow.

As you know, in chapters 6, 7, and 8, I tried to address some more specific solutions to the race problem among Christians in America. But I've also suggested in the rest of this chapter a variety of other ways—with God's help—that we can be a part of the solution. Whatever steps we take, we must learn from history.

One indication that we have learned from history is that we do not repeat the mistakes of the past. Individuals from all cultures and ethnicities have a responsibility not to stereotype other people because of the color of their skin. We must not give too much credence to our first impressions. It may take three or four encounters—or more—before we earn the right for a person to trust us and reveal to us who he really is. This may be even more difficult to do cross-culturally. But because Christ remains faithful in His love and commitment to us, so, too, can we stay committed to others. After all, we love because He first loved us (1 John 4:19–21).

## MATCHING OUR CONFESSIONS WITH OUR ACTIONS

Before we look at practical steps we can take from here, it is important to remember that Christians need to follow Jesus Christ's example of being proactive. Recent examples in the body of Christ have encouraged me that we just might be making some progress after all. For instance, certain major denominations—such as the

Presbyterian Church of America (PCA) and Southern Baptist Convention—have issued resolutions on racial repentance, producing posters of biblical people of color, and publishing various articles on developing racial partnerships. Southwestern Baptist Theological Seminary (SWBTS) has initiated a Black Think Tank. A group of African Americans meet with SWBTS President Ken Hemphill on a regular basis to address cross-cultural issues of the past, present, and future.

Prominent white leaders have *intentionally* created diverse staffs. Joseph Stowell, president of Moody Bible Institute, has initiated several friendships with Chicago African-American pastors. He also hired an African American as a vice president in a highly visible, decision-making position and promoted him to become a senior vice president. Dr. Stowell has publicly proclaimed, "We are committed to making him successful. He will not fail!"

The Orchard Foundation, associated with the Christian and Missionary Alliance, has Michael Jones, an African American, as president. The Christian Management Association featured a biblical diversity seminar in its CEO and Senior Leadership track in its annual convention for the past two years, understanding that change takes place from the top down in America. Motivated by inclusive thinking, this organization has established minority scholarships. Numerous other examples have resulted in Latinos, First Nations, and Asians coming into important evangelical leadership roles as well. No one is pretending that we don't still have a long, long way to go, but these proactive steps are far better than simply reacting to Satan's attempts to cause division among Christians.

Yet before these proactive steps could be taken, a spiritual maturity and willingness to hear and study the perspectives of people of color had to exist among white leadership. This must not be overlooked, understated, or taken for granted. Such leadership should be honored. A willingness to hear won't always result in agreement, but understanding usually will result from these efforts. Understanding usually lowers the possibility of conflict.

There are also African Americans making tremendous contributions. One such individual is Rev. Mark Pollard, president of The Common Ground Coalition based out of Atlanta. Rev. Pollard is bringing Christian Democrats and Republicans together for the sake of racial unity. This is no small feat if you know that according to most polls, in the last presidential election, 90 percent of African Americans and 70 percent of Hispanics voted Democratic and most white Christians voted Republican. Last year, Rev. Pollard was a catalyst in having Rep. Tony Hall (D-Ohio), Rep. John Lewis (D-GA.), Ron Meyers of the National Juneteenth Coalition, Jim Wallis of *Sojourners,* and others rally at our nation's capitol to support a new resolution. This new resolution, introduced on the "Juneteenth" anniversary that is recognized as the day in 1865 that the last of America's slaves learned they had been freed by the Civil War, would create a commission to study the economic impact of slavery.

Rev. Pollard was also involved in February 2002 at a prayer vigil in Jamestown, Virginia, where Christians gathered to repent for the slave trade. Susan Weddington, Texas Republican party chairman, pushed politics aside during her speech at the National Leadership Summit for Christian Reconciliation and apologized for the evils of slavery. What is interesting about Rev. Pollard is that he is initiating much of this on his own at his own expense.

Then there is Pastor Stan Long, who is co-pastoring with a white pastor, Craig Garriott, at Faith Christian Fellowship in Baltimore. For more than three years they have been alternating preaching every other Sunday, in a time when people say that it can't work.

I frequently tell people that mutually beneficial, lasting cross-cultural relationships are similar to marriage. Husbands and wives don't always agree, but if they are to have an effective marriage and serve each other, then they must at least try to understand each other! This often requires learning another language. Men and women use the same words but are often speaking a different language.

Godly husbands learn the language of their wives—and vice

versa—because the relationship is worth it. Likewise, godly white evangelicals must learn the language of people of color by understanding American history from a non-white point of view. This will help whites understand the perspectives of Native Americans, African Americans, Latinos, Asians, and other people of color on social issues and their goals. And in our increasingly international society, immigration is changing the demographics of our country, requiring us as good neighbors to understand the variety of cultures that have come to America. *Understanding*, not necessarily agreement, is crucial if trust and ministry are to come to pass. We have to remember the reality of 1 Corinthians 12:25–26, "So that there should be no division in the body, but that its parts should have equal concern for each other. If one part suffers, every part suffers with it; if one part is honored, every part rejoices with it."

People of color know the language and priorities of the majority culture in America because of the survival dynamics of majority/ minority systems. I cannot emphasize it enough: The white community must *now* learn the cultures and histories of people of color so it can demonstrate equal concern, realizing when people of color are suffering and when they are celebrating. White Christians must respond to the injustices suffered in America by blacks and other non-white citizens.

I've always found it a little strange that whites have been quick to recognize persecuted Christians in other countries, but have not displayed a similar concern for their "persecuted" black Christian brothers and other people of color at home. This lack of concern feeds, for example, blacks' distrust of white Christians. Until white Christians acknowledge the discrimination and harassment experienced by their brethren of color, 1 Corinthians 12 can't be fulfilled and it will be difficult for the body of Christ to become one in practical reality. This is one clear example as to why the term *racial reconciliation* is so troublesome to many in the analytical communities of people of color.

Of course, I realize that no race could overcome slavery and its effects on its own. And certainly, African Americans are indebted to the likes of Wilberforce, Dr. Albert Switzer, Dean Smith, Bill McCartney, and numerous white men and women, Christians and non-Christians, who have even given their lives for the causes of African Americans and other people of color. The issue here is that these heroic whites tend to be the exception and not the rule.

During diversity consulting for Christian and non-Christian organizations, I often reveal that African Americans, Asians, Europeans, and Hispanics process information differently. Knowing this is critical to effective communication, resource production, marketing, and problem-solving. It may take longer to produce something, but the outcome (or product) becomes more effective because more options have been considered. Automatically its marketability is increased because it is now cross-culturally attractive.

Again, this is not always easy. We all know how much effort and sacrifice will be required if we are ever going to see the rewards of biblical diversity. I will never forget when the late Dr. T. B. Maston, who served as a grandfather in the faith to me while I was at Southwestern Seminary, told me he received hate mail in 1959 for writing a book called *The Bible and Race,* which stated that blacks and whites were equal. Maston knew the risk he took in presenting such theology during a racially charged time in our country's history and was willing to take it! Gary Chapman introduced me to Jesus Christ and has spent much of the rest of his life discipling me. He was doing the racial partnership thing before it was in vogue. Not discounting the international pressure, white South Africans who were (and still are) the numerical minority gave the power of the country over to the blacks, knowing that they would never be in power again! What character and integrity these Afrikaners demonstrated to the world! The majority of these Afrikaners were not Christians, but as a people they realized that they had to do the morally correct thing, even if it meant sacrificing the future of their children and South Africa as they knew it. Apartheid fell at great sacrifice and cost to countless South Africans, but with the promise of great rewards for everyone.

I believe we could learn a lot from studying South Africa's Truth and Reconciliation Commission's (TRC) efforts for reconciliation in their country. Archbishop Desmond Tutu's godly leadership revealed a heavenly vision and a powerful earthly conscience to right the wrongs in his country. In a 1997 speech, he recalled many opponents to the TRC yet many victories for racial healing. In the process, he shows us the profound effects confession, forgiveness, determination, and grace have in building God-inspired relationships:

> There have been those who have been vociferous in asserting that the TRC, far from promoting reconciliation, has in fact done the opposite. It has engendered resentment and anger. It has opened old wounds and fostered alienation. I have challenged those who have made these assertions to provide us with the evidence that would support their claims, because our experience has been the direct opposite.
>
> In many ways it has been unbelievable. It has been almost breathtaking—this willingness to forgive, this magnanimity, this nobility of spirit.
>
> In Port Elizabeth at the Mtimkulu hearing, police officers testified to doing some terrible things: drugging the coffee of their charges, shooting one behind the ear and then burning his corpse. And while this cremation was going on they were having a braai —turning over two sets of meat.
>
> One of the officers confessed to lying to the Supreme Court to get an interdict that prevented the mother of one of the victims from testifying at a TRC hearing, and we had our work cut out for us to calm the people because Mrs. Mtimkulu couldn't speak. But they did not go out on an orgy of revenge; they did not attack those police officers who came on succeeding days to testify in New Brighton.
>
> No, this process has made a contribution to reconciliation, to healing, as the 1995 Promotion of National Unity and Reconcil-

iation Act says. The TRC is required not to achieve unity and reconcile our nation—it is required to promote, to contribute to it.

Let us look at some instances. In Bisho, some former Ciskei Defense Force officers testified about the Bisho massacre. One of them alienated the people with his insensitive tirade. Then another confessed his part and asked for forgiveness. In the audience were people who had been wounded in that incident, people who had lost loved ones; but when that White Army officer asked for forgiveness, they did not rush to strangle or assault him. Unbelievably, they applauded.

Yes, this is a crazy country. I said at that point, let us keep silent because we were in the presence of something special, of something holy. Many times I have felt we should take our shoes off because we were standing on holy ground. . . .

This is a crazy country. If miracles had to happen anywhere, then it's here that they would have to happen. No other country has been prayed for as much as this one. You remember the White woman victim of the attack on the golf course? She was so badly injured, her children had to teach her to do things we take for granted. She still can't go through the security check points at airports because she has shrapnel in her body.

And she said, "I would like to meet the perpetrator in a spirit of forgiveness."

That's wonderful. She goes on, "I would like to forgive him," and then quite incredibly she adds, "and I hope he will forgive me." Crazy.

Or the Afrikaner father whose toddler son was killed in the ANC Amanzimtoti Wimpy Bar bomb attack. He said he believed his son had contributed to the coming of the new dispensation; or the Afrikaner woman in Klerksdorp, who testified about the abduction of her husband by liberation army operatives, who spoke about how her grief and loss were just a drop in the ocean in comparison to what other people have suffered in this beautiful traumatized land. . . .

We are singularly fortunate, indeed blessed in this country. We could so easily have gone the way of Angola, the Sudan, Bosnia, Northern Ireland, Sri Lanka, the Middle East, which have found peace so devastatingly elusive. We have been fortunate that Mr. de Klerk was so brave in 1990 and that he had to deal with the extraordinary Madiba, so magnanimous, so forgiving. . . .

We are going to succeed—why? Because God wants us to succeed for the sake of God's world. We will succeed in spite of ourselves, because we are such an unlikely bunch. Who could have thought we would ever be an example, except of awfulness; who could ever have thought we would be held up as a model to the rest of the world?

God wants to say to the world, to Bosnia, to Northern Ireland, etc.: Look at them. They had a nightmare called apartheid. It has ended. Your nightmare too will end. They had what was called an intractable problem. They are solving it. No one anywhere can any longer say their problem is intractable.

We are a beacon of hope for God's world and we will succeed.[1]

In a version of the speech revised for publication in *Christianity Today*, Archbishop Tutu added this point:

Those who deride the TRC hardly ever refer to an amazing phenomenon—the victim's readiness, indeed eagerness to forgive. Many are seemingly taking it for granted—as something almost to which they are entitled. Dear Friends, please take this, the last but most generous offer of dealing with the past. Grab it, because once it is past it will not return.[2]

Until white Christians and people of color in the United States exhibit this same kind of commitment motivated by their love of Christ, I am afraid we will not see the same movement by God's Spirit to bring racial healing.

## WHAT PEOPLE OF COLOR CAN'T AFFORD TO DO

We cannot be like many of the blacks in South Africa who came to power and almost immediately turned all authority over to blacks simply because they were black. I certainly understand why they did it, but it was still wrong. Remember, I experienced the Jim Crow Laws as a youth. These South African blacks needed to see the big picture. In not seeing the big picture, South Africa lost a lot of resources, namely bright young white Afrikaners who left the country thinking they would not receive a fair opportunity for their careers.

Another example is of a cross-cultural church trying to maintain the balance that makes it work for everyone. One of my white prayer partners belongs to a now predominantly African-American church, and she told me about the situation in an e-mail:

My church is in a "tricky" place: In the last fifteen years it has gone from being a mostly white church to being mostly black (60% black; most of the rest of the members are white, with a handful of Asians and Hispanics). For the last several years, we have had our first-ever black pastor (our senior pastor).

In the last year, both white pastors have resigned (to work in other ministries). So now, the church is asking the question, "Who do we need to minister to us?" We have a senior pastor, but we need an assistant pastor and a youth pastor. Some people are saying that in a deliberately mixed church, it makes sense that at least one of the pastors we hire should be white, and others are saying that such a suggestion is "reverse affirmative action" and almost racist. Some are saying, in fact, that the people who "feel that way" should just leave the church, as we don't want them anyway.

As a white person who *loves* my church, has been there for more than a dozen years, and has lived in an all-black neighborhood for six years, I want the church to be as deliberate about cross-cultural ministry today as we were seven or eight years ago when "the shoe was on the other foot" and we felt it would be culturally insensitive to continue to have all-white pastoral leadership in a church that had become multicultural. Yet I feel that some have branded me, and others who think that we still need mixed leadership, by implication, as a "racist." Why? If we have three godly black pastors, it could still comfortably be my church—but some other white people might come in, see it as a "black" church that merely tolerates whites, and leave. And in that case, white people who move away from the community probably won't be "replaced" by other white people, and it will become a black church. I want this church to succeed as a cross-cultural church!! I think it says more for the power of the Gospel if it succeeds, even with some hardship and pain, than if "multicultural" is just a transition point.

We're all at different points on cross-cultural understanding. And I think white people like me, who grew up in "white" settings, need a place to *learn* . . . which we won't have if we label any discomfort as "racist."

We had a two-hour meeting at church the other day about the search process, and much of that time was on that issue. It was actually quite good—a lot of honesty, yet no raised voices or personal attacks. Still, some of the white people were going out of their way to say "no, no, it doesn't matter, if anything we prefer three black pastors" and some of the black people were saying "good, because if you feel otherwise, we don't want you anyway."

In the lobby afterward, one black woman told another that she'd heard some white people had *actually said* it would be better not to have three black pastors. The second woman bristled, and the first hastily reassured her that no one had had the gall to say it to her face. The implication was that if anyone had said something so unseemly directly to her, she'd have punched the person out or otherwise re-educated her.

Both of these women are friends of mine, and in fact I'd been talking to one of the women when the second one came over, so physically I was "in" the conversation. Yet neither made any move to include me or to see what I thought of the subject, and under the circumstances, I didn't dare speak up. Did they assume I'd agree that wanting mixed leadership was racist, or was my opinion irrelevant? I left a little sad. I don't want people to sit back and applaud that I have made a few steps toward cross-racial understanding, but neither do I want people to say *all* the work has to be on my end. If black people don't care one way or another whether there are any white people at my church, then why should we do the hard work it sometimes takes to be there?

But, ultimately, I think God cares, and I really do think the power of the Gospel is greater than the "comfort level" any of us has.

No one has asked me, but I would suggest that the church be prayerful and try to hire a white, Asian, or Hispanic pastor in order to try to maintain racial diversity. The African Americans in the church will have to work hard to remember what it was like when they were the minority in the church and be sensitive to those who are in the minority now. But as I read about this church, the real issue is how spiritually mature are the members going to be?

## STEPS TO PRAYERFULLY CONSIDER IN MOVING TOWARD RACIAL UNITY

Obviously, there are many things we can do to move forward in this tenuous arena of race relations. Our thinking and, in some cases, our theology must change. As it does, our lives must then reflect such change.

As I've traveled across the country talking with people in our biblical diversity workshops about these issues, I've seen time and time again that working through projects for a common goal seems to be a great way to improve race relations. Projects with observable problems to be solved—like building a new community center, painting Sunday school classrooms, or cleaning up the neighborhood—are a great way to bring people together in a nonthreatening manner. Working through these problems builds relationships as the process reveals how much we are alike and how our differences become assets in getting a job done. An attitude of "I'm glad we're on the same team" usually emerges. It is not the conflict with each other that is the litmus test, but rather how we work through the forgiveness process. I emphasize forgiveness because usually at some point during a project someone will say or do something that offends one or more of the participants. This is where the principle of forgiveness will need to be applied.

Therefore, I would encourage churches and/or parachurch ministries to partner as equals with (and not be paternalistic to) churches whose congregations include individuals unlike theirs and together to undertake projects that are simply dreams now. Specifically, I would encourage whites to go to the home turf of an African-American community—or Native American, Latino, Asian, immigrant, etc.—simply because, for years, people of color have been going to the whites' turf. Perhaps the thought fills you with some trepidation because you expect to meet with feelings of hostility if you do so, but most people of color are gentle toward those who voluntarily choose to be minorities in the world of people of color. Once you get there, it is essential to sit down, listen, and ask who is doing what—and can you possibly do something *better together* for the glory of God? This way, everyone can take ownership in whatever efforts you decide on together.

While this book was in page proofs, someone forwarded me this e-mail that contains wise advice for anyone teaching multicultural groups about biblical diversity. With the permission of the person who wrote the e-mail, Paul C. Gorski, I am including it here.

Subject: Re: On Being a Better Teacher for Students of Color

Jennifer,
I faced some similar tough spots with a class I teach called

Racism and Whiteness in the U.S. It's an upper-level undergraduate class.

My students are usually half people of color and half white people. I guess, in actuality, my dilemma is a little different. My students of color do not seem to be shocked. Instead, they seem to already know what I'm teaching. As a result, there are points at which in retrospect I see that I was teaching white students something the students of color already knew.

The first semester I taught the class I designed it with white participants in mind. As a result, the class sort of moved at the pace of the average white student in the class. What I realized within a few weeks was that this was just recycling racism. The students of color deserved the same opportunity to learn from the class as white students. What I find is that it's unfair on a lot of levels (social, socio-political, emotional, etc.) to put students of color in a position to do all the educating about racism without providing an opportunity for them to work through their own issues.

So, the past two semesters I've completely changed my approach. Instead of moving the class at the pace of white students, I've completely focused on moving at the pace of the students of color. The white students are lost in the class a lot, but THEY have to do the work to try to keep up instead of the students of color having to do the work to reach back and pull them along.

What I've found to my own astonishment is that this approach has resulted in more pronounced development among the white students because they're forced to do their own work and not rely on students of color to educate them. They're interrogated, challenged, critiqued and not coddled or taken care of.

I'm not sure any of this is helpful, but my suggestion is to focus on the needs of students of color in the class and let the white students do the work to find their place in the class. Try some caucus groups where students of color can have their own dialogues about the issues without white students (and even without you).

Good luck! Your self-reflectiveness and self-critique on this are inspirational to me.

Paul

I also believe the following steps should be considered as we ask the question, "Where do we go from here?"

- Be intentional in having people of color in decision-making positions. This involves risk, not because of a lack of qualifications on behalf of the minority but in possibly being rejected by others of your own race.

- Do youth missions across the tracks instead of always out of town. This creates long-term cross-cultural relationships and provides a tremendous training ground for future foreign or home missionaries.

- Strive to live, work, and play together in the integration of neighborhoods and churches.

- Learn from organizations that seek to build cross-cultural relationships such as Promise Keepers; For Faith & Family's *Light* magazine; Southwestern Seminary's Black Think Tank; Mission Mississippi (Jackson, MS), etc.

- White evangelicals need to mark Martin Luther King, Jr.'s holiday and note Black History Month and respect how important they are to African Americans (1 Corinthians 12:26). Businesses such as Coors, McDonald's, and State Farm Insurance produce calendars and other promotions marking Black History Month, Cinco de Mayo, and other culturally sensitive dates. These businesses understand that celebrating cross-cultural issues pays financial dividends down the road. They also know that people of color are typically loyal for generations.

Although these companies may well be motivated by values we

might not identify as "Christian," it is difficult to explain to thinking people of color why their white Christian brothers with so many resources do so much less than corporate America. This gives Satan a tremendous opportunity to create division.

• Work to develop an inclusive mind-set by reading periodicals produced by Christian and non-Christian people of color.

Throughout this book, I've presented plenty of African-American Christian examples from which Christian organizations could create a Christian Black History Month calendar or other promotional pieces. Asian, Hispanic, and First Nation calendars and other products could also be produced. This would be an incredible affirmation and invitation to Christian people of color across denominational lines! With many white churches experiencing decline in membership and with the exploding growth in churches of people of color, it is a biblical investment (Matthew 25:14–29).

## NO ONE SAID IT WOULD BE EASY

We have just mentioned prayer. Hopefully, prayer supplies the right attitudes, which lead to the right actions. As we seek to develop and maintain cross-cultural relationships, we must understand it will be hard work. We must go beyond good intentions as well as not become defensive quickly.

Maybe this example will help. At a Christian school, a white boy, five or six years old, calls a black girl about the same age "nigger." The girl tells her mother, who is the first African American to teach at this predominantly white Christian school. The school administrator disciplines the little boy just like he would anyone else. He makes the boy eat lunch with him and does not allow him to play at recess. He is being fair. Yet the African-American mother is still upset. Why? First of all, she said, "It was cold that day and none of the children wanted to go outside, but they had to, but this little boy didn't." There seemed to be no real consequences to his actions. The little girl doesn't want to return to this Christian school. I wonder what she thinks of Christianity now?

Was the administrator being unfair? I don't think so. What could he have done? He could have had both sets of parents, one couple at a time, come to his office to pray, discuss the situation, and try to come to a punishment that would fit the crime. Since the culprit here is a young child, the key is intervention or teaching more than punishment, as the boy most likely did not understand the effects of the word. But the little girl needs to feel that she is safe and that the adults have handled the situation justly, and the little boy needs to understand the negative impact words can have.

Possibly the administrator could ask the little boy with his parents present why he called the little girl "nigger." If the administrator believed the African-American parents could meet with the little boy with love and forgiveness, he could have them gently explain to him what the name means, its history, how it makes African Americans feel, and how God may feel about such actions. Ephesians 4:29 says, "Do not let any unwholesome talk come out of your mouths, but only what is helpful for building others up according to their needs, that it may benefit those who listen." This method has several benefits: (1) it helps the little boy to see the seriousness of his offense; (2) it helps his parents see that prejudice hurts people; (3) it lets the little girl know that she is cared for and will be protected—making her feel safe, so that the school can continue to be a place where she can learn without being distracted; (4) by having the African-American parents explain to the little boy what "nigger" means, they get to see him for what he is, a little boy, a child—it may defuse their anger as they to some extent develop a relationship with this little boy; (5) this interaction makes forgiveness and sensitivity possible; and (6) God is honored and Satan is defeated again.

Another possibility would be to have the children and parents role-play, have the blacks pretend they are white and vice versa. Since this is a Christian school, what about putting Christian principles into practice? Some of the words will need to be explained and examples given, but what a tremendous opportunity to make a God-honoring impression forever. Just think, "No need for anger or lawsuits!"

Another option could have been to sit down with the little boy and explain the seriousness of his actions, and warn him that he will be suspended if he uses such words again.

The administrator may have to learn to think holistically, seeing the big picture. One must come to understand the ramifications of certain actions and/or what appears to be lack of action. Egos need to be checked at the door. And people of color must be patient with such attempts and explain calmly and with Christ's love their concerns or lack of satisfaction with discipline, school procedures, etc.

What can such a school do *after* dealing with the immediate situation? If the administrators are serious about having the school be a safe place for people of color, they can form an advisory board that includes people of color (people who do not have children at the school). They can put together a chapel led by people of color, people with handicaps, or other adults who can explain to the student body the serious damage that can come from hurtful, derogatory words. The school can actively recruit administrators, faculty, and students of color, perhaps by using the help of the advisory group. This can be done by establishing relationships with pastors of color and asking permission to set up a booth in the church lobby with fliers and a representative from the school who can speak with parents. If educational cost is a roadblock to potential students of color, the school can recruit donors to make scholarships available and/or partner with people of color in creating the scholarships.

Developing cross-cultural relationships requires developing a sensitivity to other cultures/races. What works well in one culture may be a disaster in another.

## RECRUITING PEOPLE OF COLOR

I often hear, "We just can't find any people of color." The Christian community will need to be as creative and diligent as its secular counterpart. *Fortune* and *Working Woman* usually have some informative articles regarding diversity. The April 2001 edition of *Working Woman* gives six ways to make diversity work:

1. *Search for the Best*—Corporate America invests time in *affirmative* recruiting, and recruiters visit historically black colleges and universities; contact Hispanic students and/or labor organizations; link up with women's professional networks; create internships that lure people of color into their workplaces; and develop mentoring networks.

2. *Help Newcomers Fit In*—Having a diverse workforce is one thing; having innovation is another. The challenge is creating a climate for effective diversity—"persuade everyone to play nicely (teamwork or failure)."

3. *Educate Everyone*—Diversity doesn't work unless companies deal up front with employees' fears of change and discomfort with people from other backgrounds. (In the Christian community, this seems to be just the opposite: It is the leadership that has the fears.) People are encouraged to listen and express their views.

4. *Keep Score*—Companies that do well on diversity treat it like anything else on the business agenda. In some companies failure can result in a smaller raise or bonus, as well as slower progress up the corporate ladder. (Again, the Christian community needs an accountability system to help it in this area.) "If you are not keeping score, that's a message all in itself," says Thomas Engibous, CEO, Chair and President of Texas Instruments.

5. *Sweat the Details*—Little things really do count, such as free consulting for women and people of color who want to move beyond administration and into management.

6. *See the Future*—Business is as much about what happens next as what's happening now, so the most prescient companies are investing in people who won't be on anyone's payroll for years. (IBM has a math program for middle school students; Xerox works with kids in Harlem; some of these companies help at-risk children of color get into college and then secure jobs with them. This may be where Christian organizations and Christian schools could learn

a lot from secular organizations.)[3]

My friend John Kobara, Sylvan Learning Systems, Inc., Online Senior Vice President, writes: "What can we do as individuals and communities to reconnect to one another, to appreciate what each person has to offer, and recognize that diversity is necessary for us to survive and flourish? I think the future is so bright and filled with countless opportunities. We have come so far as a society to appreciate one another, but yet we have so far to go." He suggests:

### 1. Awareness and education

The more we can learn about ourselves the more we will appreciate each other. Whether white, black, Asian, or Latino, our backgrounds and ancestries are multicultural, multireligious, multiethnic, and multiracial. Understand that Asians, Africans, Latinos, and Europeans are all so extraordinarily diverse in their appearance, backgrounds, and cultures that they defy categorization. We must resist the temptation to put everyone into a neat little box—to limit who people are by labeling.

### 2. Take an interest in other cultures and communities

Be open to learning about others and their unique stories and their unique ways of viewing things. You will find a world of difference and a universe of commonality.

### 3. Reconnect with your network

We must recommit ourselves to spending time to interact, listen, and share with those around us. We have to stop being so busy and offer one of our most valuable and precious resources—our attention —to those around us. We will discover a tremendous diversity of interests, backgrounds, talents, needs, and resources that are right in front of us.

### 4. Intolerance for intolerance

If we want to make a difference, if we believe in a diverse society, if we value treating each other with dignity—then we must commit ourselves to helping others learn about and value differences. We have to be open to corrections to characterizations and pronunciations. This is not political correctness; this is understanding one another. In short, how we conduct ourselves every day, how we model our behavior, how we attempt to foster a supportive, respectful, and educational environment defines the quality of our community and whether we will be the beneficiaries of it.[4]

Secular organizations want a diverse workforce so that they can compete globally. The world outside of the United States see people of color as brothers. People of color comprise two-thirds of the world's population.

### 1 CORINTHIANS 12:25

This verse states that the members of the body of Christ should have equal concern for all members. This verse also says that when one member suffers, we all suffer. If we understand this, then issues that are important to other members of the body should become important to us. We may not always agree, but we need to be aware and try to understand. For African Americans, it is often the issue of justice or the lack of it that bothers us, making it difficult to "get over it."

For example, it has been documented that even for people of color who have insurance, there is a better than average chance that they will receive inferior medical care. An Institute of Medicine (IOM) panel study of Medicare beneficiaries, for instance, found that blacks were 3.6 times as likely as whites to have their lower limbs amputated as a result of diabetes. "Some of us on the committee were surprised and shocked at the extent of the evidence," said the chairman of the panel, Dr. Alan R. Nelson, a former president of the American Medical Association. He added, "The evidence is overwhelming."

Racial bias, albeit subconscious, may be at work, the study found. Although the panel said most health providers were well-intentioned, it cited "indirect evidence" that doctors' decisions were influenced by their perception of race. As an example, the authors cited the study of major medical centers in New York State that found African Americans were 37 percent less likely to undergo angioplasty and other heart procedures, including bypass surgery, than whites. In 90 percent of the cases in which the patient did not get the surgery, the doctor had not recommended it. In interviews with the doctors, the researchers found "classic negative racial stereotypes," the report said, such as assumptions that black patients would be less likely to participate in follow-up care.[5]

Another concern for African Americans, according to an article in the *Washington Post,* is that researchers found that "black boys living in wealthier communities with better schools and more white class-mates were at greater risk of being labeled mentally retarded and sent to special classes than those attending predominantly black, low-income schools." The article said, "Black children are almost three times more likely than white children to be labeled mentally retarded, forcing them into special education classes where progress is slow and trained teachers in short supply." This article says that other children of color are also at risk. This study was released by the Civil Rights Project at Harvard University. More than 24 million students were researched in the data.[6]

It would be tremendous if these issues became a rallying cry for all Christians, especially the Christian watchdog organizations. And these are just two of numerous documented concerns for people of color.

## NO MORE EXCUSES

In my neighborhood as a child, fighting was common. It was a good neighborhood, but boys will be boys. There were no guns or knives in these fights, just fists. If both parties wanted to fight, there was no problem. Sometimes, if someone was trying to get out of a fight, an expression was used to ensure a fight would occur. It was: "Ain't nothing but the air and opportunity." This meant that none of the previously given excuses satisfied the crowd. Therefore, if you didn't fight, you were considered a coward. To be labeled a coward in my community would end all of a kid's athletic and social activities. He would be ostracized.

I believe the evangelical community has come to the point where God is saying, "Ain't nothing but the air and opportunity." We all know God always prepares us for battles and often fights them on our behalf, but each battle requires faith on our part. Some people thought that if the older generation just died out, race relations would automatically get better. One need only watch the evening news to know the race problem has not been getting better; people of color are still usually portrayed negatively, because a negative legacy is being left. Because racism is taught by verbal and nonverbal communication, our children learn and respond to people of different races the way their parents do. We say we are afraid, unaware, or unavailable to reach out across cultures. I say the evangelical church has given enough excuses.

Unfortunately things don't always seem to get better even when we start to move in the right direction. But one thing is true: Things will get worse if nothing is done. We as Christians must demonstrate to the world the better alternative Jesus has given us—or be willing to accept the consequences.

I'll say it again: We must be proactive in living God's vision for diversity on earth, or the consequence will be race wars among Christians. And so the question, "Where do we go from here?" becomes, "What will you do as an individual, a church, or a parachurch organization to improve race relations?"

## MOVING AHEAD

If we are going to improve race relations in the church, each Christian must take a racial audit. We must honestly ask the Holy Spirit to examine our hearts to reveal any racial prejudice and how it might be manifested. Then we must agree with God that this kind of thinking and acting is wrong. Next, we must tell God that we don't ever want to think or act that way again. You know the drill. If we aren't convicted by the Holy Spirit that we have offended another person, then we need to confess to God any underlying racial prejudice. If we have offended someone, we need to go to him or her and ask for forgiveness. Racial prejudice has no place in Christ's church, even if everyone in the room is of the same culture or race.

My former Sunday school teacher, Tim Stephenson, took our class through the book of Acts. One particular Sunday, he reminded us of Paul's commitment to spread the Gospel no matter the personal cost. That same Sunday, my former pastor, Dwight Brown, showed a brief video of a missionary to Cambodia who had recently died. The missionary in the video said the same thing Paul did. Both men said they would gladly give their lives if it would mean more people would come to Christ.

Tim really drove the point home by asking us to get alone and look in the mirror. While looking in the mirror, we needed to ask ourselves the same questions that I believe apply to our work for racial unity: What is the price I am willing to pay for the proclamation of the Gospel? How far is too far?

Am I willing . . .

- To be inconvenienced?
- To stay an extra few minutes on Sunday morning?
- To walk across the street to make friends with my neighbor?
- To let someone see the real me without the artificial barriers?
- To change my plans and dreams for my life?
- To relocate?
- To understand someone who isn't just like me?
- To humble myself?
- To shed tears for someone's salvation?
- To pray?
- To go?

• To die?

How much is too much? In 2 Corinthians 6:3–10, Paul talks about dying for the sake of the Cross, remembering the death Christ suffered for his sake. Now more than ever, I believe it is a critical time to remember Christ's sacrificial death, look to His resurrection life, and ask ourselves in the process if are willing to make the personal sacrifices that must be made to improve racial relations and celebrate biblical diversity.

Will we do it, even for our Lord's sake?

*Lord, I know it is time for action now. Help us not to give You any more excuses. Please enable us through the power of the Holy Spirit to have the courage to do what is right in Your eyes.*

*Amen.*

### THOUGHT QUESTIONS

1. Is there a first step that you personally need to make to help improve race relations among the body of Christ? If you do need to do something, is it practical, measurable, and obtainable?

2. If you do need to do something, have you counted the cost? What will your family think? What will people of your own race say about you? Do you think you can handle possible criticism or rejection?

3. Can you help your church, school, or organization to make a positive step toward biblical diversity? What do you think that first step should be? Will the board, leadership, etc. support it or object to it?

4. Christian schools and ministries have notorious reputations for being worse than secular organizations when comes to racism. How can you as a student, an employee, a member, or an administrator make a difference that will glorify God? If you have a library, does it reflect Christian contributions from people of color (not

just African Americans)?

## NOTES

1. Archbishop Tutu's speech was given to the South African press club on October 21, 1997. The full speech can be found at http://www.futurenet.org/7Peacebuilding/tutu.htm. The official Website for the Truth and Reconciliation Commission is http://www.doj.gov.za/trc/.

2. Desmond Tutu, "Between a Nightmare and a Dream: If Reconciliation Can Happen in South Africa, It Can Happen Elsewhere," adapted from a speech he gave to the South African Press Club, 21 October 1997, *Christianity Today,* 9 February 1998, 25.

3. Annie Finnigan, "Different Strokes," *Working Woman,*26, no. 4 (April 2001): 42.

4. This text was written by John Kobara at my request for this book.

5. *New York Times,* 21 March 2002. See also http://www4.nationalacademies.org/onpi/webextra.nsf/web/minority?OpenDocument.

6. Jay Matthews, "Report Finds Special-Education Bias," *Washington Post,* 3 March 2001. The article can also be accessed at http://www.racematters.org/specialeducationbias.htm.

# Questions You May Have Wondered About But May Not Have Had The Opportunity to Ask

### Clarence Shuler and Pastor Mark Brewer
### Discussing the Race Game

PASTOR BREWER: Clarence, I know your heart is for marriage and families to be strong, but secondly, I believe you want to see race relations improve. You live in two worlds. You work for a predominantly white Christian organization, yet you are black. How do you do this?

CLARENCE: Living in two worlds is not optional for minorities. Many times, our success in the world is directly linked to our ability to master both worlds.

PASTOR BREWER: Clarence, where were you raised? Did you grow up in the South?

CLARENCE: Yes, I grew up in the Promised Land—North Carolina.

PASTOR BREWER: Did you experience segregation?

CLARENCE: Yes, I did. There were some advantages. The teachers really cared about you and made sure you learned. There were also more male teachers who provided good role models. Many of these men left when integration came because there was usually little room for advancement. Men who were previously head high school coaches found themselves as junior coaches, etc. Blacks in the South were usually better educated than those in the North.

PASTOR BREWER: Paint a picture for an Anglo or suburban church of what is going on in the heart of the black church as it looks at the white church. I realize that you can't speak for all blacks, but generalize for us. I know I don't like it when someone tries to speak for all whites and doesn't call me, but help us out here.

CLARENCE: First of all, it may be difficult for the Anglo or suburban church to understand the black church because the suburban church is not impacted by the black church. I see a misunderstanding because the suburban church has no history of the black church. Part of the frustration of the black church seems to be a cry for equality.

Another frustration is when a suburban church says it wants to help an urban church—which is basically fine, and usually sincere—but often, there seems to be a paternalistic slant to it. There is an unspoken standard which the suburban church wants the black church to meet in order for the suburban church to deem the experience successful. I think it is difficult for people to understand simply why people are different without the difference being translated into inferiority. We focus on the effect, but not the cause. Just exchanging pulpits won't make this change. I think sometimes the urban church looks at the suburban church as being full of money. Therefore, share the money with us.

PASTOR BREWER: Let's just say I'm the average white guy, Joe Suburbanite. I say, Clarence, why not give it a rest? What have I done against blacks? My life has been hard. I worked hard. No one helped me out. What do you communicate to a person like that?

CLARENCE: Well, first of all, to help his or her argument, he could also say that some blacks have done really well, so how come the rest of you don't do well?

PASTOR BREWER: I've never heard that before.

CLARENCE: You've got to hang out with me. One must understand that very few people are leaders, but leaders will always survive and will rise to the top regardless of color. That is the nature of being a leader. But most people are followers. When people say "give it a rest," we need to think of elephants when they are small. Their legs are chained to a stake—which means they can't move. By the time the elephant is grown, even though it is strong enough to move the stake, it has long since stopped trying. When people are oppressed or feel oppressed, there is a tendency to give up. The question they ask of the person who says, "I haven't done anything wrong," is "What have you done to make things better?" As Christians, we are to go the extra mile and be servants to anyone. [Chapter 5 has a section on this subject titled "Can the Evangelical Gospel Minister to Minorities?"]

# Bibliography

Aptheker, Herbert, ed. *A Documentary History of the Negro People in the United States*. Vol. 1–4. Secaucus, N.J.: Citadel Press, Carol Publishing (an imprint of Stuart, Lyle), 1989.

Beals, Ivan A. *Our Racist Legacy: Will the Church Resolve the Conflict?* Notre Dame, Ind.: Cross Cultural, 1997.

Bennett, Lerone, Jr. *Before the Mayflower: A History of Black America*. New York: Penguin, 1988.

Cameron, Robert J. *The Last Pew on the Left: America's Lost Potential*. Lafayette, La.: Prescott, 1995.

Chideya, Farai. *Don't Believe the Hype: Fighting Cultural Misinformation About African-Americans*. New York: Penguin, 1995.

Cuffee, Paul F. *Memoirs of Captain Paul Cuffee, a Man of Colour: The Epistle of the Society of Sierra Leone in Africa & etc.* New York: W. Alexander, 1812–1817.

Du Bois, W. E. B. *Black Reconstruction in America: [An Essay Toward a History of the Part Which Black Folk Played in the Attempt to Reconstruct Democracy in America, 1860–1880]*. 1935. Reprint, with an introduction by David Levering Lewis, New York: Atheneum, 1992.

Ellis, Carl F. *Free At Last: The Gospel in the African-American Experience.* Downers Grove, Ill.: InterVarsity, 1996.

_____. "The Gospel, the Black Man and Slavery." *Body of Christ* 9, no. 3 (November 1997) (Denver): 3.

Falconbridge, Dr. Alexander. *An Account of the Slave Trade on the Coast of Africa.* London, 1788.

_____. *A Narrative of the Life and Adventure of Venture, A Native of Africa.* New London, Conn., 1798; expanded ed., Hamden, Conn., 1896.

Gates, Henry Louis, Jr., and Nellie Y. McKay, eds. *The Norton Anthology: African American Literature.* New York: W. W. Norton, 1997.

Gutman, George H. *The Black Family in Slavery and Freedom, 1750–1925.* New York: Pantheon, 1976.

Harley, Sharon. *The Timetables of African-American History: A Chronology of the Most Important People and Events in African-American History.* New York: Simon & Schuster, 1995.

January, Jerald. *A Second Time.* Franklin, Tenn.: Cool Springs, 1996.

Kunhardt, Philip B., Jr., Philip B. Kunhardt III, and Peter W. Kunhardt. *Lincoln: An Illustrated Biography.* New York: Knopf, 1994.

Perkins, Spencer. *Reconcilers Fellowship: Reconciliation Wednesday for Leaders* 1, no. 14 (15 October 1997).

_____. "Plain Vanilla Christianity." *Ministries Today,* November/December 1996, 34–41.

Skinner, Barbara Williams. "Been There, Done That." *The Reconciler.* Jackson, Miss., Winter 1996.

Stewart, Jeffery C. *1001 Things Everyone Should Know About African American History.* New York: Doubleday, 1996.

Tapia, Andrés T. "After the Hugs, What?" *Christianity Today,* 3 February 1997, 55.

Terkel, Studs. *Race: How Blacks and Whites Think and Feel About the American Obsession.* New York: Free Press, 1992.

Usry, Glenn, and Craig S. Keener. *Black Man's Religion: Can Christianity Be Afrocentric?* Downers Grove, Ill.: InterVarsity, 1996.

Weary, Dolphus. *I Ain't Coming Back.* Wheaton, Ill.: Tyndale, 1995.

Williams, Gerald. *History of the Negro Race in America from 1619 to 1880,* vol. 2, 1800–1880. *American Negro: His History and Literature,* no. 1. 1883. Reprint, Philadelphia: Ayer, 1968.

Wilson, Joseph T. *History of the Black Phalanx.* Hartford, Conn.: 1890; New York: Da Capo, 1994.

Terkel, Studs. *Race: How Blacks and Whites Think and Feel About the American Obsession.* New York: Free Press, 1992.

Usry, Glenn, and Craig S. Keener. *Black Man's Religion: Can Christianity Be Afrocentric?* Downers Grove, Ill.: InterVarsity, 1996.

Weary, Dolphus. *I Ain't Coming Back.* Wheaton, Ill.: Tyndale, 1995.

Williams, George. *History of the Negro Race in America from 1619 to 1880.* vol. 2, 1800–1880. American Negro: His History and Literature, no. 1. 1883. Reprint. Philadelphia: Avon, 1968.

Wilson, Joseph T. *History of the Black Phalanx.* Hartford, Conn., 1890; New York: Da Capo, 1994.